THE EVERYTHING®
Resume Book
3rd Edition

Dear Reader,

To the inexperienced eye, the difference between an average resume and a great one is minimal. To the sophisticated eye of the corporate recruiter or prospective employer, the difference is enormous. It translates into getting the interview or simply being dismissed, even if your credentials and work experience are strong.

This book is meant for all readers—the ones who are writing their resume from scratch and the ones who are eager to improve it. You always want to present your best version of yourself so that hiring authorities are eager to meet you. The *Everything*® book format makes creating a great resume easy for all levels of job candidates. It will also help you navigate the technology and methods today's job seeker uses to get noticed.

Use your resume as your key to a world of job opportunities! Good luck with your career!

Nancy Schuman

Certified Staffing Professional

Welcome to the EVERYTHING Series!

These handy, accessible books give you all you need to tackle a difficult project, gain a new hobby, comprehend a fascinating topic, prepare for an exam, or even brush up on something you learned back in school but have since forgotten.

You can choose to read an *Everything*® book from cover to cover or just pick out the information you want from our four useful boxes: e-questions, e-facts, e-alerts, e-ssentials. We give you everything you need to know on the subject, but throw in a lot of fun stuff along the way, too.

We now have more than 400 *Everything*® books in print, spanning such wide-ranging categories as weddings, pregnancy, cooking, music instruction, foreign language, crafts, pets, New Age, and so much more. When you're done reading them all, you can finally say you know *Everything*®!

QUESTIONS?
Answers to
common questions

FACTS
Important snippets
of information

ALERTS!
Urgent
warnings

ESSENTIALS
Quick
handy tips

DIRECTOR OF INNOVATION Paula Munier

EDITORIAL DIRECTOR Laura M. Daly

EXECUTIVE EDITOR, SERIES BOOKS Brielle K. Matson

ASSOCIATE COPY CHIEF Sheila Zwiebel

ACQUISITIONS EDITOR Lisa Laing

DEVELOPMENT EDITOR Elizabeth Kassab

PRODUCTION EDITOR Casey Ebert

Visit the entire Everything® series at *www.everything.com*

THE
EVERYTHING
RESUME BOOK

3RD EDITION

Create a winning resume that
stands out from the crowd

Nancy Schuman
Certified Staffing Professional

Adamsmedia
Avon, Massachusetts

For Tommy Czizik, who has *always*
done it his way and never with a resume.

An Everything® Series Book.
Everything® and everything.com® are registered trademarks of F+W Publications, Inc.

Published by Adams Media, an F+W Publications Company
57 Littlefield Street, Avon, MA 02322 U.S.A.
www.adamsmedia.com

ISBN 10: 1-59869-637-8
ISBN 13: 978-1-59869-637-0

Printed in the United States of America.

J   I   H   G   F   E   D   C   B   A

Library of Congress Cataloging-in-Publication Data
is available from the publisher.

This book is available at quantity discounts for bulk purchases.
For information, please call 1-800-289-0963.

Contents

PART 1: Resume Writing

Resume Writing and the Job Search / 1

Writing Your Resume / 19

Seven Steps to Resume-Writing Success / 000

Acknowledgments

Many thanks to my colleagues and friends who have provided support and resources for this project. I want to particularly thank the Banks Team (Merrill, Keith, and Jason), Cheryl Pagliuca, Sharon Miller, Drew Petrillo, Barbara Cohen Farber, Linda Matias, Mac Ismail, Ellen Schechterman, Janet Pushee, and the entire Czizik family.

Thank you to all my business associates at Lloyd Staffing for their input on resumes and job seeking in the Web 2.0 world. Sincere appreciation to my editors, Lisa Laing and Elizabeth Kassab, for their guidance, flexibility, and valuable input every step of the way. And finally, heartfelt thanks to my friend and agent, Grace Freedson, for her energy, enthusiasm, and for making all things possible.

Top Ten Reasons to Update Your Resume

1. You've been promoted!

2. Economic ups and downs in your industry mean you might be subject to downsizing or a layoff.

3. You can do the job better than your boss.

4. Your contact information has changed, or you have a new cell number, married name, address, or e-mail provider.

5. You are thinking about moving to a new city, state, or industry.

6. You have new career goals, aspire to a better position, or want to transition to a different field.

7. Your education has changed; you've just gotten a new degree, taken new classes, or been trained in a new skill.

8. It's been more than two years since your last update.

9. You've been asked for your credentials for an award, board position, membership, or networking opportunity.

10. You might be recruited when you least expect it.

Introduction

▶ THE PHRASE, "IT'S time to get your resume together" sends shivers down many a spine, causing headaches as well as heartaches. Graduating from college, hunting for a new, more responsible position, and losing a job can all cause nervous palpitations. It is possible, however, to be invigorated by a review of your achievements and to look forward to a challenging and rewarding future.

There is something very positive about seeing your education, experience, and achievements presented in a visually appealing document. Creating this document need not make you anxious or uncomfortable. Resume writing is not as difficult as you might think, and by following the rules and advice outlined in this book, you will be on your way to getting the job you want. The first step in this process is a well-written resume that calls attention to your strengths and skills and makes the prospective employer want to interview you. That's really the main purpose of a resume—to get your foot in the door.

To do this, you need a great resume, one that sets you apart from your competition. Of course, times have also changed, so you need to make sure that you pay attention to keywords, consider today's technology, and follow new methods for job seeking and personal networking. *The Everything® Resume Book, 3rd Edition* is designed to help you conduct an effective job search using both traditional techniques and those associated with the Web. Read and act upon the powerful ideas presented in this book to create a dynamic resume, which will inspire and facilitate an effective job search.

For centuries, we have used documents to confirm our identities, make introductions, and inspire others to see us as useful, valuable, and capable. Regardless of its origins or the new formats and methods used to present the modern resume, it still is one of the most important tools necessary to getting or changing jobs and advancing your career.

Resume Writing

Chapter 1

Resume Writing and the Job Search

A resume is an important tool in your search for employment. Internet advances have vastly altered the realm of job searching in a few short years. Technology has also changed the way job seekers write and transmit their resumes. Job seekers need to keep pace with the technology and hiring methods of today's employers, and their resumes must reflect the new recruiting practices and the ways employers identify and consider talent. The right resume will help you get the job, while the wrong resume will completely eliminate you from the competition.

Resume Writing for Today's Job World

The vast number of books written on the subject of resume writing is mind-boggling. Over the years, there have been almost as many suggestions for format, content, and approaches as there are resume books in print.

Books published only a few years ago are already out of date. As technology changes, so do the concepts that have always applied to resume writing. While books once detailed how to prepare a resume suitable for scanning, today's resumes are typically transmitted by e-mail or posted on the Web. That means greater focus on developing strong content and a resume that can be viewed easily by the reader, regardless of platform or application, and increased attention to keywords for online searches. Many employers now target the passive job seeker—someone who isn't currently seeking employment, but whose work experience makes him or her desirable for hire. Such candidates are often identified via the Internet.

This book addresses traditional resumes as well as e-resumes. Samples like those included in these chapters should inspire you. Resume illustrations can often appear intimidating, as presentations of perfect job candidates. Don't worry! You aren't competing with these mythic people for jobs, but you can use their examples to make your resume as dynamic as theirs.

Seeking Inspiration

One search of an online book retailer's inventory returned more than 1,000 results on the keyword search "resume." You, too, have probably encountered the confusion of shelf after shelf of titles in the career section of your local bookstore. No matter how, where, or why you purchased this edition of *The Everything® Resume Book,* you have taken a solid first step toward new employment. You are now ready for education as well as motivation. Knowing the latest trends in resume design and delivery tells your prospective employer that you are aware of contemporary practices. It enhances communication opportunities between the Gen X/Gen Y and baby boomer generations, regardless of which one is the candidate and which one the hiring manager.

The Old Approach: Resumes Any Way

For years, resume books have established and advocated a "resumes any way" attitude. No matter the title, these books all espoused the same belief: "There is no one perfect resume." Ironically, even those authors who did promote the so-called "perfect" resume did little more than echo the others. Most, if not all, of those books focused on creating the resume that potential employers (the infamous "they") would want to see.

Readers were encouraged to assume the thoughts and preferences of their prospective employers. Energies and attitudes were focused on what they—meaning human-resources professionals, managers, recruiters, and executives—wanted to see in job-search documents like resumes, cover letters, and other supporting material. The resumes any way approach covered too many bases and included long, often contradictory, laundry lists of what they wanted.

Such an approach has an obvious disadvantage. There's no way that you, the job hunter, can possibly know what they want to see in your resume. A far more sensible—and effective—approach is to focus on what you do know: yourself. A successful, useful resume presents you as a person who knows the job and has the skills and abilities to do that job better than anyone else. It's that simple!

The New Way: Web 2.0

Web 2.0 is generally understood to be the second generation of how computer users relate to and utilize the Internet. This matters to job seekers because the venues associated with Web 2.0 impact how you conduct your job search in this age of technology. New tools include Web logs (blogs), videos, podcasts, social-networking sites, and more. These tools allow personal opinion and general information to be shared by various Web users in ways that were not possible before.

Do you really need to know this techie stuff?

Absolutely. This know-how will give you greater opportunity to direct your resume to the employers of your choice and will demonstrate that you are Internet-savvy and familiar with sources and methods used by organizations to locate candidate talent.

For example, a blog, which is a kind of online diary or commentary (typically interactive between writer and reader), can help you identify names of people who work at your target company and what they think about the organization's corporate culture. You will learn more about these new techniques in Chapter 5.

Focus on Yourself

With the proper attitude, guidance, and communication tools, anyone can successfully look for a job. You don't have to be a hotshot Ivy League graduate. Whoever you are, and whatever you have done to date, you can develop a powerful resume that will help you achieve your career goals. As your resume will reveal, you are the best candidate for the job.

Your Personal Brand

Some resume professionals currently advocate creating a personal brand for yourself and using your resume to convey this strategy. Your brand is what differentiates you from the next candidate, the same way one product is set apart from another. Why do some people spend $4 on a cup of coffee? It is because of the perceived value of that coffee and what it says about image, taste, and quality. You can make the same principle apply to yourself.

To have a clear brand, all of your job search materials must be consistent with each other. This starts with simple design. Your resume and all correspondence must be on the same type of paper with the same letterhead and the same font.

You can probably think of real people who have their own personal brand. A few good examples include Madonna, Tiger Woods, Oprah Winfrey, and Bill Gates. You can identify who they are and what they do in 100 words or less. After looking at a cover letter and resume, prospective employers should be able to do the same for you. The key to successful branding is making yourself stand out from the other candidates in your field.

Your resume brand must showcase your unique skills and the value you can bring to the employer. What makes you different from the next candidate? You must be able to articulate your unique value by detailing your distinctive talents, skills, and abilities. This will come across in your resume and during your interview.

You want the prospective employer to invest in you, the same way the coffee company wants you to invest in their high-priced beverage. Additionally, the design, format, and content of your resume, cover letter, and any other correspondence must be consistent and appealing. They create an image for you the moment the employer sees them. In essence, they presell you before you even walk through their door.

Simplified Steps to Job-Search Success

Great resumes are the beginning of job-search success! Through the process of resume writing, you will also be empowered to do the following:

1. Set and articulate professional goals.
2. Create or update a goal-directed resume.
3. Develop a target list of potential employers and a network of advocates both through one-on-one contact and through the Web.
4. Respond to job postings in all mediums, as well as apply directly to desirable employers.
5. Submit your resume, cover letter, and any appropriate supporting materials by the employer's preferred method (Web posting, e-mail, fax, or snail mail).
6. Follow up, assess strategies, follow up, enhance competencies, then follow up again and again.
7. Interview using your resume for guidance.
8. Receive offers and accept one.

Set and Articulate Professional Goals

Your resume does not have to state your lifelong goals. But it should express the aim of your immediate job search, and you should understand how this goal fits into your long-term career plan. Preresearch is the key to goal setting. Before you officially kick off your job search, take an inventory of your achievements and qualifications. Use your inventory to update your resume and other important documents. A successful, goal-oriented resume projects focus and mirrors self-knowledge. The most powerful resumes make clear statements of the job hunter's objectives.

Preresearch, the time before putting your resume together when you investigate your chosen job field, is conducted using four techniques:

- Paper and pencil or eyes to screen (using printed and Web resources)
- Person to person (conducting information conversations)
- Exploration by academics (taking courses or seminars)
- Exploration by experience (including internships or special projects)

An objective like, "I'm looking for anything, anywhere" is not focused enough to be effective. As you create and update your resume, focus will become easier, and it will be easier to project the confidence you gain from self-assessment. Goal setting often begins by assessing yourself and identifying your values, interests, and skills.

Next comes research into careers, job functions, and academic options. When you write your resume and other job-search documents, you project the knowledge you've gained about yourself and your chosen field, creating a powerful self-presentation. The interview, at that point, is your opportunity to flesh out in person the image you've already created on paper or onscreen.

The list on page 5 spells out eight steps to a successful job search. You must be able to articulate your goals and qualifications in order to complete all eight—in other words, to get the job you want. Career counseling is available from a variety of sources that can help you with your self-assessment.

Looking in the mirror is self-reflection for some, but it's not the kind of assessment you need for job-search success. Don't confuse introspection with assessment or active exploration. Meditation rarely yields goal articulation, but reading a book or two might help. Printed and online resources also help. Reference librarians and Web search engines are excellent and often underused resources.

If you are a college student or graduate, your college career center may provide services to address your needs. There are also private counselors or career coaches who can work with you one-on-one to help you personally manage your job search. Many career guidance books include do-it-yourself assessment exercises designed to help you find your chosen career. Some Web sites also provide assessment exercises.

One of the best and simplest ways of focusing your career goals is to read the trade magazines and other publications of a few industries. In as little as a few hours of reading, you can learn enough about job requirements and your own skill set to contribute to a powerful and clear statement of professional objectives.

Goal-Directed Resumes Your Way

Not coincidentally, the steps for creating or updating your resume run parallel to the steps you take toward identifying and articulating your professional goals. In turn, a strong resume inspires you to write dynamic cover letters and follow-ups. This chapter prepares you to complete a fast, effective resume. (Chapter 6 provides more guidance and inspiration for painless resume writing.)

Develop a Target List of Potential Employers

Just as important as your resume is your target list of people, places, and organizations that might be potential employers. You develop this list starting with professional directories and other printed and online resources. Online resources especially can provide a wealth of contact information.

Your colleagues, friends, family, faculty, and fellow graduates can also help with preresearch, networking, and actual job-search efforts. When you ask around for assistance and job referrals, always include a copy of your resume with your request. This is a good way of both projecting your potential and inspiring continued support from your advocates. Go online. Read a prospective company's home page.

Explore opportunities listed under "Employment" or "Careers" on Web pages. If there is a "Media" section, review current and archived press releases, particularly those that reference department heads or corporate leadership. Once you've collected some names and numbers, it's time to do some detective work online. Use a search engine like Google to see if your contact's name appears with any helpful information. You should also see if the individual is listed on social networking sites like LinkedIn, MySpace, or Facebook.

Then take a deep breath and pick up the phone. Telephone calls are your best way to confirm the proper contact people and, if possible, to clarify the nature of any jobs available. Keep updating your list, and maintain clear records of your contacts. Know whom you've talked to, when you talked to them, and what you talked to them about. Follow-up is critical, so you must always know the status of your interactions with those on your hit list.

QUESTION?

What is a job-search advocate?
Job-search advocates are those people who actively support your efforts to find your ideal job. They offer ongoing advice and regularly refer you to postings and, when possible, to prospective employers. Advocates are most often nurtured, not just found. Some people call them career mentors. Often, they are simply regular people in your life who are well connected to the career, industry, or company you seek. Tap into your resources!

Talking to people is the best way to gather, analyze, and prioritize information regarding employment options and referrals. Initiate the networking process with a call or an e-mail. When you e-mail, introduce yourself and state that you will soon follow up with a call. Always be courteous and clear about why you're getting in touch. You can ask for specific referrals or informal information dialogues. Conversations like these are a good way to learn about the careers of people in your chosen industry and to solicit their help in your job search. These contacts can act as advocates within their organizations, offering direct referrals and providing recommendations. They can also introduce you to associates in other companies, thus increasing the scope and power of your network.

Building Your Network

The purpose of networking is twofold. First, you want to know as much about your chosen field as possible. You network with as many people as you can in that field to get all of their input and points of view. Second, you want to become known in your chosen field. The more people you meet, the more your name and your qualifications become known. Networking is a powerful component of any successful job search.

Professional groups and online resources like field-focused Web sites or mailing lists are good ways to begin networking. Go slowly. Instead of introducing yourself right away as a job seeker, ask for a business card. Then, in follow-up communications, you can identify your career goals and ask for guidance. Once the person has responded to your request, share your resume as an effective way of presenting your goals and qualifications.

Today's job seeker should also explore social networking Web sites. Some popular ones at the moment include LinkedIn, Facebook, and MySpace, particularly with Gen X and Gen Y candidates. These sites allow you to create a personal profile and to opt in to one or more of the many networking groups on their sites, some relating to shared pursuits such as schools attended, employment/industry, or personal interests. By doing so, you are able to communicate with members, read public profiles (or blogs), view photos, and meet people you might never have come into contact with previously. Your contacts might be able to assist you in your quest for your ideal employment. Additional information about social networking sites will be discussed in Chapter 5.

End each networking conversation by getting guidance on what you should do next, whom you should contact, and, of course, with a resounding,

"Thank you!" Keep communications current by dropping a line every now and then to keep your contact informed of your progress.

Successful job seekers often cite networking as one of the most important factors in their success. Most polls of experienced job candidates rank networking as a top tool. Even in this Internet age, person-to-person networking is still important, yet few people do it effectively.

Finding Job Postings and Advertisements

Many people fool themselves into thinking they are conducting a comprehensive job search just because their resumes are uploaded onto a few of the big-name job boards. It's true that Web-based job postings are part of an effective job-search strategy. But answering these ads is a reactive effort—that is, a reaction, rather than an action—and that's just part of a comprehensive campaign. An effective job search must also include proactive strategies, including networking. In later chapters, you will learn some effective proactive strategies. You will also be directed to some excellent Web sites as well as more traditional resources.

Comprehensive job-search campaigns include proactive as well as reactive strategies and resources. No matter how proactive you are, you should still be prepared to maximize your reactive efforts. Newspaper classified ads can't be discounted as a good source of information about potential jobs. And don't forget about postings printed in general and subject-specific periodicals or niche Web sites. Professional newsletters and journals are also too often ignored.

Get Your Resume into the Marketplace

Your goal is to inform as many people as possible about your goals. Keep the flow of communications persistent, but make sure they're appropriate, too. Here are some communication tips for strengthening your network and approaching others effectively:

- Don't ever wait to communicate! First, call to confirm your contact person. When possible, request detailed information regarding available positions and posting methods.
- If you are told not to contact someone directly, respect this request.
- Submit documentation as instructed, confident that it will be processed and forwarded appropriately.
- After making the initial call, submit your resume. Attach a resume to your initial correspondence as well as any future follow-up e-mails, faxed notes, or printed correspondence.

Don't worry about how your initial inquiries are interpreted; it's okay to ask for basic information. In fact, if you fail to take those courageous first steps, you will be unlikely to succeed at all. Typical first contacts might sound like the following.

"Hello. I would like to speak with the person in charge of hiring for your firm. Could you provide me with his/her name and title, then forward me to him/her? Thank you."

"Hello. My name is Chris Smith. I am interested in a position with your firm. I would like to submit my resume. What is the most convenient method, and to whom should I address my inquiry?"

Be prepared for the employer to tell you to apply online or to review the firm's current openings on their Web page. If you have seen a posting that interests you, you might ask if it has been filled, or if you can submit your resume to a manager directly, rather than generically applying online or to an anonymous e-mail address.

The best way to view your job search is to think of it as a communication process. You initiate the communication reactively when you answer postings; you are proactive when you contact the people on your target list. Don't hesitate to communicate, and be polite and respectful when doing so.

Use the Web as a navigational tool to identify employment opportunities. According to the National Association of Colleges and Employers (NACE), 90 percent of employers prefer to receive electronic resumes via e-mail or on their company homepage instead of print versions through the mail.

Follow Up, Follow Up, Follow Up

There is always an appropriate way to follow up. E-mail has become the most widely acceptable format. It's usually easier to be clear in writing, and you can send your message after hours, when you have time to clearly pose questions or convey your appreciation. You can also e-mail a thank-you note, but don't fax one. However, a hand-written mailed note shows a personal touch and attention to detail. Continue to build your relationships with prospective employers, and reinforce your existing networking relationships via a well-crafted series of e-mails or phone calls.

Enthusiastic and upbeat questions and comments are obviously much more effective than impatient and demanding inquiries. Be sensitive and creative in your follow-up communications. Be persistent, but don't pester.

It's sometimes difficult to pick up the phone or compose yet another friendly follow-up e-mail. But remember that each follow-up effort increases your chances of reaching your goal and getting that job. Regularly assess the effectiveness of your follow-up efforts (did your follow-up lead to another conversation? a return letter? an interview?) and refocus if you need to.

Be polite and persistent. Always call to confirm whether materials were received. This gives you a chance to ask your contact what will happen next and when you should take your next step. You can ask whether you should communicate again within a designated time period. If the answer is, "Be patient," don't make a pest of yourself by calling back anyway. However, others in your network—particularly your job-search advocates—can support you with calls or e-mails to a potential employer.

It is your responsibility to communicate effectively during your job search. Don't expect prospective employers to follow up with you, and don't expect your resume to get you in the door all on its own. Your resume is a crucial part of your job search, but it is the personal follow-up that fuels a job seeker's success.

"Phone-a-phobia" can be fatal. E-mail may be state of the art, but the telephone is still a powerful communication tool. In fact, it's essential to your job search. Decide what you will say before you call. Your call can offer you a distinct advantage over your competition since many job seekers never think to go beyond hitting the send button.

The Interview

Chapter 8 provides detailed preparation for interviews, with specific questions and answers. The first and most basic thing to remember about interviewing is to project confidence, whether the interview is in person or over the phone. To be confident, you need to be prepared.

Your resume is the focal point and foundation for interview preparation. Be confident in the abilities you describe in your resume and in your qualifications to perform the job. It is best to know as much as possible about the interview situation.

In preparing for your interview, don't memorize answers to typical questions, and don't practice too much or else your responses might sound false or canned. Role-playing is a good way to become familiar with topics and build confidence, while still improvising as you go. Use your resume as a checklist, but be prepared to talk about other topics and concepts.

Offers and Acceptance

You are going to get a job offer, and you will need the skills to analyze and appropriately respond to it. Remain focused. Comparative salary data is available online and in books.

Here's where your network comes in really handy; ask around to see what kind of offer you should expect and how to negotiate, if necessary. Try to get a sense of salary range for the position you seek and determine if your target number falls within that range. Once you accept an offer, stop your job search. Period. Do not take another offer and renege on the first one.

If you need to know about the validity of an offer, conduct your research before you accept. If you are wavering between two companies and have an offer from one but not the other, you can always try to leverage the opportunity to your advantage. With an offer in hand, it is much easier to call other prospective employers and talk about your chances of their offering you a position to determine if an offer might be forthcoming. Don't hesitate to make those calls if you think their input might help you make a good decision.

Psychological Barriers

For some, the idea of updating or creating a resume generates a counterproductive attitude. These negative beliefs include the following:

- I can't create a resume if I don't have anything to offer.
- Even the sample resumes look better than mine.
- I haven't done much, so I shouldn't update my resume.
- If I don't have an ideal job in mind, I can't create or update my resume.
- I don't know what employers want to see, so I can't start or finish my resume.
- I've heard they don't really read resumes, so why bother.
- It's not really the right time to look for a job, so I don't have to create or update my resume.

Resumes Created in a Day

The search for the perfect resume and the ideal time to create or update one may last forever for those suffering from self-doubt and lack of focus. You know you need a resume to start and complete your job search. In fact, you should have a current resume whether or not you are currently seeking new employment because you never know when you might be approached or recruited by an employer who desires your skills and experience. Ironically, if you delay your resume writing and subsequent job search, you also delay the ultimate positive reinforcement that comes with interviews and, yes, offers.

Some Excuses

The reasons and excuses for avoiding creating and updating a resume are too numerous to name. The following examples show how futile and pointless these excuses are in the face of such an important need, the need for a powerful resume.

- I can't find my old version, and I don't have time to create a new one.
- I don't have enough money to pay for one of those professional resume developers, so I'll wait.
- I can't seem to get it to one page, so it's hopeless.
- I missed the deadline for that job posting, so I have some time before I need to finish my resume.
- I don't know what employers want to see, so I can't start or finish my resume.

Creating a resume is frustrating work, and it is easy to procrastinate. At this early stage, though, you have already begun the journey toward updating or creating a powerful resume. You will soon have travel papers in hand for the voyage that will end with meaningful employment.

Easy Steps to Get You Started

Even people who think of the job search as difficult and fraught with anxiety must agree that it ends with success! You will attain your goals! It all begins with a few easy steps. Chapter 2 describes the seven steps to a successful resume, which are illustrated throughout this book (especially in the sample resumes). Here's how you get your start:

1. Review some samples, including your old resumes and the examples in this book. Pay particular attention to those related to your goals.
2. Pick the approach that you want to model. Imitation is more than flattery. It is the best strategy in writing your resume.
3. Determine the format, content, and order of your resume. Will you use headlines? What entries will be presented within these categories? In what order will these sections appear?

FACT

Most experts agree that a job search takes at least three months. Be surprised if it takes only a few weeks, and remain determined and upbeat if it takes longer than the estimated three months. Everything starts with the proper attitude. Eventually, all true job searches end with success.

Next, if you have not already done so, identify your objectives and target audiences. What is your job-search target? This is not necessarily the same as your career goal. Can you clearly and concisely articulate your goals? If not, don't fret. Chapter 4 will take you through this step with minimal pain.

Once you've defined your goals, you can really create a resume in just one day. Put your goals on paper, then list your relevant qualifications and achievements. Examine your general qualifications, and present your specific competencies and capabilities in terms of their importance. Once you have a draft together, read it over with an eye to the person (you) it represents. Your aim is to present yourself as qualified, knowledgeable, and self-confident. By following these steps, you can create a resume in just one day. Why not make it today?

Your Job-Search Foundation

Resume writing happens through a series of cognitive and behavioral steps. These steps also form a foundation for your effective job-search campaign. Each of the eight steps toward job-search success (the steps outlined earlier in this chapter) depends on a powerful, goal-oriented resume. The only way to write a focused, targeted resume is to set and articulate your goals. For many people, goal articulation is the missing link in their resume writing and job search. Those seeking anything, anywhere often find nothing, nowhere.

With focus, you will create or update goal-directed resumes—you can have more than one targeted resume, each reflecting a different goal. These are your tools for initial contact, follow-up, interview prep, and interviews themselves.

When you call first, then fax or e-mail, and, finally, mail your resumes to potential employers, you begin a communication process that includes your resume at every step. As you follow up and assess your strategy, you refocus your job-search efforts. This includes updating your resume. Ultimately, when your efforts yield an interview, your resume will be your preparation tool. Throughout the process, your resume is your key communication device. It presents your past performance and your future potential; it is the reference point for potential employers to use in selecting you as a worthy job candidate.

Here's a confidence-building exercise. Take out a piece of paper or open a new file on your computer. At the top of the page, write your name, address, telephone number, and e-mail address. You've just started your resume.

After you ace the interview—using your resume as a powerful tool— and accept an offer, update your resume right away. No, you don't have to begin your next job search so soon, but entering your new position on your resume makes a bold, confident statement.

Chapter 2

Writing Your Resume

During the years that the "resumes any way" attitude prevailed, authors echoed the belief that there is no one perfect resume. This mentality made it difficult for resume writers to find the focus necessary to present themselves successfully on paper. The focus of this chapter is on creating resumes your way, following a methodical approach to creating successful resumes.

The Seven Key Steps to Writing a Resume

Gaining focus and creating a strong, content-rich resume is easy when you follow these seven simple steps:

1. Review as many resume samples as you can. Look over old versions of your own resume, and ask friends and associates if they'd mind letting you take a look at theirs. This book includes many samples of many different resumes, designed for many different fields. You can also find a wide range of resume samples on the Web.

2. Analyze those resumes. Think about what makes them work (or not work). Effective elements might include things like format, content, typeface, and the order of information.

3. Identify your job objectives and your target audience. This doesn't mean you need to include a career objective on your resume. It does mean that you need an understanding of the field you plan to pursue. Be sure you know the proper terminology, the job functions that will make you valuable, and how to present yourself as a viable candidate.

4. Perform an inventory of your qualifications and achievements. Knowing yourself and being confident in your abilities is key to creating a powerful resume.

5. Analyze your competencies and capabilities as they relate to your job goals and your chosen field. This is another aspect of the "know yourself" mantra. How do you see yourself contributing to this field? Remember your unique value proposition and identify what makes you the most desirable candidate for the job you seek.

6. Draft your resume and critique it. Compare your draft to the samples you've analyzed and admired. How does it compare in terms of format, content, and order of information? Fix those elements you see that can be stronger. Proofread it carefully, and after you're sure it's perfect, ask a friend to look it over.

7. Make plenty of copies, and distribute your resume whenever appropriate. Try sending it by e-mail to several friends. See if any of them have trouble opening up the document or if your layout or fonts become altered.

The Resume Your Way

If there is no perfect resume, how can you hope to create a document that all employers would want to see? The answer comes from a change in emphasis. Stop thinking about resumes any way, designed to present yourself as you think an employer would want to see you. Start writing resumes your way.

A good resume presents your past achievements as well as the assets and capabilities that qualify you for this new job. As you get better at communicating your qualifications, you will approach the job of writing your resume with confidence. The seven steps to success are good guidelines, and they should inspire confidence. But before you start writing, it is also a good idea to understand the different types of resumes and the purposes they serve. The following sections describe some traditional types and formats of resumes.

Chronological, Functional, and Combined Resumes

Chronological resumes present information in reverse chronological order, starting with the present and working backward. Students and recent graduates usually list education first, and all other job seekers list experience first. They traditionally use one-word headers to identify content sections. As you've read and heard again and again, they are usually no longer than one or two pages in length.

Functional resumes present candidate skill sets and discussions independent from job descriptions, if those descriptions are included at all. In this resume type, skill listings come before all other content. Such summaries tend to be lengthy, presented with hope that some broadly chosen phrases might stick in the minds of readers and encourage interviews. In this model, it's employers, not the job seekers, who define the job being sought. Most resume guides recommend functional formats for career changers or for those who are keeping their options open, while the chronological format is usually recommended for all others.

Combined resumes contain skill or qualification profiles, like the functional format, but they also incorporate the chronological format by presenting work history, educational background, and other content in reverse chronological order.

Be careful about using a functional resume. Almost all inquiries to prospective employers reveal that this format is ineffective and difficult to review. According to studies and polls, the pure functional resume format is the least preferred. To strengthen your functional resume, link each of your job skills to a particular position or responsibility. Tell your prospective employer where and how you used your skills.

Targeted and Customized Resumes

Recent resume guides use words like *targeted* and *customized*. Targeted resumes include either a branding statement or a clear objective and/or description of professional goals. They are aimed at a specific job opening and allow you to address your skills and qualifications in regard to the position. Like targeted resumes, customized resumes are often created for a specific job title or employer, particularly when you know the desired skills and hiring criteria. These are the most powerful resumes because they speak directly to potential employers.

Many large employers now use software programs to help them sort through the volume of resumes they receive. A targeted approach will help your resume appear in keyword searches done by recruiters or the services they employ. Post a targeted resume on job boards; recruiters often search the boards for potential job candidates.

Combinations, Permutations, and Confusion

Some guides advise you to include all the schools you attended. Some suggest you include only those schools where you were conferred a degree. Many books and articles emphatically suggest that you list courses, while as many others strongly urge you not to because your potential employers will already have a good idea of what courses someone with your major took. Some suggest you present all scholarships and honors, no matter how small, because the longer the list, the more impressive it is to potential employers. Still others encourage you to present a selected list of scholarships and honors. But when it comes to grades, everyone agrees: Only include good grades and averages!

Advice regarding experience is equally conflicted. Some say describe all jobs—no matter how small—in active terms, in hopes that some of those verbs will catch a prospective employer's eye. Others state with conviction that you should only include impressive jobs. Should you list volunteer and community service experience? Some say yes, but some say no; the same goes for personal interests. In years past, the phrase "References available upon request" indicated the standard close of the resume. Most resume professionals now omit this phrase and see it as unnecessary.

The Modern Resume Your Way

As you focus on your chosen career field and articulate your abilities, your resume writing and your job search will be inspired. A resume that projects "me and my goals" will strengthen the rest of your job search; it will also have an impact on the outcome. Keep your goals firmly in mind; they will enhance the power and purpose of your resume. Plan and implement strategic actions.

Goal setting is critical to all resume-writing and job-search efforts. Overall, goal development and articulation are the most crucial components of resume writing and your comprehensive job search.

State-of-the-Art Documents Focused on You

A resume that focuses on you makes you the central figure in the resume-writing and job-search process. You must clarify and articulate your goals on paper but also in person. If anyone asks how you created such an effective resume, you can tell them you place a high value on your career goals and have a good understanding of what will mutually benefit you and your employer.

The first sample resume (shown in **FIGURE 2-1**) is an adaptation of the "Harvard Business School Resume." For generations, this was the required

Sample Resume: Harvard Business School Format

FIGURE 2-1

CHRIS SMITH

100 Main Street, Apartment 1 • Hometown, NY 00000
csmith@company.com • H (555) 555-1234 C (555) 555-5678

education

2005–2007   HARVARD GRADUATE SCHOOL OF BUSINESS   BOSTON, MA
Candidate for Master in Business Administration degree, June 2007.
Vice President of Marketing Club. Codirector of Marketing Project. Outreach 2006
Volunteer Program. Tutor first-year students.

1997–2000   CORNELL UNIVERSITY   ITHACA, NY
Bachelor of Arts degree, double major in American Civilization and French, May 2000.
Studied international relations and political science in Paris at L'Institut d'Etudes
Politiques. Freshman Advisor. Chair, Visiting Prospective Students Program and Student/Alumni Network.

experience

Summer 2006   UNIVERSAL STUDIOS   LOS ANGELES, CA
Summer Assistant Marketing Manager, Consumer Products/Interactive Division:
Worked with Vice President of Sales and Marketing to create business vision and
branding strategy for introduction of new brand in educational interactive products
industry.
- Developed brand elements and positioning statements and contributed to brand-name generation.
- Created preliminary marketing and communications programs for brand launch and national product rollout, targeting both home and academic markets.
- Analyzed economic and consumer trends and conducted competitor analysis, resulting in entry strategy recommendation.

2002–2005   THE MAXIMUM MARKETING GROUP   NEW YORK, NY
Associate Supervisor: Directed marketing communications activities for Nikon, agency's largest account, representing 65% of annual billings at start-up firm specializing
in consumer products.
- Created strategic plan to increase brand awareness and loyalty in consumer and professional photography markets. Addressed shrinking market share and increased competition.
- Managed new product launches from concept development to market for existing and new products. Led multifunctional team responsible for product positioning, competitor analysis, media coverage, and dealer/sales education.

2000–2002   PUBLIC RELATIONS ASSOCIATES   NEW YORK, NY
Account Coordinator: Developed and implemented national media campaigns in
support of new product launches for Nikon Lite-Touch, Reebok Pump, and Step Reebok aerobic workout program.

personal   Fluent in French. Active Cornell alumni interviewer and volunteer for youth hockey
program.

format for graduates of this prestigious school, and it illustrates a frequently copied and generally effective resume.

The Harvard Business School format was generally considered appropriate for investment banking and consulting positions. However, no single resume format is specifically required by any particular field. The samples presented in this book are aimed at many popular fields. It's up to you, the job seeker, to establish your targets and create or update the formats you deem appropriate.

This format is a multipurpose chronological resume. Note the use of one-word headers and the condensed presentation of educational information. Work experience is first described in general terms, and specific achievements are then highlighted using bullets. The format efficiently uses space and highlighting techniques, including capitalization, bold, and italics. In some ways, this resume is still employer oriented, presented to meet the (unknown) expectations of the potential employer. This is a solid example of this type of resume, but it's not quite evolved to the approach suggested in this book. Samples shown later in this book illustrate techniques for building a stronger resume, including the following:

- Headlines or objective statements that clearly project focus. Well-crafted headlines advertise the nature of your content and reinforce your stated job goal or career focus.
- A comprehensive summary of qualifications section, including appropriate terminology and field-focused verbs and nouns, which projects a knowledge of self as well as a knowledge of the field (and is critical for keyword searches).
- Information is presented to highlight the most important information first rather than chronologically.
- Relevant courses, academic accomplishments, and other pertinent activities are listed briefly.
- Descriptions of work experience appear under headlines in order of significance. They project your capabilities and industry knowledge, as well as your accomplishments.
- Left-justified and text block formats are easy to e-mail and to upload into PDF-based resume banks and job board sites.

When you're reviewing these resume samples, examine those that match your field(s) of interest, but don't limit yourself. Review all the samples, and pick out the formats and contents you'd like to model. Be analytical and curious. Your background may be different from the fictional Chris Smith, whose qualifications are presented over and over, but you and Chris are not in competition. Avoid focusing your resume on the faceless employers who will be reading it. Project your knowledge of field and functional goals. Focus on you, because when you do get the interview, the hiring manager will use your resume to establish a dialogue. Your resume must say everything important to help you get the offer.

FIGURE 2-1 shows an effective resume for a soon-to-be business school graduate. If it inspired you to think about what your resume should look like, this book has already been effective. Remember that the first two steps in resume writing involve review and analysis of samples.

The best resumes have common components. They use headlines rather than headers. They include qualifications summaries, lists of courses and projects, and highlights of specific accomplishments. The best resumes use field-focused terminology and present information in order of importance.

The College Graduation Benchmark

The people who most need resume guidance are those who have little or no experience preparing a resume. Many of those who find themselves in the market for their first "real" job belong in the college grad category, which includes the following:

- First- and second-semester college seniors
- Recent graduates
- College juniors, seniors, and others seeking internships

Campus career centers offer counseling and job-search coaching, and seniors are the most likely to take advantage of these services. First-semester seniors spend a lot of time on resumes for on-campus recruiting, career fairs, and other job-placement offerings. On-campus counseling usually produces resumes focused on what the recruiter expects, rather than the candidate's qualifications and focus. In their urgency to create and update their resumes, first-semester seniors often overlook the assessment and research steps that lead to goal setting. Fear of focus often motivates them to avoid these critical steps to college resume-writing success.

New job candidates usually hope that a large quantity of data will overcome any issues of quality. Anxious about what recruiters want to see and hoping that something in their arsenal will get them interviews, they include everything. Myths about recruiters seeking well-rounded individuals inspire this kind of unfocused volume. Ironically, candidates are actually screened with narrow, rather than diverse, criteria. Reviewers of college resumes are mostly on the lookout for field-focused majors, high grade-point averages, and pertinent internships.

FACT

An Internet poll of more than 500 top entry-level employers revealed that hiring employers ranked a student's major as most important (42.8 percent), followed by interviewing skills (25 percent), and internship experience (15.9 percent).

Second-semester seniors are either inspired by reactions of recruiters during the fall, or they become anxious and pessimistic because few recruiters responded favorably to their resumes. Those with goals matching the fields and functions that recruiters are looking for often use the same resume and reactive strategies through the spring semester and beyond. Those whose goals do not match recruiters' needs, and those who cannot express their goals, get very anxious around commencement time. This anxiety often inspires unfocused, multipurpose resumes or leads to procrastination that lingers well past commencement day.

Approximately 30–50 percent of college graduates keep looking for a job after commencement. About 15–25 percent did not set goals or start their job search before graduation. For these candidates, like anyone else looking for a new job, it's important to work through the seven steps to resume success. The assessment and research steps are particularly effective for gaining and projecting focus. This is critical; a complete, effective job search mirrors the candidate's knowledge of qualifications and field-specific competencies.

FACT

College graduates are commonly confused by misunderstood job-related data and statistics. Many feel that the top students take all the good jobs, with nothing left by commencement. In reality, recruiting seasons are on-campus anomalies. In the real world, the job search goes on well after June. Many, many candidates get their jobs three to six months after they graduate.

Here are a few common questions among recent or soon-to-be graduates:

▶ **How do I make my resume stand out?** Flawless spelling, punctuation, and sentence structure. Use an appealing visual format. Emphasize professionalism. Write strong content that plays up work experience while in school, internships, coursework, and extracurricular activities, as well as any honors.

▶ **What if I don't have related experience or education?** Emphasize the contributions and skills you can make or possess that are universal to all employers, and focus on transferable skills such as coordinating events, customer service, computer skills, or budget planning. Find the common thread between what you've done and what you want to do. Talk to a professor or mentor to see if they can help you bridge any relevancy gaps based on their knowledge of the workplace.

▶ **Should I include education or experiences from high school?** If you are an entry-level grad, it is permissible to do so if you were a stellar student who received awards or scholarships or held officer titles in school clubs or community groups. Otherwise, focus on college experiences.

▶ **When and how do I present my most significant work experience?** Lead it off directly under the "Employment" heading, but recent grads need to list education first. Use descriptive keywords that illustrate actions taken and any important on-the-job achievements.

▶ **If I had one very relevant course and project, how do I highlight both, or either?** It can be set off under "Education" as "Thesis" or "Case Study." Treat it like a work experience.

▶ **If I haven't been successful getting an interview, should I change my resume?** Probably—or maybe your methodology. Ask for some critical feedback from any senior-level business professionals you know. See if anything strikes them as problematic. Compare your resume to others you can view on the Web. Assess whether you are being proactive enough in your approach or are just being a passive job seeker, waiting to be called.

▶ **My GPA in my major is higher than my cumulative average. Should I include it?** Include a GPA in your major or overall GPA only if it is 3.5 or above. Otherwise, leave it for discussion at the interview should it come up.

More than any other kind of job candidate, if you are a soon-to-be or recent graduate, you must work hard on identifying and articulating your goals. Identify and analyze what you learned in the classroom and beyond. Pick out your most significant courses, labs, and projects, and present those in terms of their potential for making you valuable and effective on the job. Focus your resume and your search for a job or internship on your academic achievements, but don't forget to analyze what you've learned in terms of your personal exploration and your choice of a career field.

Intern Candidates

About 75 percent of college students use resumes in their search for an internship. Internships are difficult to define. In general, an internship is more sophisticated than a summer job. There are both paid and unpaid positions.

Some internships offer academic credit, while others are more project-focused, offering the opportunity to build skills and explore a field of interest. Some internships are promoted through large, well-publicized, and structured programs, and others are identified through networking and self-initiated efforts. Internships are growing in importance. Students in search of an internship should use their resumes to project their curiosity, competence, and awareness of the field.

As college students become more sophisticated about their career aspirations, internships have grown in importance and popularity. A 2007 poll by MonsterTrak showed that 78 percent of college students plan to complete one or more internships before interviewing for their first job.

Just like any other job candidate, those seeking internships must project focus, since competition is high. You're probably looking for an internship to get a deeper knowledge of your field of interest, but—in an ironic twist—you need to project focus and some familiarity with the field before you can get that internship. Do that on your resume!

First Jobs

Many college grads do not get their dream jobs right away, nor do they usually start out on a clearly defined career path. Often, these young men and women lack the focus to begin their true career development or to implement a goal-directed job search. So, naturally, they find transition positions.

These positions include a variety of experiences. Some people plan to enter graduate school, so they seek something meaningful to do. The jobs can be for experience or adventures, such as the Peace Corps, Americorps, Teach for America, or a job teaching English in another country. The job might also be something practical, such as a retail sales job, just for a paycheck. Still others might be in positions unrelated to their majors, but are with a well-known employer and offer name recognition and prestige.

No matter what the position is, the resume must support and inspire a first step onto a true career path. In these cases, it is best to avoid the reverse-chronological format, as experience is still limited and the format will make it difficult to project any sense of goal or focus. It's most important to present your potential and identify your goals for the future.

Here are some common questions that new job seekers generally ask:

▶ **If what I am doing now has nothing to do with my goals, how and where do I present my experience?** Spend some time on self-assessment. Find some commonality between your goals and current or past experience. If there is no connection, employers will not view you as qualified for their opening. Consider taking additional coursework with your goals in mind. Or, take a step back and go for a lower-level job in the area of your goal to gain some credible work history.

▶ **What about education; specifically, my major?** Build this up as it applies to your job target. Show how your education and recent training will be advantageous to the new employer.

▶ **Do I highlight what I have been doing for the past few years?** Yes—but focus on specific responsibilities that are similar in scope or typical of what you will be doing in your new job. What can you bring to this position that others cannot?

▶ **Where and how do I present my most recent experiences?** Any job candidate except a recent college graduate should place work experience above education, near the top of the resume and/or a qualification summary. Follow the examples in this book on formatting and presentation.

▶ **If I wasn't given enough responsibilities to yield achievements, how do I leverage my current job?** Surely, something you did makes you proud—what is it? Did you streamline a process? Did you generate more reports than your predecessor? Did you volunteer for any committees? If you think you haven't had any notable achievements, you need to re-examine your work and the challenges you've faced. Almost all employment experiences can be positioned to showcase the job seeker in some way. Additionally, consider your present employer's reputation. A position with negligible responsibilities at a company that is a household name may generate interest simply because of the kind of environment or leadership interaction you faced on a daily basis.

Candidates seeking their first jobs must focus their resumes, job-search correspondence, and interviews on the qualifications they already have and those they will need to succeed in the future. Resumes must target the newly identified goals. Your objective must be presented clearly and supported with powerful summaries of your qualifications.

Focus here is critical. You must use the resume writing process to identify and articulate your goals. Working through the first five of the seven steps will help. You must abandon the attitude of leaving your options open if you're going to focus on future goals.

Beyond Entry Level

Some people take their first steps (or giant leaps) on their career paths right after they graduate. Two or three years later, they're ready for more responsibility. Job advice from career centers is easy to come by for college seniors, but sound guidance is much less accessible later on. Entry-level workers, those with two to five years of experience, can become confused and anxious; as with anyone, fear of change plus fear of focus yields procrastination and anxiety.

Some recent graduates seek change in a subconscious effort to recapture their college experience. In college, you got to choose your courses. Your life changed from semester to semester, always offering something new. As a new member of the work force, either seeking promotion or a new position, you must decide what is driving you. Do you miss the cyclical changes of academic life or are you motivated by ambition and the need to develop your career?

Steps four and five of the resume-writing process encourage you to analyze your accomplishments so far and to assess your capabilities. This proactive approach is positive. It motivates you to present your experience dynamically, in terms of what you've accomplished. As you consider your past achievements, your performance potential for the future becomes clearer.

Resumes for All

Whether you're called an hourly worker, nonexempt personnel, or—more traditionally—a blue-collar laborer, you may be working in an administrative, food-service, customer-service, or manufacturing position. People in these fields often do not create or update resumes that reflect their potential for continued success. Too often, when it's time to look for a new job, they depend upon applications, references, or word of mouth. Everyone needs and deserves a powerful resume. Word of mouth can be translated into words on paper, creating an effective resume that mirrors capabilities and projects a clear future focus.

People at the other end of the professional spectrum are also often guilty of overlooking their resumes. In most cases, those we call senior management have old, vague resumes or no resume at all. Though they're responsible for large operations and organizations and generally supervise many others, these people may not be as ready for the job search as they should be. However, with our culture focusing more and more on career advancement and reinvention of self, many senior leadership professionals are taking the time to keep their resumes current in anticipation of being recruited or finding new ways to use their talents and enjoy meaningful job satisfaction.

Anyone, on any rung of the job-success ladder, should use the resume-writing process to identify and articulate their goals. No matter how diverse your interests or background, creating a powerful resume will enhance your focus and effectively project your qualifications and commitment for your future performance.

Resumes Between Generations

As baby boomers age and Gen X and Gen Y advance within the workplace, it is important that the generations understand each other's skills and strengths as denoted by their resumes. The younger millennials tend to like electronic resumes, and some do not even possess paper versions. On the other hand, baby boomers may feel more comfortable with printed resumes, and might be reluctant to post their resumes online or unsure how to format their resumes for readability by computer users. Each generation must be sure that their resume can be understood and appreciated by the other, even though the mindsets of each group might differ.

FACT

According to the U.S. Bureau of Labor Statistics, more than 25 percent of the working population will reach retirement age by 2010, resulting in a potential shortage of nearly 10 million workers. The number of people who are over age fifty-five will increase by 73 percent by 2020, while the number of younger workers will grow only by 5 percent. This means it will be a candidate's market, with employers competing hard for talent.

Baby boomers must be sure that their resumes don't date them unnecessarily or to their detriment. They can't keep adding to a resume that was originally written twenty years ago. If you're guilty of this, it's time for a rewrite. Go online and review newer job descriptions, even for some of your old titles.

Update your terminology. Industry speak is critical for keyword searches and to demonstrate you have kept pace with your field. Remove the "References On Request" close—that's old school. Have you included jobs that have no bearing on your current position or the one you desire? Go back only as far as your current employment objectives, and use the rule of relevancy to determine which jobs to highlight.

If you've been with one employer for many years, separate your tenure by positions and changes in responsibility. Remember, one resume doesn't fit all. It may be necessary for you to have two or three different versions, each with a different focus. Maintain several formats to accommodate different users: a standard Microsoft Word-formatted resume, a PDF version for downloading, and a plain text version to paste into an e-mail message.

Gen Xers and Gen Yers tend to hold more jobs with more employers than baby boomers. You might need to communicate the reason behind your multiple moves to the baby boomer hiring manager, who could perceive your job hopping as restlessness rather than growth. Millennials, who use text messaging and casual e-mails as a way of life, need to remember to be more formal in their approach to prospective employers by watching their use of abbreviations. Not everyone knows Web speak such as PTMM for "please tell me more" or NRN for "no reply necessary."

The Video Resume

The latest trend in the employment marketplace is the video resume. These presentations waver between homemade versions from job seekers equipped with Web cams and movie-making software to versions that are professionally produced by videographers, executive search firms, or special video resume services. While the popularity of such resumes is growing, they remain uncharted territory for most job hunters and employers, many of whom are wary of the potential discrimination based on race, age, or other factors that would not be obvious from a more traditional resume.

You can view a variety of video resumes online by doing a simple search. You will also find sources for these productions in Appendix B. Be sure to view several samples before creating your own so that you have a good idea of what works and what doesn't and whether this format is a good fit for you. Many of them seem a little bit like infomercials, but it is usually the individual's overall appearance and comfort level speaking on camera that give some candidates leverage in their job hunt.

FACT

Eighty-nine percent of employers said they would watch a video resume if it were submitted to them, with the primary reason being to better assess a candidate's professional presentation and demeanor. Only 17 percent admitted to actually having viewed this kind of job search technology.

No doubt the usage of video resumes will continue to grow as technology permeates all facets of our workplaces, but just like the traditional resume, you may want to have several versions depending on your target audience. What can you convey in video that would not be possible in print? Are you truly making yourself a more desirable candidate on screen or will your credentials be better represented in a traditional format? Be careful not to get caught up in a trend that isn't advantageous to your personality or skill set. You don't want your video resume to seem like a bad TV audition. However, if you are comfortable on camera, speak well, and have good stage presence, a video resume may give you a leg up on the competition.

Tips for preparing an effective video resume:

- Dress as though you were going to the interview
- Talk into the camera; make good eye contact
- Smile and speak clearly, without pauses, and not too fast
- Introduce yourself by your first and last name
- Outline your skills, experience, education, and what you can contribute
- Eliminate background noises or other distractions
- Keep it short—two to three minutes maximum
- Conclude with a thank you and your contact information

Some of the major job boards and specialty sites now have sections for you to upload your video. You can also create your own page and link to your video resume. Have others screen it to get their opinion. If the reaction is favorable, include a link for viewing on your e-resume.

The Vitae Alternative

For professors, physicians, and scientists, resumes are not enough to present accomplishments and experiences. Vitae, or curriculum vitae, are comprehensive documentations of academic and employment performance. Still, it isn't a bad idea for these professionals to prepare a powerful resume that encapsulates their goals and abilities on a single page.

ALERT!

Don't be confused or delay your response if someone asks for a vita. Unless you are seeking positions outside the United States or within special fields, respond to requests with your resume. If applying overseas, create a vita by adding information including date of birth, sex, height and weight, marital status, and all educational experiences, including high school.

Even though vitae are usually lengthy documents listing publication citations, research projects, presentations, affiliations, and educational and training experiences, they don't have to be passive collections of data. The same qualities that make for a powerful resume—self-knowledge, goal focus, and clear statement of objectives—also apply to a quality vita.

Chapter 3

Seven Steps to Resume-Writing Success

Just like those popular home-repair shows that teach you to follow well-conceived plans to minimize costs, eliminate errors, and maximize outcomes, this chapter provides you with the blueprint for a great resume. It details do-it-yourself steps, identifies quick fixes, and addresses issues for job seekers who might need special tools.

The Process

Resume writing is not as difficult as many believe. Creating your resume is an opportunity to identify the positive things about very important aspects of your life. The process can be simplified to seven easy steps (those outlined in Chapter 2) that you can use to update or create resumes in just a day. Here are the steps again, in brief:

- Review samples.
- Determine format, content, and order of information.
- Identify objectives and target your audience.
- Inventory your qualifications and achievements.
- Analyze your competencies and capabilities.
- Draft and critique your resume.
- Duplicate it, post it, and distribute it.

Chapter 2 also outlined which steps are most important for certain job seekers. Pay particular attention to those steps, but don't ignore any of the steps.

Reviewing Samples

Break out the pens, highlighters, and sticky notes and start examining the samples that appear throughout this book. Analyze them like the knowledgeable and focused job seeker you are. Instead of thinking critically, identify the qualities you like.

Prospective employers look for certain things as they review resumes. (You can read some of their comments in Chapter 10.) The first thing employers and recruiters do when they want to fill a position is to list the qualifications the job requires. They list these traits in order of priority, according to which are essential, which are optimal, and which are merely desirable (or optional).

Once the employer decides on the qualities he or she is looking for—such as capabilities, areas of expertise, character qualities, employment history, and educational background—candidates are encouraged to apply, screened, and, ultimately, interviewed and selected. Sometimes job descriptions and postings include detailed qualification criteria. More often, however, these preferences are expressed vaguely in broad descriptions.

FACT

It is helpful to understand the employer's perspective, and it is a good idea to review other resumes. Just remember, this is your resume. You, and not anyone else, are responsible for success.

No matter how inaccurately they express their defined criteria, employers are always aware of them. Employers review resumes and cover letters, conduct interviews, and make their offers with those qualification criteria clearly in mind. In particular, they use written profiles of their desired qualifications for keyword scanning (described in Chapter 5) and behavioral interviews (Chapter 8).

While the job seeker might wish otherwise, employers almost never share detailed qualification criteria, nor do they thoroughly analyze the resumes they receive. The employer is not responsible for digging through a mass of poorly organized, badly written resumes to find the perfect job candidate. As the job seeker, you are responsible for conveying your goals, objectives, and a clear sense of job purpose. You must create a powerful resume that mirrors your qualifications and follow that up with an interview that impresses the employers with your capability to perform the job.

Format, Content, and Order of Information

Pick out your two or three favorite sample resumes. Examine them from top to bottom. Here are some basic questions to consider:

- What first impression does the resume generate? How is it formatted?
- What appears first on the page?
- How does the resume identify the candidate? Does it include a street address, an e-mail address, and a phone number?

- Does the resume include a brief yet effective objective and a qualification summary?
- Does the resume present educational information before or after a qualification summary? Before or after experience? How will you present this information?
- How does the resume order information about the candidate's work history, qualifications, and objectives?
- Does the resume use as few lines as possible, reserving most of the page for critical content?
- Does the resume use columns, with dates on the left and descriptions on the right, or a block format?
- Are headlines centered or left justified?
- Does relevant information appear under clearly phrased and focused headlines?

ESSENTIAL

You may have been told that it was bad to write in books, but in this book you should write your response to the sample resumes as you review them. Anyone's first response to a resume is often purely visual; therefore, as you read, note the ways in which you can give your resume a greater visual impact.

Look at the answers to these questions, and let them guide your resume writing. The resumes you selected jumped out at you for a reason, and you can use the aspects you like to form your own resume.

Formatting Basics

The font you choose is the key to a well-formatted resume. Fonts should be traditional, easy to read, and common. You don't want to create a beautiful resume in some obscure font that will be replaced on your reviewer's computer by an automatic bad font substitution (probably destroying all your careful line spacing and other formatting work as well).

The Best Fonts and Point Sizes for Resumes

Bookman Antiqua, 9-Point

Bookman Antiqua, 10-Point

Bookman Antiqua, 11-Point

Century Schoolbook, 9-Point

Century Schoolbook, 10-Point

Century Schoolbook, 11-Point

Garamond, 10-Point

Garamond, 11-Point

Palatino, 8-Point

Palatino, 9-Point

Palatino, 10-Point

Times, 9-Point

Times, 10-Point

Times New Roman, 9-Point

Times New Roman, 10-Point

Times New Roman, 11-Point

For headlines, increase the font size two points at a time until the headline is emphasized but not disproportionate. You can highlight important elements with CAPITALIZATION, **boldface,** and *italics,* as well as with indentations, line spacing, and bullet points. At one time, e-mailed resumes had to be formatted so they could be easily scanned. Today, PDF is more common. PDF, or portable document format, is a file format that anyone can read using special viewing software (free from software maker Adobe).

Most current word-processing systems let you save documents directly as PDFs. Your software should explain how you can do this. The beauty of PDFs is that they allow you to use more creative formatting, such as graphics. Just keep in mind that a cluttered page will confuse your reader; use only those elements that help you present yourself effectively.

Consistency is the key to readability and effectiveness. Resumes are rarely read very thoroughly at all. Most employers say they review each resume for less than a minute before keeping it live or filing it. You want employers to be able to pick up important information just by scanning your page. Review the samples for illustrations of effective and not-so-effective highlighting techniques.

Identify Yourself

Maybe you don't need an eye-catching logo, but you do need to begin your resume consistently. Letterhead is the best and easiest way to do this. You can design your own very simply, using the features in any word-processing program. Letterhead features your name on the first line.

Letterhead includes your full mailing address, the telephone number(s) where you can be reached during business hours, and your e-mail address. By the way, lose any cutesy or gimmicky e-mail monikers like Partyall-night@ or Muscleman@; it's hard to take such names seriously. Set yourself up with a free address at a major search engine to keep your job search correspondence easier to track. This keeps it separate from your personal e-mail or your work e-mail.

Never use a current employer's e-mail address. You don't want your prospective employer to think (or know) you aren't giving 100 percent to your job while you're working. Also, take the time to review your voice-mail messages on the phone numbers you include on your resume, both home and cell. While you're in the job market, refrain from music, clever hellos, or other weird greetings. Try not to think of this formality as stifling your personality, but rather as improving your chances for getting the interview.

The point is to make it as easy as possible for your reader to recognize you and to contact you with minimal effort. Use the same letterhead for all your job-related documents, including cover letters, thank-you notes, or submissions of reference information. This is also part of creating your personal brand, as defined in Chapter 1.

Summarize Yourself

Targeted resumes use qualification or achievement summaries to present objectives and goals. Summaries follow or even replace the statement of objectives, depending on what you learn in your self-assessment and goal research (steps four and five). Sometimes these sections come at the end, providing the resume with a solid bottom line. Chapter 4 details issues related to objectives, as well as qualification and achievement summaries.

Putting Your Experience in Order

The best resumes present the job seeker's most significant experiences first. Entries are grouped under headlines. They include undergraduate and graduate degrees, specialized training, and work history. Education can come at the top, as the first or second category, or last. Candidates with plenty of valuable on-the-job experience generally list that first, saving the bottom of the page for a summary of their education.

ALERT!

Most recent graduates put their education at the top of their resumes. Your academic achievements may be significant, but you should think about where and how you want them to appear. Don't list education first just because you think you should; you might make important work history, projects, and other achievements look less important by bumping them farther down the page.

Academic achievements and honors can be presented in a bulleted list. To figure out what belongs on this list, think about courses, papers, and projects with special relevance to this field. You might also have pertinent extracurricular or community experience. In general, these activities should follow your education and employment entries. Most good resumes do not have a personal interests section. Include yours only if you're sure it emphasizes your goals and qualifications in the field.

Finally, it is important to note that your resume does not need to end with "References available upon request." That's a given.

Identify Your Objectives and Your Audience

This critical step is too often overlooked. You *must* identify your objectives and your target audiences. What do you aim to achieve with your resume? Answer that question, and you will define your goals. You must also define, as best you can, who will read your resume. Your reviewers belong to the field. They use particular words, phrases, and other field-focused terminology when they talk about their work. By using the proper language, you project the sense that you can do the job.

Your resume should clearly state your career objectives, but not necessarily with a designated career objective line. Instead, the content of your resume should convey the career objective. Too often old-fashioned career objectives were pure fluff. They were vague or did little to enhance the job seeker's qualifications or goals. Look through the samples in this book. When a sample resume includes a career objective line it is very targeted, meaning it clearly focuses on a specific field and, within that field, on a certain job function.

Inventory Your Qualifications and Achievements

Why do so many resume-writing and job-search guides ask you to list your ten most significant achievements? The answer has to do with the power of positive thinking. With your greatest achievements in mind, you are more likely to think about—and represent—yourself as a valuable job candidate, full of potential.

It's not so easy to draft a summary of your qualifications, and don't worry if it takes some time. Start by asking yourself this question: What skills have I demonstrated in the past that will make me valuable in my chosen field in the future? Think of problems you have solved, instances of collaborative teamwork, or projects you managed with great success.

The best way to pick out your important achievements is to think in terms of the job or field you're aiming to enter. Freeform lists of random accomplishments are not as effective. You don't want to rely on your reviewer to figure out or analyze the significance of anything in your resume; it's your job to make your value clear.

Achievement summaries are the heart of any good resume. That's what makes a resume content-rich. They should be enough to convince the reviewer of your commitment, your qualifications, and your obvious value. It's important not to skimp on the time or energy you put into summarizing your past accomplishments; to a potential employer, your past has everything to do with the future.

Analyze Your Competencies and Capabilities

It may be physically impossible to look backward and forward at the same time, but the world of resume writing follows different rules. Great resumes reflect past achievements and, via qualifications summaries, look ahead to future roles and responsibilities. You are not limited to talking about what you have achieved in the past. Instead, your resume is the perfect platform to express your confidence and competence in tackling the future.

Drafting and Critiquing Your Resume

Your first draft should be inspired by the sample resumes you've reviewed and analyzed. They will probably influence your choice of content and the order of your information. Let them. Later on, you can go back and determine the best order of presentation, and omit unnecessary entries.

Resume Software

You'll find plenty of resume-building software to tempt you as you create your draft. Resist the temptation and use a basic word-processing application. Most, like Microsoft Word, come with resume templates. While attractive, these lock you into a format, and that can limit how you present yourself. Also, prospective employers have seen these templates used over and over. You might eliminate yourself from consideration just because a hiring manager dislikes a particular format. Give yourself the greatest control over your resume by starting with a blank page.

FACT

The Internet has hundreds of listings for professional resume writers. Do your best to resist! Your resume is your responsibility; nobody can present you better than you can. If you are still dissatisfied with your finished product, you may consider a professional resume writer (see Chapter 6 for guidance). Your drafts will be a good basis for your consultation with an expert.

The First Draft

As you put your first draft together, don't worry about keeping it to any particular length. If anything, it is better to start long and edit it down later. Write as spontaneously as you can. Don't rewrite as you go; that's a sure way to inhibit your creativity and there will be plenty of time for rewriting when your draft is complete.

Your finished resume should be concise. If it is still longer than one page after your best editing efforts, so be it! Employers do read two-page resumes as long as they are well organized, with the most important information on the first page. The one-page resume rules are part of the old way of job hunting.

When drafting, aim just to get the information down. Jot descriptive phrases to help you capture your thoughts quickly. You don't have to use articles (*the, an, a*), and you can leave the pronouns out. It's unnecessary to say, "I completed the survey" in a resume—"completed survey" gets the point across. Without shocking your English teacher, you can feel free to use sentence fragments.

Reviewing the Draft

Begin your critique only when you have a complete draft in hand. Some people like to see their resume on paper, and they edit with the old red pen technique. Others revise and edit onscreen. Work the way you're most comfortable, being sure that your method helps you polish your draft to perfection. Critiquing does not mean criticizing. Your revisions are meant to transform your resume into its most powerful form. Be positive. Make immediate changes as you need to, and be prepared to make future changes as your job search progresses.

Mass Production, E-mail, and Distribution

At one time, people worried about things like typesetting and having a clean ribbon in the typewriter. Then it was a good laser printer, picking the right paper, and finding matching envelopes. That eventually moved into fax machines and now e-mail. Each era comes with its own advantages and pitfalls.

Most of your resumes will probably go out via e-mail or be posted to the Web, though you will still need a printed version as well. In either case, it's important to make a good first impression. Make your resume effective with strong format, very simple graphics (as long as they contribute to your statement), and an attractive design.

Most resumes are created or updated using word-processing software and duplicated on paper using quality printers and photocopiers. It's best to use standard portrait orientation (with the resume reading top to bottom on the page), and while you've probably seen creatively formatted resumes—horizontal style, foldouts, or brochures, for instance—it's really best to stick with the standard.

For paper copies, use a top-quality laser printer or photocopier, and use bond or linen paper. White, ivory, natural, and off-white are your best color options. The content and format of your resume will make your document stand out; the color of your paper does not matter. If you have your resumes copied, get extra paper and matching envelopes. Use the same paper for your cover letters and other correspondence. Brand yourself; a professional image contributes to your marketability.

Chapter 4

Goals, Qualifications, and Achievements

Your potential employer meets you for the first time in the first few lines of your resume. A strong statement of your professional objectives (that is, your goals) and a convincing summary of your achievements to date assure your reader that you're worth the time it will take to keep reading. This chapter shows you how to give your resume the power it needs to hold your prospective employer's attention.

Meeting the Employer's Criteria

When an employer decides to fill a position, she must write up an accurate job description if she hopes to attract qualified candidates. That means listing job functions along with requirements such as years of experience, education, training, and any specialized skills or knowledge. As you now know, employers establish and use lists of essential, optional, and desired qualifications to identify, recruit, interview, and select candidates. Your potential employer will use your resume and supporting correspondence to determine how well you meet the defined criteria.

FACT

Career counselors say that lack of research is the reason most job seekers can't articulate their professional goals. Even those professionals who rely on standardized tests to identify their clients' values, interests, personality traits, and skills agree that research is a key component to knowing your goals and what it takes to reach them.

It's important to know as much as you can about your chosen field and function. The more you know, the better you can focus your objectives. If you name a particular job title, or if a certain job function is your goal, be sure you know the responsibilities that come along with it. Some job hunters use the big job board sites to read employer job descriptions to help them better define their own positions or to update their language and improve the way they relay their duties.

Field Descriptions

When it comes to an effective job search, the only question you have to answer is "What field do you want to enter, and what job are you looking for?" Many industry publications compile long lists of criteria to help workers assess their career compatibility and evaluate their potential goals. For you, as a job seeker, simplified field and functional perspectives are enough to help you check whether your qualifications meet an employer's qualification criteria.

The following sections provide brief descriptions for a variety of fields. With this general idea of what comprises a field, you can more easily determine your particular focus and your qualifications for performing a particular function.

Administration

The administrative field involves general office management as well as oversight of facilities and systems associated with day-to-day organizational activities. No matter their titles, many employees in this field work in administrative, customer service, or general office positions. Those serving within these functions are also responsible for large operations and organizations. They generally supervise many individuals, projects, and resources. Job functions include office services, facilities, security, management, and project management roles.

Architecture, Construction, and Engineering

This field is dominated by the principles and theories of science, engineering, mathematics, and design. Those in this field solve and carry out initiatives within research, development, manufacturing, sales, construction, inspection, and maintenance.

Arts and Media

This field includes the performing and fine arts; broadcast, print, and Internet media; and communication-oriented organizations. Settings include—but are not limited to—galleries, museums, radio and television stations, dot-com organizations, publishers, newspapers and magazines, public relations firms, and advertising agencies.

Business

This sector includes almost any profit-driven activities. Most often, the business world is associated with large publicly or privately held companies that provide services or market products.

Communication

The communication field involves writing, graphics, public relations, publicity, and promotions. It includes all activities associated with creating, distributing, and transmitting text and graphic information via varied print, video, audio, computer, and Web-based media.

Education

The education field includes private and public preschools, elementary schools, middle and secondary schools, colleges and universities, and tutorial and training operations.

Finance

This field involves accounting, budgeting, treasury, auditing, and information systems activities. It includes collection, documentation, and analysis of financial data and the use of this data to make strategic decisions and share pertinent information with investors, regulators, and government entities. It also includes allocation and growth of capital required for annual operations as well as growth.

Government

Government includes all local, state, federal, and multinational organizations that pass legislation, offer and regulate services, lobby, and promote specific programs and resources.

Health and Human Services

Usually considered a part of the service sector, this field includes both individuals and facilities that offer medical, psychological, social, and related services. Practitioners can be private, government affiliated, or have nonprofit status. Hospitals, clinics, residential treatment facilities, agencies, and special programs all fit within this field.

Hospitality

This is a service sector that encompasses a broad variety of industries such as hotels, restaurants, casinos, travel, and tourism.

Human Resources

This field involves recruiting, retention, and staffing; compensation and benefits; training and development; and employee relations efforts. It includes all hiring, career development, compensation, and personnel management activities.

Law

The legal field includes services and systems associated with enforcement of laws, such as judicial, regulatory, corrections, investigation, and protection organizations. Employers include government and private agencies, law firms, nonprofit entities, and courts and mediators.

Marketing

Marketing involves new product development, product management, marketing analysis, research, product and sales support, advertising, promotions, public relations, and customer services. These functions can take place in consumer and industrial product manufacturers or at specialized consulting firms or agencies.

Sales

The sales field involves direct sales, representative sales, distribution and arbitrage, and retail sales. It includes all activities associated with sales of raw materials used to create products or the sale of products directly to consumers. It can also involve sales of financial or other services.

Science and Technology

The tech sector includes organizations and businesses associated with research, development, manufacturing, and marketing of new technologies.

Activities can be purely research and development-oriented or they can be product or service-oriented. Government, business, and education entities all fit within this specialized category.

ALERT!

The popular job board Web site *www.careerbuilder.com* cited the following occupations among the top ten "cutting edge jobs" based on Bureau of Labor Statistics data, consumer need, changing technology, and shifting demographics: radiation therapist, nurse paralegal, genetics counselor, computer forensic expert, and animal defense lawyer.

Technology and Operations

This field involves production, materials, traffic, and management of information systems. It includes overseeing or participating in the activities associated with producing tangible products and with purchasing, receiving, and storing raw material, components, or finished products. It is also associated with the allocation of human resources to specific assignments and with the operating, programming, or servicing of computers.

Talk the Talk to Walk the Walk

Conversation is easy with almost anyone, as long as the people talking have something in common. In your job search, including your resume, correspondence, and interviews, you must speak the language that is common to your field of interest. The employer speaks to you in that language in the form of job descriptions and job postings. Your response is in the form of your resume and, later, your interview.

You don't need to limit yourself to a single resume for one field. Objective statements are not difficult to create or update, and it is equally easy to recast your qualifications summaries to meet the criteria of different employers. Many candidates create multiple resumes and tweak them as needed based on the position they are applying for.

Courses and seminars are another way of learning the criteria for success in your field. If you can devote the time to an internship, or even arrange to spend time shadowing someone who performs your chosen job function (sometimes called an externship), you can learn through day-to-day experience.

A good way to focus and state your goals to meet the employer's criteria is to check out a few professional publications. After just a few articles, you should start to notice some common factors. The terminology of the field should become clear, but you should also be able to tell something about individual job functions. Look for interviews or profiles of successful people in the field. What qualifications did they bring to their jobs? Even more general information, such as articles about processes or innovations in the field, should still contain clues. What you're looking for is the collection of characteristics that people share who already work in your chosen field. It is likely that those will be on your employer's list of qualification criteria.

Now is the time to think about the qualification criteria associated with job titles that raise your curiosity. Take out a pad or open a new Word document. For each job function that interests you, list the job title, field, and function. Think about the qualification criteria for each. If you were a prospective employer screening resumes, what would you look for? Jot down every qualification you think of. Don't write vague statements like "experience within the field and related education." Be specific and behavioral. **FIGURE 4-1** lists some sample criteria for an entry-level Assistant Account Executive. Notice how each can be worked into a resume or used in follow-up correspondence and in your interview. Together, they form the basis of your common conversation with your potential employer.

Figure 4-1: Sample Criteria

Qualification Criteria	Assets Sought and Interview Questions to Ask
Knowledge of the field	• Previous experience via internships or jobs • Courses in Advertising or Marketing • Vocabulary used in resume and cover letter • "What ads do you like the most and why?" question • "What agency has gained the most significant accounts last year?" question
Curiosity regarding consumer behavior and market research techniques	• Selected courses in Psychology, Anthropology, Marketing, or Sociology • Independent study or research, specifically in social sciences or marketing • Experience with questionnaire or survey development and analysis • "What ads do you like the least, and why?" question
Research and project management skills	• Diverse research or term paper topics, methodology, and outcomes • Multiple extracurricular roles or jobs while in school • Leadership within group projects • Examples of multitasking in internships, jobs, or academic roles • "When were you in charge of a project?" question
Blend of quantitative and qualitative analytical skills	• Diversity of courses, including mathematics, science, social sciences, and humanities • Economics, Business, Psychology, Anthropology, or Liberal Arts Curricula • Independent study or research experience revealed through papers and projects • "What are your strengths and weaknesses?" question
Group communication and task management abilities	• Extracurricular membership and leadership • Independent study, research support, or term-paper research experience • Semester-by-semester analysis of courses taken, motivation, and outcomes • "Describe your most impressive paper or presentation" query
Persuasive oral and written talents	• Majors and courses completed • Research and term paper topics • Cover letter and resume content • "Briefly describe your most impressive paper or presentation" query
Flexibility, curiosity, and ability to accept criticism	• Transcript analysis • Major choice, course selection, research, term paper topics • "Lessons learned from mistakes?" question • "What if I put you on the dog food account?" question • "What have you learned from your mistake?" question

Sample Statements of Objectives

Your professional objective does not have to state your long-term or lifelong career goals; it is simply a statement of the job title you are seeking. It provides focus for reviewers and influences how they perceive all subsequent content. Your statement of objectives is like a label that names the professional door you seek to enter. When you knock, seeking entry, you introduce yourself via a resume and cover letter. Ideally, after interviewing, you will receive an offer to stay.

As illustrated in samples throughout this book, resume objectives should be simple and stated in as few words as possible. They are best composed of a few nouns, not complex adjective- and verb-filled statements. No fluff. Top off your powerful page, literally, with the answer to the question: "What is the title of the job you seek?"

As you examine the format, content, and order as well as the objectives of the many sample resumes in this book, think about their simplicity. Think about how they mirror a powerful knowledge of self and of a chosen career field and job function. Though the samples use different approaches, they still have much in common. Some probably have objectives and qualifications that match your goals, and it may be possible for you to adapt some of that content for your own resume. Your goal, here and throughout your resume-writing and job-search progress, is to show hiring managers that you know what it takes to succeed within your chosen field and function.

Think of a career objective like the thesis statement of a term paper. By putting keywords to your resume, you are trying to prove your knowledge of a particular area. Avoid pat phrases like "organizational skills" or "team player." Usually, the keywords you need to get your resume noticed are in the desired job description. Here is a sample objective:

Web Management professional with skills encompassing marketing, design, development, and programming using Web 2.0 technologies including .net, AJAX, J2EE, WebLogic, and traditional HTML and JavaScript.

Qualifications: The "Q" in You

Now that you have an objective, you can focus on more nitty-gritty aspects of your chosen field. Here's another resume-writing mantra for you to repeat:

"I can get any job I can describe—as long as I can describe it well." The rest of this chapter explains the all-important skill of writing good qualifications summaries that articulate and support your career goal. Qualifications are critical. In your work (or education or volunteer commitments), you have probably performed the very functions prospective employers are looking for.

Plenty of your achievements are relevant to your goals. To decide which are important enough to include on your resume, think like a knowledgeable member of your target audience. From this perspective, you can see the criteria that would qualify you for the job. If the field is veterinary science, for instance, your volunteer work in the local 4-H club teaching kids how to care for their livestock would count as a qualification. Review your achievements from a field-oriented perspective. Pick the ten that are most relevant to your current goals; they will be the foundation for your qualification and achievement summaries.

FACT

E-resumes are often analyzed electronically with database keyword searches. The more of these keywords you use, the more likely it is that your resume will make the cut. You can make a good start at figuring out the keywords in your chosen field by visiting any of the big online job boards, like *www.monster.com, www.careerbuilder.com,* or *www .hotjobs.com.*

Thinking about past achievements makes you take one step back so you can take two steps forward. Summaries of qualifications talk about the past, but they project your abilities and goals into the future.

Bringing Out the "Q"

Take out three pieces of paper. Title each as follows:

- Employment Achievements
- Service Achievements
- Educational Achievements

Starting from the present and working back in time, list your achievements in each category using the following guidelines:

- Note when you accomplished this achievement, including month and year.
- For the employment category, think about full-time and part-time jobs, internships, and other project-by-project roles. The service category should include volunteer work and memberships in service organizations. In the education category, in addition to degrees earned, note important papers, publications, fellowships, or other awards of excellence.
- Think in particular about leadership roles you might have had. The proven ability to lead is an important achievement in any category.
- Name your title, if you had one. Be specific about the context of your achievement (were you an undergraduate when you got that paper published or a busy grad student?).
- Phrasing should be brief. Edit later for style and to make your descriptions active.

When you finish, your three pages will list past achievements under each heading. But the lists on their own don't make for a thorough inventory, and it's an inventory you're after. The next step is to analyze your past.

Making a Self-Inventory

Take out a fourth piece of paper. Title it "Most Significant Outcomes and Accomplishments." Review the achievements you listed on your three earlier pages, and pick the ten that were most significant. Add them to this final page, and include the outcome that resulted from each one.

Finally, transform these accomplishments into bullet points using an active, outcome-focused style (illustrated in the following samples). Refer to the samples for inspiration, if necessary. You can use these bullet points on your resume (under headlines like "Experience," "Community Service," and "Education"), or, with a little more work, you can transform them into your qualification summary.

Action Verbs and Action Statements

The following lists include action verbs and sample statements for describing qualifications. Boldface is used in the sample statements for emphasis, but it should not be used this way in your resume.

Most keyword searches scan for achievement-focused nouns in addition to action verbs. Those might include the names of software applications, new technology, industry-specific phrases, specialized techniques, conceptual models, or analytical tools.

Action Verbs				
Accommodated	Achieved	Activated	Adapted	Adjusted
Administered	Advertised	Advised	Advocated	Affirmed
Altered	Analyzed	Applied	Appraised	Approved
Archived	Assembled	Assessed	Assisted	Assumed
Attached	Attained	Audited	Augmented	Authorized

Statements
• **Analyzed** procedures to **assess** overall efficiency and monitor outcomes relative to goals for Quality Assurance and Quality Control.
• **Assessed** proposals to determine **accuracy** of financial projections and prioritize strategies.
• **Applied** theories to research data, generated hypotheses, **analyzed** data, and then presented trends via written and oral reports.
• **Appraised** value of properties as well as risk **associated** with prospective buyers and mortgage options.
• **Audited** financial and manufacturing performance records to identify cost-sensitive variables.

Action Verbs				
Balanced	Branded	Built	Calculated	Calibrated
Chose	Classified	Collected	Combined	Commanded
Communicated	Compromised	Conceived	Condensed	Conferred
Confirmed	Consolidated	Consulted	Controlled	Converted
Coordinated	Counseled	Created	Credited	Curtailed

Statements

- **Built** and **tested** actual and virtual prototype model of bridge and off-ramp.

- **Conceived, implemented,** and **improved** promotional campaign using Web, direct mail, posters, and print media strategies.

- **Conferred** regularly with supervisors, peers, and clients to determine effectiveness of programs.

- **Coordinated** the activities of more than 100 volunteers, focusing on serving approximately 5,000 meals.

- **Counseled** students regarding academic performance, class scheduling, test preparation, career options, and college admissions.

Action Verbs				
Debugged	Decoded	Deducted	Deemed	Delegated
Deleted	Delivered	Demonstrated	Derived	Described
Designated	Designed	Determined	Developed	Dictated
Digitized	Directed	Disclosed	Discontinued	Discovered
Dispatched	Displayed	Distributed	Documented	Drafted

Statements

- **Designated** specific tasks to individuals, **motivated** maximum performance, and **monitored** outcomes.

- **Described** products and services accurately over the phone, via e-mail, and in written proposals.

- **Designed, implemented,** and **documented** experimental procedures.

- **Demonstrated** effective customer service and relationship sales skills targeting varied consumer markets and demographics.

- **Documented** achievements via attendance, sales, and profit figures, all in excess of established targets and quotas.

- **Drafted, edited, finalized, duplicated**, and **distributed** promotional materials and media packets.

Action Verbs				
Economized	Educated	Eliminated	Employed	Empowered
Encoded	Encouraged	Engaged	Established	Estimated
Evaluated	Examined	Exchanged	Executed	Expanded
Expedited	Extended	Familiarized	Forged	Formulated
Galvanized	Governed	Grouped	Guaranteed	Guided

Statements

- **Evaluated** program effectiveness using predetermined criteria, then **cited** findings using PowerPoint presentations and written reports.

- **Expressed** views in persuasive yet appropriate ways via verbal and written arguments.

- **Formulated** and **implemented** questionnaire designed to clarify problem areas and assess attitudes.

- **Generated** trust and confidence of clients, parents, peers, and supervisors.

- **Guided** families and prospective students, **answered** questions, and **served** as spokesperson for the university.

Action Verbs				
Headed	Heard	Highlighted	Honored	Hypothesized
Illustrated	Implemented	Imposed	Improved	Increased
Informed	Initiated	Installed	Instructed	Interpreted
Introduced	Invented	Inventoried	Investigated	Joined
Judged	Justified	Lectured	Listened	Localized

Statements

- **Headed** committee that **inspired** revision of mission statement, strategies, and methods used to measure adherence to stated goals.

- **Identified** key issues and alternatives, and **detailed** strategies to achieve desired outcomes.

- **Improved** methods used to register clients, retrieve files, and initiate counseling sessions.

- **Investigated** past strategies, resources, and services to establish and implement improvements.

- **Listened** to concerns of customers and **responded** in ways to maximize loyalty and repeat sales.

Action Verbs				
Maintained	Managed	Mandated	Matched	Measured
Merged	Minimized	Modernized	Modified	Motivated
Named	Negotiated	Noted	Observed	Obtained
Operated	Organized	Originated	Planned	Prescribed
Procured	Produced	Programmed	Publicized	Published

Statements

- **Managed** time, personnel, and finances efficiently, maximizing impact with minimum resources.

- **Motivated** colleagues to complete program planning, implementation, and evaluation efforts.

- **Marketed** products and services to target audiences using specialized strategies and promotional materials.

- **Organized** projects to ensure accurate completion within existing deadlines.

- **Procured** materials donated to renovate living space for the homeless.

Action Verbs				
Queried	Quoted	Recommended	Rectified	Reduced
Regulated	Reorganized	Repaired	Replaced	Reported
Represented	Researched	Restored	Revised	Rewrote
Shaped	Simplified	Solved	Sponsored	Stabilized
Strengthened	Studied	Supervised	Supplemented	Surpassed

Statements

- **Queried** users regarding customer service, effectiveness of displays, and desired improvements.

- **Reported** findings in PowerPoint illustrated presentations and written reports containing charts, graphs, and spreadsheets.

- **Revised** training manual, including role-play interviews, interactive scripts, and inspirational quotes.

- **Suggested** options to improve performance and profitability.

- **Simplified** client greeting and payment procedures to expedite check-in process.

Action Verbs				
Taught	Terminated	Tied	Took	Tracked
Traded	Trained	Transcribed	Transferred	Transformed
Transmitted	Tutored	Typed	Uncovered	Underscored
Unified	Updated	Uploaded	Used	Utilized
Verified	Vetoed	Voted	Waged	Wrote

Statements

- **Taught** new paralegals to use LexisNexis and other computerized search systems.

- **Trained** peer career advisors to greet students, conduct quick assessments, and address residence needs.

- **Verified** effectiveness of promotional strategies via attendance profiling and attitude questionnaires.

- **Used** state-of-the-art CADD techniques to design and test prototypical manufacturing equipment.

- **Wrote** creative promotional materials and **designed** advertising materials in Spanish and English.

Back to the Future

With your inventory of significant accomplishments in front of you, it's time to create a timeline to link those past achievements to the present and on into the future, where your desired job awaits. Your significant accomplishments don't only belong to the past. They were significant because you made changes. Like a stone dropped in a still pond, the effects of your work create a ripple effect of energy that keeps moving, long after the stone has left your hand.

Your goal is to create a resume that, at a glance, gives a potential employer a powerful picture of your job worthiness. You do that in steps:

- A clear statement of **objectives** targets your resume.
- A summary of **past achievements** tells your employer about your abilities and qualifications.
- A description of **outcome** tells your employer about the continuing impact of your achievements.

You can see that it makes sense to talk about outcome. Your next employer is going to hire you as an outcome of your previous achievements; when you make outcome a theme of your resume, you're helping that employer think of a future that has you in it. That's exactly what you want your resume to do.

The following examples are taken from the action-verb statements given in the previous section, with outcomes in boldface. Compare the two versions to see how an outcome description can add impact to your qualifications:

- Counseled students regarding academic performance, class scheduling, test preparation, career options, and college admissions. **Three of these counseled students completed freshman year with honors. One started a successful business straight out of high school.**
- Marketed products and services to target audiences using specialized strategies and promotional materials. **Sales increased 20 percent across the board, with polls attributing success to marketing-campaign focus, collateral literature, and Web branding.**

- Simplified client greeting and payment procedures to expedite check-in process. **On basis of positive customer feedback, won "Employee of the Quarter" award. Received personal recognition at annual meeting from vice president of customer relations.**

The difference is dramatic. Reviewing these qualifications summaries, it is obvious that the information about outcomes is important. If you were the reviewer, wouldn't it make a difference to know that your candidate was not only qualified, but had proved some success?

Not all resumes are targeted resumes. You've seen that some resumes are prepared as open-ended introductions, without career objectives or branding statements. Both types of resumes are accepted by employers. Use the format that best suits your goals, content, and field of interest.

Chapter 5

Your Web Resume

Recruiting these days could just as easily be called e-cruiting. Resumes today are e-mailed, sent as attachments, posted to job boards or Web sites, or uploaded to resume banks. You must be able to transmit your resume electronically so that a reviewer can open it easily without jeopardizing your content or layout. After that, your concern, as usual, is with quality. No matter who (or what, in the case of a database search engine) opens your resume, it must be clear that you are goal-oriented and qualified for the job. This chapter describes how to create a resume suitable for the technology that dominates today's job market.

Uploading Your Web Resume

Many potential employers use the Internet to list their job postings. Some use their own corporate Web sites. (For example, the *Everything*® book publisher, Adams Media at *www.adamsmedia.com*, has an Employment link on its home page.) Many also use targeted recruiting sites, where the Web site organizes and displays an employer's opening or advertisement and also makes sure qualified applicants come to the employer's attention.

FACT

The process of uploading a resume from your personal computer is simple. Web sites walk job seekers through the process step by step. The process may vary a little, but in all cases you are using your Internet connection to send the electronic file containing your resume directly to an employer or to the job board's online job bank.

File Format for the Web Resume

Uploading is easy, and it is a very effective way of making your resume easily available to many potential employers. However, the electronic file that contains your resume must be in the correct format. Your uploaded resume is useless if the database can't store it or your recipient can't open and read it.

All online job banks specify the file format you should use. The following are some common formats:

- **Microsoft Word.** Almost everyone in almost all professional fields uses Microsoft Word. This is the application most preferred by hiring companies and job boards. If you create your resume using another software application, see if your software has the option to save your file as a Word document.
- **PDF.** PDF files retain the formatting of the original file, and they tend to not get corrupted in their travels across the Internet. You can create a PDF from almost any file format. PDFs cannot be edited or altered, making them a good way of keeping your content exactly as

you created it. They are created through Adobe software, which you can download for free.

- **Web page input.** Some job banks ask you to create a resume by filling in the fields of a resume form. In this case, you are not really uploading a file at all. The information you enter into the various fields gets saved directly into the job banks database. Instead of storing resume files, this database contains the information directly.

No matter what format you use, you should do a quality check before uploading your file:

1. Make sure your resume file can be opened, and that it is formatted correctly. Word files can be corrupted, and PDFs can substitute fonts and change things like font size or margins. Do not assume that just because you saved the file or created the PDF that it will meet your requirements.
2. Name your file correctly. Check the requirements of the job bank: They might have a system for naming files. In general, your filename should be short and descriptive.
3. If you are filling in a Web form, take your time entering your information in the fields. Keywords here are essential. You might need to edit your resume, aiming to keep things short while using as many keywords as possible.
4. Test it yourself. E-mail your resume to several friends or family members and ask them how it looks on screen, and ask for a sample printed version to review yourself.

Keywords Are Essential

Many job seekers upload their resumes to Web job banks or job boards. These are true Web resumes, sometimes referred to as e-resumes. The potential employer only sees this electronic version, only printing a paper version at his or her own preference. Often, before any human being lays eyes on these Web resumes, they are subject to review by a search engine. This tool is loaded with certain keywords that the employer has defined as critical to any applicant's qualifications. Regardless of your abilities, if your qualifications summaries or general content does not use these keywords, it is likely that you'll never make even the first cut.

Here is where your research pays off. In defining your goals and drafting your resume, you learned the terms and phrases used in your chosen field. When possible, in your statement of objectives, you should name a particular title that you know is used in your field. The verbs you use to describe your qualifications and experience should mirror those terms as closely as possible.

Here are two statements of objectives that could be used for the same resume. See which one would yield the more fruitful keyword search:

- **Objective:** Position designing logos and graphics for state-of-the-art Web sites.
- **Objective:** Position as Web Designer for software design firm, using skills in XML, DTML, streaming video, Flash animation, Oracle database design, and Web site maintenance.

Chances are that you are uploading your resume into a job bank in answer to a specific job posting. The smartest thing to do, therefore, is to compare the job description to your resume. Does your resume, particularly your qualifications summary section, contain the key verbs, terms, and phrases used in the job description? If this job description is short or vague, search the Web for other descriptions of similar jobs. You will notice that they use a common vocabulary to define job functions and desired qualifications.

Check the rules of the online job boards. Most allow you to regularly update your resumes. When you do an update, take the time to upload it so all potential employers always see the best and most accurate depiction of your job skills.

Keep an Inventory of Keywords

As you continue to search out new job postings, you will learn new industry-specific ways of phrasing your qualifications and summaries. Rather than rewriting your resume every time you find a new, more appropriate term, keep a list. Update your resume when you have a collection of these terms. In this way, your update will not only be more efficient in terms of time, you may come up with better ways of phrasing whole sections, instead of changing a word at a time.

E-mailing Your Web Resume

Some job postings ask you to e-mail your resume directly to a contact person. The process here is very simple: Your e-mail message is your cover letter, and your resume gets included as a file attachment. An e-mail cover letter should be short and direct. The first line should state your purpose ("I am writing in response to your posting for an experienced Web Designer"). Any subsequent text should state your qualifications bluntly ("I have five years of freelance experience designing Web sites for independent movie studios, sometimes using GoLive and Adobe Design software but mostly writing my own code to incorporate movie clips and other complex elements").

QUESTION?

How much information should I include in my e-mail?
It's a good idea to say what made you respond to this posting ("I use links to your site to give our visitors access to real-time industry news, and I would love the opportunity to work for you"). E-mails are quick and informal by nature. You know from experience that an overwritten e-mail is hard to read. Be polite, but don't be stuffy. Be specific so that the recipient knows it is not generic.

E-mail Etiquette

In this case, the question of file formats is particularly important. Pay attention to the stated format requirements, and do not bother submitting a resume that doesn't meet them. You may think PDF is much better than Word, but if Word is what the contact person requests, he or she will not appreciate your substitution and it immediately signifies that you don't take direction well.

The common question with an e-mailed file of any kind is whether the recipient got it in a legible form. If your resume file is huge, with graphics or other special features, it will take a long time to transmit and to open. Nobody appreciates being made to wait, so for e-mailed resumes, it's a good idea to keep things very simple.

Regardless of your care, file attachments do sometimes get mangled. That gives you an automatic excuse for a follow-up. Ask the recipient to let you know if your file did not come through. Take the opportunity to slip in another quick selling point. There's no harm in sending a follow-up, as long as it is very brief and not demanding in any way.

Addressing the E-mail

Job postings often ask you to reference a job number in your subject line. Be sure you include this information, as it is unlikely your e-mail (or resume) will reach its destination without it.

Most job postings include a link to the contact person's e-mail. All you have to do to address your e-mail properly is to click on the link. You must also use a personal address, however, in your cover e-mail. Online job postings are notorious for giving little to no information about the contact person. Sometimes all you have is an e-mail address and no name at all. Use whatever information you have. If you don't have a contact name, start the letter immediately after the address, using no salutation at all.

Web-Based Research and Job Search

The Web is full of all the information you could ever need to know about your chosen career. Chances are that your dream job is out there somewhere—if only you could find it.

In doing research on the Web, the best place to start is with what you know. It doesn't matter whether you start off in the exact right place. The Web is a job seeker's paradise because it is so easy to follow any trail in whatever direction you choose. Here's an example. We'll let our Web Designer friend Chris Smith take a quick look around the Internet to see what's happening in the working world.

1. Chris is just beginning a job search, so he starts at his favorite all-purpose search engine (we'll say that's *www.google.com*).
2. Chris types in his chosen job title, "Web Designer," in the search field and narrows the search just a little by adding "employment."
3. The Google search engine returns nearly 2 million Web sites that are related somehow to the phrase "Web Designer employment." Some of these sites belong to other Web designers looking for employment. Chris ignores these for now, although later they might be a good way of networking with others in his field. He wants actual job postings. He doesn't have to look very hard to find them. The second link on the page lists a job board specializing in Web designer and other graphic-oriented opportunities. These are sometimes known as niche job boards.
4. In the next five minutes, Chris finds the following information, just by clicking links that look promising:

   - Dozens of job postings for Web designers, containing plenty of keywords.
   - Several big job boards or niche sites specific to graphics and Web professionals. These contain not only job postings for Web designers, they give Chris an idea of what companies are hiring, what industries in his part of the country are seeking Web designers, and what qualifications employers currently expect.
   - Salary information. Some job postings include a salary range. But these are not often reliable, so Chris clicks around a little and finds salary statistics on an employment-related government Web site, as well as on salary sites.
   - Sites of individual companies with pages devoted to current openings, all with contact people listed.
   - Online forums and blogs maintained by people just like himself, experienced Web designers of all kinds. Their discussions cover topics ranging from "Freelance Survival" to "Making It Big in the Corporate World."

These are the results of a real Web search, using these keywords, conducted during a quick coffee break. As you can imagine, the real key to getting useful information from the Web is knowing when to stop. Five minutes can easily yield more information than anyone could use in a week; one page links quickly to another. The Web is a huge, chaotic haystack of information. But as long as you don't worry yourself about hunting for one in particular, you'll find more needles there than you can possibly use.

Vistas for a Web-Based Job Search

Here are a few avenues for beginning your online job search:

- Check with your local librarian to see whether your state or geographic region sponsors a job bank or whether individual listings can be found online.
- Check the Web sites of companies in your chosen field or marketplace.
- Use a Web search engine to visit the three current major job boards: *www.hotjobs.com*, *www.monster.com*, and *www.careerbuilder.com*.

Your local newspaper may also list its help wanted ads online. Online listings are usually much easier to search than the printed version. Also, ads often include a link to the company's Web site, where other suitable postings may be found.

Reactive and Proactive Web Strategies

It is easy to think of the Web as a giant fishing pond. You, as the job seeker, have a certain kind of bait on your pole, and you dangle your line in hope that the right fish is out there, waiting to bite.

This is a reactive job-search strategy, where you react to postings and try to model yourself as the best candidate for the job. Sometimes that's all it takes, but a truly effective job-search campaign incorporates proactive techniques as well.

You have already begun using the Web in a proactive manner. When you research your chosen field, for instance, to find the Web sites of the top companies, you are engaging in proactive research. Maybe the company you would most like to work for has several postings that are close to what you're looking for, but nothing that you feel qualified to apply for. You plan to keep checking back, but in the meantime why not write a quick e-mail to the contact person listed for that job. Tell him or her of your interest. Explain briefly how you believe you could be a real asset to the company. Close by saying you will keep in touch, and do it.

FACT

The 2007 User's Choice Awards, compiled from an online poll by the Internet recruitment site *www.weddles.com,* named thirty favorite job boards as chosen by job seekers and recruiters. Among them were *www.careerbuilder.com, www.indeed.com, www.theladders.com, www .militaryhire.com, www.net-temps.com,* and *www.vault.com.*

Another proactive technique on the employment e-frontier is a twist on our old favorite, networking. Online forums and bloggers cover almost any topic imaginable. They are easy enough to search out (try Yahoo!'s e-group listing, at *www.groups.yahoo.com*) and to join. You may not get any job offers, but you are likely to learn a lot about your chosen field and the function you hope to perform in it.

Job Board Giants and Niche Sites

The job seeker who fails to make use of the Internet's most popular job boards and niche sites is doing his or her job search a major disservice. These Internet resources have become a major source of recruiting for almost all employers. A job board is a Web site that lists job postings by employers and resumes offered by job seekers. Although each site has different methodologies, both the employer and the candidate can identify good prospects based on their need. Some job boards are generic and offer a wide range of employment opportunities by industry, job title, location, and earnings.

Job Board Giants

At the time of this writing, the three most popular general job board giants are: *www.monster.com, www.careerbuilder.com,* and *www.hotjobs .com.* You can visit *www.topjobsites.com* for an up-to-date ranking of job boards that are categorized under General, College, Executive, Diversity, Niche, and International.

Many job seekers choose to set up a search agent at the boards, which means they are regularly e-mailed openings that match a specific criteria according to parameters they set up for themselves. If you see a position that appeals to you, click the link that allows you to reply to the opening and send your resume. Do not rely on the job board or the employer to find you on the site, even if you have a resume posted there. Be proactive and go after the openings that seem the best match for your skills and career goals.

Niche Sites

The niche sites are exactly as they sound and are typically sites that are devoted to an industry, earning capacity, or geographic region. Some popular niche sites include: *www.absolutelyhealthcare.com, www.allretailjobs. com, www.jobs4hr.com,* and *www.talentzoo.com* (this last one for advertising and media professionals). If you want to make your job search more focused, you might find greater success with the niche boards.

Online Networking

Everyone knows about networking face to face. You meet someone, you chat, and you build contacts and learn about employment leads or the names of other people who can assist you with your career goals.

Social Networking on the Web

Now social networking sites on the Internet are changing how people communicate and gain information about employers and job candidates. Sites such as *www.myspace.com, www.friendster.com, www.facebook.com, www.jobster.com, www.ryze.com,* and *www.linkedin.com,* to name a few popular resources, provide personal Web pages and personal and professional information about individuals which can include their job titles and where they work.

Online networking is very proactive and means you actively seek out and introduce yourself to someone who might work at a company you aspire to be part of. You can also seek people with a certain title to learn more about their professional duties or their company and perhaps give you an inside edge on getting your foot in the door at their firm.

FACT

Estimates regarding how many resumes are stored on or transmitted via Web-based resources vary. Some believe that the numbers of resumes stored in resume banks and connected to postings via mega job-search sites doubled each year over the past five years. While actual totals are difficult to confirm, almost all agree that millions of resumes are stored annually and tens of thousands are transmitted by e-mail daily.

Typically, you can join a social networking site on your own, or someone already a part of the network invites you to join. Joining simply means you set up a profile viewable to others who then have the opportunity to contact you as well. Social networking sites that are not business oriented often showcase an individual's hobbies and lifestyle. Be careful what you include on such sites since many employers now go to these sites to see if a candidate is profiled there. On some occasions, individuals have included inappropriate photographs or comments that may reflect poorly on their consideration for employment. Be careful what you include on such sites, since you do not want to be blind-sided by digital dirt. Additionally, do yourself a favor and Google your name. Simply type your name into the search engine and see if you or others with your name show up. You can remove anything of your own that might jeopardize your search. This also allows you to discover if there are others with your name that might be mistaken for you if an employer goes through this same process.

Blogging

Blogs are online journals. Some bloggers write about their lives, some about their jobs, and still others write about interests or simply the mundane. You can go to *www.blogger.com* to read blogs and gain a better understanding of their wide scope and subject matter. For job search purposes, you might visit a blog site and read what someone has to say about your anticipated line of work or a prospective company as an employer. Recruiters sometimes search blogs to target candidates with special interests or expertise in a specific field. The same way some people like to read a daily column or someone else's diary, blogs have loyal fans, and the community of bloggers continues to grow. Again, if you choose to maintain a blog, be sure that what you write won't jeopardize your chances of getting the job you want. You never know who will be reading it!

Sample Web Resumes

The following sample resumes were all specifically formatted and written for digital presentation.

Common elements of most successful Web resumes include the following:

- E-friendly fonts
- Left-justified block text formatting, with minimal tabs or columns
- Detailed, comprehensive qualifications summaries containing key phrases and industry-specific vocabulary
- Ability to be cut and pasted into e-mails or the fields of Web-based forms

While a print resume and a Web resume may differ, very often they are now one and the same. Acceptable formatting and technology have caught up with one another and employers now typically print a Web resume as a candidate's official resume. Generally, it is a Microsoft Word document.

Advertising Account Executive Web Resume

Chris Smith

123 Main Street, Hometown, NY 00000, (555) 555-1234, csmith@company.com

ADVERTISING ACCOUNT MANAGEMENT QUALIFICATIONS

Marketing research, strategic planning, promotions, customer service, and sales talents nurtured by in-depth and diverse advertising, promotions, retail internships, and employment. Technical skills gained via courses including: Principles of Marketing, Marketing Projects and Cases, Psychology of Human Motivation and Emotion, Business Administration, Public Relations Writing, Advertising, Mass Media, Persuasion, and Consumer Behavior. Confidence serving on account team and interacting with client colleagues. Special interest in using and enhancing talents associated with market research, segmentation, demographic and media planning, business forecasting, break-even analysis, product strategy development, pricing analysis, financial planning, and publicity concept creation. Capacities to understand four Cs: context, company, consumer analysis, and competitor analysis; and the five Ps: people, product, price, place/distribution, and promotion. French, Dutch, and Farsi fluency, and conversational Spanish capabilities. Word, Excel, PowerPoint, Quark, PhotoShop, and Internet skills.

ADVERTISING AND MARKETING EXPERIENCE
DAYS ADVERTISING, INC., Pittsford, NY
Account Management Intern: Assisted with design of television and radio ads and proposals for varied clients, including Wegmans and Bausch & Lomb. Summer 2005

ADEFFECTS, Rochester, NY
Account Management Intern: Researched and developed promotional materials for retail, manufacturing, and restaurant clients. Suggested changes in advertising materials, consumer outreach strategies, and marketing literature. May 2004–July 2005

PEARLE VISION CENTER, Pittsford, NY
Sales Representative, Summer 2005

IT HAPPENS, Antwerp, Belgium
Marketing Intern: Determined target markets and developed advertising budget for concert, event planning, and entertainment agency. Conducted and analyzed surveys to determine market penetration. Assisted artists with ads, posters, and brochures. Summer 2002

BUSINESS, ECONOMICS, AND LANGUAGE STUDIES
UNIVERSITY OF ROCHESTER, Rochester, NY
Bachelor of Arts, French, with a major GPA of 3.5, May 2006
Bachelor of Arts, Psychology, with a major GPA of 3.3, May 2006
Minor: Economics, with a minor GPA of 3.4
Management Studies Certificate, Marketing and Finance/Accounting Tracks, May 2006

FINANCE EXPERIENCE
THE FINANCIAL GROUP, INC. DISCOUNT BROKERAGE FIRM, Pittsford, NY
Operations Management Intern, January–May 2005

- Times New Roman font is Web friendly.

- Bullets and special formatting, like bolding, are omitted to make resumes easy to upload and/or scan. Boldface, italics, bullets, and other formatting techniques do not interfere with keyword search, retrieval, or printing capabilities.

- Because line spacing and overcrowding are not an issue, spacing was eliminated between headlines and first entries.

- Paragraph-style qualification summary is descriptive and full of keywords.

- This version can easily be cut and pasted into e-mail or a Web-based form and easily retrieved.

Financial Planner Web Resume

Jamie Brown

123 Main Street • Hometown, NY 00000 • (555) 555-1234 • jbrown@company.com

Financial Planning Qualifications and Credentials

- Over a decade of progressively significant roles and achievements within planning, portfolio management, and client services.
- Personal responsibility for more than $210 million client assets.
- Regularly recognized for asset-based performance and customer service.
- Asset collection, asset allocation, asset management, risk management, tax deferment and minimization, portfolio management, generational wealth transition, trust and estate planning, and private placement funding competencies.
- Experience hiring, training, and supervising newly hired FCs and FPs.
- Served as trainer and curriculum developer, using traditional lectures, audiotapes, videotapes, and simulation exercises.
- Licensed Series 6, 7, 63 and health and life insurance.

Financial Planning Accomplishments

ABC FINANCIAL CONSULTANTS, Princeton, NJ
Financial Consultant/Financial Planner, 1996–Present
Serve within comprehensive financial planning roles. Oversee individual and group portfolios. Serve as senior manager, supervisor, and trainer within corporate headquarters of firm responsible for over $800 million in client assets.

- Developed $210 million client asset base via prospecting and targeting.
- Successfully built portfolio that includes stock, bonds, options, and insurance products for more than 450 clients.
- Implemented financial plans through account development and growth.
- Gained estate planning, asset allocation, and wealth succession expertise.

Sales Associate, 1992–1996
- Worked directly with firm's top producer, profiling high net-worth individuals.
- Generated $90,000 for top producer through new account openings.
- Analyzed existing portfolio, assisting in development of accounts.

Account Executive Trainee/Intern, 1991–1992
MAPLEWOOD INVESTMENTS, Maplewood, NJ
Prospecting Intern, Summers 1990 and 1991

Education

IONA COLLEGE, Iona, NY
Bachelor of Arts degree in Economics, 1992
Concentration in Business Management, with courses in: financial accounting, managerial finance, corporate treasury, insurance, statistics, and financial services.

Pharmaceutical Sales Web Resume

DANA JOHNSON

123 Main Street • Hometown, NY 00000 • (555) 555-1234 • djohnson@company.com

PHARMACEUTICAL SALES QUALIFICATIONS

Familiarity with the following conditions and/or treatments: AIDS, Antidepressants, Antihistamines, Arthritis, Cancer, Cholesterol, Diabetes, FDA Approval Stages, Heart Disease, Osteoporosis, and Aging. Knowledge gained via research of: Antiulcerants, Antidepressants, Calcium Antagonists, Plain Antirheumatic Non-Steroidals, ACE Inhibitors, Plain Cephalosporins and Combinations, Antipsychotics, Non-Narcotic Analgesics, and Oral Antidiabetics. Record of success within direct marketing and information-driven sales roles. Capacity to understand and share pharmaceutical product and protocol knowledge. Abilities to blend qualitative and communication talents as well as analytical skills to set goals, document impact of sales efforts, and maximize output. Bilingual English-Mandarin abilities and cross-cultural sensitivities.

SALES AND SALES SUPPORT ACHIEVEMENTS

SSG PHARMACEUTICALS CORPORATION, San Francisco, California, 2003–Present
Sales Associate for Prescription Drugs Division: Promote and market pharmaceutical products for an international prescription drug distributor and manufacturer. Sales methods include appointments onsite, telemarketing, physician visits, and tradeshow exhibiting.
Directly involved in sales to house accounts totaling $2.5 million in 2005.
Indirectly involved in sales to salespersons accounts totaling $3 million in 2005.

COMPUTER ASSOCIATES INTERNATIONAL, San Jose, California, 2001–2003
Quality Assurance Analyst: Analyzed business applications and RFPs (Request for Proposal) for marketability. Implemented quality assurance for an inter/intranet-enabled, multiplatform, enterprise management solution used worldwide. *Supported customer service and sales representatives in refining product to match customer needs.*

BUSINESS EXPERIENCE

BANK OF HONG KONG, Hong Kong, Spring 2001
International Securities Dealing Room Trader: Communicated with customers' desires to execute orders in the areas of American and foreign equities, bonds, and options. Received training in and gained working knowledge of Bloomberg and Reuters information systems.

BANK OF HONG KONG, San Francisco, California, 1998–2001
International Lending Department Credit Analyst: Prepared proposals on prospective customers for credit committee. Conducted business and industry research using Bloomberg, Moody's, and S&P analysts and publications.

BUSINESS, ECONOMICS, AND LIBERAL ARTS EDUCATION

UNIVERSITY OF CALIFORNIA, BERKELEY, Berkeley, California, 1994–1998
Bachelor of Arts, Political Science, with minor in Economics
Served as Intern for Member British Parliament, London, England, Fall 1996. Served as Intern for Senator Barbara Boxer, U.S. Senate, Washington D.C., Summer 1996.

HAAS SCHOOL OF BUSINESS ADMINISTRATION, Berkeley, California, 1998
Management Certificate for completion of Marketing, Accounting, Economics, Statistics, and Computer Science courses. Developed detailed and fiscally sound marketing plan.

- Times New Roman is a Web-friendly font.
- Bolding is used as a highlighting technique.
- Qualification summary is placed first.
- Industry-specific phrasing is used, as are specific sales achievements.

Chapter 6

High-Speed Resumes

If a picture is worth a thousand words, you would think that a snapshot of your own perplexed face, struggling to update or create your resume, would be worth even more. Smile! This chapter directs you on developing new or revised resumes quickly and painlessly.

The Seven Steps Revisited

You should look forward to the opportunity to identify and then describe your most significant achievements. It can be an empowering experience if you think about it: You get to write a true story of yourself as a qualified, achievement-oriented person. Don't let yourself be intimidated by thoughts of what people expect to see or how they will judge you. Your job is simply to present yourself as effectively as you can.

At this point, you should be grounded in the fundamentals of resume writing for success. You should understand the importance of stating your goals, supporting them with a qualification summary, and then spelling out your significant job experience. This chapter is designed to take that confidence and apply it, with the concrete goal of creating or updating a useful resume in the shortest possible time frame.

Maybe the sample resumes in this book have already motivated you to revise your existing resume or draft a new one. In that case, you will be ready to put the finishing touches on your work. Later discussions on critiquing your first draft and preparing your resume for distribution will come in handy.

Assumptions and negativity aside, great resumes can be created in a day. In truth, they can be drafted and finalized within an hour or two. Your frame of mind is critical to resume writing as well as every part of your job search. Remain positive and everything will fall into place painlessly.

As you work through this chapter, think about the seven steps to resume-writing success. Gauge where you are on the continuum and how close you are to completing a powerful resume. Go down your internal to-do list. Experience the relief and sense of accomplishment that comes from a mental "done that" check. Look forward to the next step. Don't worry or wait—go for it! Each resume-writing step means you are closer to achieving your job-search goals. After you finalize your resume, you will be empowered to reactively and proactively complete job-search undertakings.

The Seven Steps as Critical Questions

To inspire action, let's examine the seven steps through a series of questions. Your answers will reveal your readiness to take steps and how close to completion you really are.

- Have you identified two to four sample resumes that you wish to model? Do they match your goals, or do they just appeal to your sense of style?

- Do they have objectives, qualifications summaries, and/or achievements summaries? When does specific content appear? What is first, and what is presented last? Is education before experience, or vice versa?

- Can you state your objectives concisely? Will they appear first on your draft? If your resume will begin with a qualifications summary, will the headline clearly project your goals and can it be easily identified by specific target readers? To whom will you be sending resumes, and why?

- Do you have a collection of your most significant achievements? Do they appear under academic, experience, or other headlines, or do they appear in summary sections? What did you do to achieve these outcomes? What skills, perspectives, or knowledge were involved? Can you list the headlines for all sections that will compose your resume?

- Can you describe the job you are seeking? What qualification criteria would be associated with the position? What fields, functions, and titles best characterize your targets? Have you circled or highlighted relevant summary entries that match your accomplishments and capabilities or criteria for specific jobs? Do you have a collection of keywords associated with field- or job-focused goals? Do you have a listing of accomplishments associated with each?

- Have you typed a draft? Is it longer than a page? Did you do spelling and grammar checks? Did you have someone else proofread and comment on the draft?

- Will you e-mail, post to the Web, snail mail, or hand deliver the distribution-ready version? Did you double-check spelling and usage? Do you have a cut-and-paste e-mail-friendly version?

If many of your answers are "No," "Don't know," or "Huh?" you should think about why. Review the previous chapters to get your bearings again, but don't worry. Most resume writers are overly self-critical and analytical. Begin or keep drafting; you'll have the opportunity to be more critical during the critiquing process, which doesn't start until you type the final words at the bottom of your page.

If your answers were mostly "Yes!" you are ready to go or, better, almost done! Start on that page you made that has your name and identifying information written across the top. Start writing! Go for it! Finish your draft right now!

Drafting, Critiquing, Duplication, and Distribution

Don't worry if your first resume is more of a multipurpose than a targeted resume. That might be the best way to get started; that is, by starting from a broad, general base. Later, as you revise, you should aim to create a more targeted version. Remember, writing targeted resumes and taking initial job-search actions are not commitments to specific fields. These are simply important first steps in a particular direction. These steps will, if you choose to proceed, ultimately lead to offers. Once you receive an offer, you will have the power to accept or decline; then and only then are you actually making a commitment.

They say the eyes are the windows to the soul. Your resume, with its clearly stated objectives and qualification summary, is your prospective employer's window into your job goals. A resume allows you to display your assets; it also gives others a way to learn about your capabilities and interests. Don't underestimate the two-way powers of targeted resumes.

You should create your resume as a Microsoft Word document. This will make it easy for you to share electronic copies, whether by uploading or by e-mail. Spell check your resume every time you make revisions. The grammar check tool can be helpful, but remember that in resume style, you are allowed to use sentence fragments. You also commonly leave out personal pronouns (such as "I") and articles (*the, a, an*).

As you write, stay focused on the aspects of yourself that you want to present. Don't fall into the trap of trying to please some potential employer. In almost all cases, the person who reads and reviews your resume will be a stranger. No matter how hard you try, you have no way of knowing what that person wants or expects to see. All you can do (and it's actually a lot) is put your best foot forward. Show them what you can do.

Additional Inspiration for Action

If you are hesitant or insecure about your ability to create a powerful resume, you are most likely suffering from fear of focus. In your day-to-day life, you may have many interests and possibilities, and you may not be ready to choose one at the cost of any others. That is excellent news. It means you are engaged in a serious investigation of your abilities and of just the right career for you.

In the meantime, however, you probably need to get a job of some kind. To do that you need a resume, and to write a resume, you need to define a goal. Don't worry that you're being untrue to all the options in your life; just choose one goal, define it, and use that as your statement of objectives. You can create as many resumes as you like, so if it makes you feel more in control of your future, you can create a resume for each and every one of your professional objectives. The important thing is to use your interests and ambitions to move forward.

Twenty-seven percent of human resource managers report receiving more than fifty resumes on average for each open position. More than one in ten (13 percent) say they receive more than 100 resumes per opening. When evaluating resumes, these same HR managers indicate relevant experience as the most sought-after consideration.

When you write your resume, and even when you send it out to apply for certain jobs, you are not committing yourself to any field or job function. You might consider this a way of conducting research about the fields you are most qualified for. Any response you get from your resumes will tell you how professionals already working in that field judge your qualifications. If a resume lands you an interview, you can consider yourself a qualified candidate in that field for that position. This is important feedback for anyone just entering the job market who is unsure of how their talents and experience can be valuable. It's also good feedback for the job seeker who cannot decide on any one field. Often, the most attractive field is the one where others consider you an asset.

You are free to submit all the resumes you like and to take any interview offered you. But you should only accept an offer if you are prepared to take the job. Research into that particular position, in other words, ends when and if you are made an offer. If you cannot commit yourself to performing those job duties to the best of your ability, thank the employer for their consideration and graciously decline their offer of employment.

Qualifications Summaries

Steps one through five of the resume-writing process all target completion of statement of objectives and achievements summaries. These elements are the cornerstone of powerful and effective resumes and are critical components. Very few (fewer than 10 percent) of the samples presented in this book do not include some form of qualifications or achievements summary.

Start out by reviewing the sample resumes to gain a sense of how these sections are presented. Mark any statements that match your goals or mirror your achievements. You can use them as a foundation for your own achievements summaries. Refer to the list of action verbs in Chapter 4 for inspiration, if needed.

Decide whether you prefer the bullet-point format or paragraph style. Try both to see which one makes your qualifications stand out. You might decide to use your achievements summaries directly after your statement of objectives to begin your resume, or you might choose to put them at the bottom of your page. If you present them first, they will serve as a preview of your work experience. If you choose to put them last, they will summarize your talents, skills, and experience.

Competence and Confidence

The most critical of all your job-search tools is your ability to project your own competence and capability. You must know that you are a qualified, competent worker before you can write a resume that creates that impression in others.

You rely on your resume to convey your abilities to people you most likely have never seen or met. This may seem uncomfortable and embarrassing, but remember that there are two sides to the job-search proposition. You are looking for a job. Your potential employer is looking for someone to do a job. It is unnecessary to think of yourself as inferior in this relationship. The two of you need each other.

When you draft your statement of objectives and your qualification summary, think of them as messages you're sending to potential employers. The message says, "I know what you need. I understand the job and its importance to your company. I am confident that I have the skills and ability to meet your needs and be an asset to your company."

Reflective and Projective Phrases

You must be able to look back over your life in order to write summaries that reveal to readers that you have clear goals in sight. Your qualifications summaries must reveal to all that you know a great deal about roles and responsibilities of targeted jobs. This is where you talk the talk that will give you the chance, whether in interviews or on the job itself, to walk the walk. Your aim, at first, is projected toward the interview. Later, your aim will include job offers and career success. Effective, action-oriented phrasing, in both your statement of objectives and your qualifications summaries, will be what shows you are capable of doing more than just talking about the future; you're prepared to make a contribution.

Special Issues for Special Circumstances

Candidates can overcome limited experience by learning as much as they can about their target fields and functions. Research is key. It's difficult to take one logistical step back before taking two forward, but this is in many cases the best approach. Take the time you need to create very detailed qualifications summaries and supporting correspondence that show how much you really do know, whether your knowledge comes from on-the-job experience, school, volunteer work, or other means. Use the correct terminology to show your familiarity with the field.

This advice holds true for recent graduates, those preparing for graduation, people in the middle of a big career change, and for undergraduates looking for part-time job internships. Focus on making your resume show how much you do know, and don't worry about what you don't know. Use your academic achievements to represent the experience you've gained in your field. Take the time to write a clear statement of your job objectives. Follow that up with a carefully crafted qualification summary, and you will have created a powerful resume.

If you choose to include your volunteer work with your paid work experiences to save space and make your work history more continuous, make sure to title the section "Experience," rather than "Employment Background" or "Professional Experience."

Resumes for recent graduates must clearly project their goal-focused qualifications. If you wish, create and use one multipurpose and several targeted versions of your resume, but don't allow fear of focus to diffuse your goals or strategies. A job search can be frustrating; don't let yourself lose the focus you need to present yourself as a talented, committed employee. Continue to assess your strategies and enhance your competencies when needed. It's amazing how one or two goal-specific courses taken at a local community college, in addition to a subscription to a field-focused professional or trade journal, can ignite a somewhat passive, if not dormant, job-search campaign. Keep track of whom you contact in your job search. Follow up, then follow up again.

People in the under-experienced category of job seekers usually have an excellent record of success, yet they can be the most frustrated and easily overcome by self-doubt. A powerful, targeted resume is a sign to yourself and others that you are engaged in a serious job search. It is powerful as a direct contact tool and as a means of networking. Use it with great pride.

Putting It All Together

Whenever possible, you should create or update your own resume, or at least attempt to do so. You will need to edit and revise until you are satisfied. It should read well to you, as well as to others whose judgment you trust. However, if you are not confident in your final version, or if the resume you have created does not generate interviews, a professional resume writer may help to increase your chances of success.

Working with a Resume Professional

The key to working with a good resume writer or resume service is finding someone whose finished product—your resume—will positively reflect who you are in a way that you can also communicate verbally. A good resume can open doors, but you still have to go on the interview yourself. In other words, if you outsource the writing of your resume to someone else, you will still need to be able to articulate your experience and background as it appears on your resume. A good resume writer will understand this concept.

Time needed for the finished product and the overall pricing often depends on your work experience, career, marketplace, and other personal factors. Typically, you will help the writer by providing information on worksheets and via one-on-one communication, in person, online, or by telephone. Most writers provide a final resume in a digital file saved in Microsoft Word format that you can print and/or update as needed.

There's no shame in seeking out the services of a professional to improve or write your resume. Not everyone can create a document that showcases their talents and education to their best advantage.

How can you find someone to do this job? There are two major reputable associations in this field. Check out the National Resume Writers' Association at *www.nrwa.com* and the Professional Association of Resume Writers and Career Coaches at *www.parw.com*. Both groups provide membership information to help you find the specialist that is best for you. A few things to consider in choosing your resume writer include:

- **Credentials.** How did this person become a resume writer? Does she or he have an employment background? What is their success rate? Ask for references and review samples before making a commitment. A great way to find a resume writing professional is often by referral, so ask around or call a staffing service and see if they can make a recommendation for you.
- **Methodology.** Ask about the process. How will the two of you accomplish your goal? What will you be required to do?
- **Chemistry.** Are you comfortable working with this person? This is a collaborative process. Do not work with someone who treats you condescendingly, displays poor customer service, or appears unprofessional.
- **Product.** Ask about the end product. What will you receive? What format will your resume be in? Can you make changes or updates yourself, or does the resume writer require you to work only through her?
- **Delivery and Price.** Fees vary widely, but you should be quoted a price based on your experience and need. Prices generally range from $150 to $1,000, and turnaround time is usually a week or more.

Spell Checking and Critiquing

Use, but don't solely depend upon, spell-checking tools within word-processing software. After you have completed your draft, print out a copy. Proofread the old-fashioned way. Read it aloud. When you do, your eyes slow down, and your ears identify potential corrections or changes. Make changes, and then repeat this process one last time. Distribution-ready resumes must be free of typos.

Seek the comments of others, but don't feel obligated to make suggested changes immediately. Many still believe in the old-style tenets, but they might not be best for you. Solicit the feedback of those you respect, particularly those within your field of interest, and seriously consider their advice. When it comes time to make final editorial decisions, however, you are the one responsible.

FACT

There is no better way to review and revitalize a job search and facilitate follow-up than by distributing a revised resume. Whenever you desire, revisit the Resume Checklist (page 100) and Resume Before-and-After Review (page 101) to determine if you are due for a new resume. Three cheers for the inventors of word processing. Thanks to them, you can easily and quickly update your resume whenever you want.

Revising Your Resume

In many ways, the first task you complete for a new employer is your resume. At the very least, this document shows those who review it your project management and communication talents. Resumes and correspondence reveal your ability to collect, analyze, and present information in the most appropriate formats, using the best phrasing and tone. They are like the first business letter you send important clients, colleagues, or customers. Put your best metaphorical foot forward. Show all who review your resume your potential for effective and dynamic communication.

Of course, resumes are not permanent. While seeking constantly evolving perfection, feel confident to make changes or additions when situations warrant. Job-search circumstances may inspire you to revise strategies and fine-tune specialized tools. The process often requires that you revise resumes for specific jobs, maybe as often as every few weeks.

Your Resume Checklist

Here is an actual step-by-step review of what you must do to create or update your resume today. This list simplifies the actions already outlined and clarified previously. Have your legal pad or, better, your laptop or desktop computer ready. You should soon be writing or typing, not just thinking. The time for action is here. Without delay, you should be able to create or update your resume in less than a day.

- ✓ Identify at least two sample resumes to model. This should now take no more than fifteen minutes.
- ✓ Reflect upon how and when these samples presented their information. Create a draft listing of headlines you might use, in the order you want them to appear. This step should take about ten minutes.
- ✓ Concisely state your job-search goal as it will appear in a statement of objectives or as the headline of a qualification summary. This step should also take ten minutes.
- ✓ With this goal in mind, make a list of significant related accomplishments. This should take about thirty minutes.
- ✓ Review significant related accomplishments to link past accomplishments with future potential via a qualification summary. It is recommended that you actually draft your entire resume, including the objective, before you take on this task. No matter whether this section is presented first or last, this section should be your last, most important, and, perhaps, lengthiest task. This could take about an hour, but it can be done in less time.
- ✓ With model resumes in view, type a draft of your version. Don't think, just type. Later, you will complete self-critiquing and copy-editing. This should take an hour at most.
- ✓ Conduct software-linked spell-checking and grammar reviews. Have someone else review for typos and format questions, then make revisions and complete the final version. Complete the Resume Before-and-After Review. It should take about fifteen minutes for the self-contained responses to specific questions, but it takes a bit longer to receive the comments of others. While you should respect comments of colleagues and friends, remain

confident that you are the best and ultimate judge regarding what
should appear in your resume and how it should be presented.

✓ Draft and finalize your cover letter. Distribute your resume. The
time it takes to complete this step will depend on whether you e-
mail your resume or deliver it by hand.

Resumes Before-and-After Review

Appendix A contains several before-and-after illustrations, and Chapter 9
includes some critiques, illustrating the transformation of a resume from
draft to finished version. Once you complete your draft, you must next complete your critique. Your silent or spoken answers to the following questions
will reveal whether your resume is ready for distribution.

If answers to the following queries are all "yes, yes, yes," your resume
has evolved from "before" to "after" status, and it is ready for distribution. If
some answers are "no," keep working. You're on the right path.

Identifying Information

✓ Is your name in larger font and bolded?

✓ Are your address, phone, and e-mail presented as part of the header?

✓ If more than one address or phone appears, is there a logical reason why, and are they presented using as few lines as possible?

Overall Appearance and First Impression

✓ Is the resume neat, easy to visually scan top to bottom, and in a
first-glance logical format?

✓ Are the font type and size easy to read and professional in
appearance?

✓ Can you scan down the page and identify a logical pattern of headline placement as well as highlighting techniques?

✓ Are capitalization, boldface, italics, indentation, and page placement used to highlight specific information in easily identifiable
patterns?

✓ Can the resume be cut and pasted into an e-mail message and still
retain logical formatting?

✔ Objective

✔ Does this statement project knowledge of your desired field and use field-specific phrasing?

✔ Is it presented in as few words as possible?

✔ Qualifications or Achievements Summary

✔ Does this paragraph or, better, bullet point listing support the stated objective?

✔ If no objective appears, does the headline used for this section clearly project your goal?

✔ Does this paragraph or bullet point listing reveal that you understand the qualifications criteria, specialized terminology, and keywords associated with your target job?

✔ Does the headline used inform the reader quickly that you have a sense of focus?

✔ Does this section reveal a thorough projection to the future as well as reflection to the past?

✔ Does the statement reflect competence as well as confidence?

✔ Are the most significant goal-related qualifications statements presented first, and less important last?

✔ If viewed independently from the resume or within a cover letter, does this section project focus and an impressive knowledge of target-specific field and functional roles?

✔ Education and Professional Development

✔ Do special headlines reinforce objective-related focus?

✔ If a traditional header is used, does it downplay the importance of this section?

✔ Does the order of appearance accurately portray significance, with most important information presented first and least important later, if not last?

✔ Does this section present school(s), degree(s), area(s) of concentration, courses, or honors?

✔ Do courses, papers, and project listings appear as subheadings or as independent headlines?

✓ For soon-to-be or recent grads, do complimentary (over 3.0) overall or subject-specific GPAs appear?

✓ Is specialized, goal-focused training and development presented under a specific headline?

✓ If specifically related to job-search target, are experiences referred to in a qualification summary?

Experience

✓ Do special headlines reinforce objective-related focus and impact order of presentation?

✓ Do the headlines project knowledge of targeted fields and draw attention to related achievements?

✓ Do headlines catch the eye, revealing through quick review the nature of entries that follow?

✓ If a traditional header is used, does it downplay the importance of this section?

✓ Are entries described using active and accomplishment-oriented phrasing, including facts and figures when possible?

✓ Are goal-specific experiences grouped under appropriate headlines, presented in order of significance?

✓ If specifically related to job-search target, is a special headline used and are experiences referred to in a qualification summary?

✓ If entries are simply cited with no descriptions, are they obviously of less importance than others?

✓ Are organizations, titles, and dates easy to see, revealing an obvious pattern and logic?

✓ Have you, for space as well as goal-directed strategies, presented only the most significant experiences, with most important appearing first and least important later?

Community Service, Cocurricular Activities, and Special Categories

✓ For soon-to-be or recent college grads, are leadership roles and achievements cited?

✓ If specifically related to job-search target, is a special headline used and are experiences referred to in a qualification summary?

✓ Do all entries seem relevant to stated goal? Do they project a logic for appearing at all?

✓ Are activities presented in easy-to-read and easy-to-follow patterns, avoiding acronyms and an overly lengthy listing of detail?

✓ If specifically related to job-search target, are experiences referred to in a qualification summary?

Overall Presentation, Last Glance, Final Details

✓ Are most important headlines presented first, with most significant information appearing under each?

✓ If your resume is more than one page, is the most important information on the first page and does the second page have your name and a page number header?

✓ If you have more than one targeted resume, are the objectives clear, did you change order of presentation for each, and are summaries of qualifications target specific?

✓ Does the resume present a professional image, with easy-to-recognize highlighting patterns, with a top-to-bottom and last-glance logical format?

✓ If a qualification summary appears last, does it summarize goal-directed competencies and capabilities accurately and dynamically?

✓ Can you elaborate upon the resume in a cover letter?

✓ Would a prospective employer sense goal-oriented competence and confidence even without an accompanying letter?

✓ Can you elaborate upon the resume and use it as a clear guide during an interview?

✓ Are you ready to duplicate and distribute your resume?

Your answers must be affirmative to all these questions, or you are not ready for the final steps. Don't be overly analytical or self-critical. Finish and use your resume. If needed, you can always update it, and it will only take another day!

Duplicating and Distributing

Resumes can be printed each time one is needed or they can be copied using a quality photocopier. Good laser and ink jet printers create copies on quality bond paper in conservative and easy to duplicate colors (white, off-white, and ivory). Traditional laid or linen bond (not parchment) paper is best for mailing, faxing, and hand delivery. Use blank pages and envelopes that match for job-search correspondence and for personal branding purposes. If you create a master copy on plain paper, photocopy on better paper; duplicates must be clean and toner residue-free.

FACT

Today, most resumes are electronically transmitted in some way (largely by e-mail), so issues related to duplication have changed. Anxieties and old causes for frustration and procrastination have been diminished if not eliminated. You have no excuse to delay creating, updating, duplicating, and distributing your resume today.

Circumstances will dictate whether you e-mail, post, fax, or mail your resumes. While you can combine two approaches to the same employer, it's not a good idea to do all four unless you are specifically requested to do so. Eventually, you will use the telephone and other letters as you follow up on your resume distribution. As you can see in the closing comments of almost all our cover letter samples, it is always appropriate to proactively follow up a resume with a phone call confirming its receipt and, if possible, requesting an interview or clarifying strategically sound next steps.

Common Resume Blunders

Sixty-three percent of human resources managers surveyed in a resume poll reported that spelling errors are the most annoying mistakes they see. Other gaffes include:

- Resumes that don't fit the position (30 percent)
- Lies (23 percent)
- TMI—too much info! Don't include insignificant details about duties performed.
- Resumes that are more than two pages long (21 percent)

Remember, sending resumes is only one of the eight steps to job-search success. These powerful pages must be used as part of a comprehensive strategy. You will use your resume to get interviews, and you will use it during your interviews. You will get offers and make good decisions. In behavioral and motivational terms it's the person—not the page—that succeeds.

Chapter 7

Resumes, Cover Letters, and You

You've heard all your life that you can't tell a book by its cover. While this may be metaphorically true for some publications and people, it's not the case for resumes. A cover letter is the basis for your employer's first impression. It invites your reader to examine your resume thoroughly. From glancing at your cover letter, your prospective employer gleans information about your personality, your communication style, your attention to detail, and your professional qualifications. This chapter examines the relationship between your resume and the letter that accompanies it.

Always Send a Cover Letter

It's easy to focus too much job-search attention on resumes. But the cover letter is just as important. Regardless of the means you use to submit your resume, and regardless of who the prospective employer is, never send your resume without a cover letter. While a complete letter may not be necessary in all circumstances, at the very least a quick note should accompany your resume, especially if you are sending your resume via e-mail.

Your cover letter represents you. It tells your readers what you most want them to know about you and your goals. Just like your resume, your cover letter mirrors your knowledge of self and your knowledge of qualification criteria associated with specific positions or functional areas.

In the old days, a standard cover letter included a line asking readers to "assess my candidacy and determine the most appropriate fit." Today, you must quickly and clearly state your goals, briefly present your qualifications, and then refer your reader to the resume. While cover letters are most definitely written for others to read, they are in many ways personal tests of your abilities to state and support job-search targets. They are the preassessment tools that help you make it to the job interview.

Always cover your resume with a letter or a note. If you are told to "just send a resume," what you should hear is, "Send a resume and a supplemental document focusing the reader's attention on your desired goals." While you may not actually hear that lengthy phrase, you should always send some form of letter. Resumes should, in good taste, never be naked.

Ideally, every cover letter you send will be addressed to a particular person. "To whom it may concern" or "Sir or Madam" are never appropriate salutations. If you don't know the recipient's name, start the letter immediately following address information, or use a memo format. Correspondence-style or memo-formatted documents can be faxed, e-mailed, or physically mailed. Know your target readers and write accordingly.

The best cover letters and resumes can stand alone, soliciting and supporting consideration. Readers can look at either independently and have enough information to judge the candidate's worthiness for an interview. But when they're combined with a resume, the impact of the two is much greater.

Ironically, the most common mistake made by job seekers is overdependence on resumes. No matter how powerful the words on this page, they must be continually supported by your assertive and appropriate actions, reactions, and continued interactions.

Types of Job-Search Correspondence

You will write many different types of letters as you progress through your job search. The following sections describe a few of them.

Letters of Introduction

A letter of introduction does just what it says; it introduces you and your circumstances to readers. You also clearly identify what you would like the reader to do next and what you will do next. You can seek assistance, specific information, or referrals. Most often, readers are prospective network members and advocates or persons who can offer answers to specific questions. Less often, they are potential employers from whom you solicit consideration.

Letters of introduction are most effectively used as research and information-gathering tools. They ask readers to conduct conversations or to give referrals to people, organizations, or Web sites that might be of assistance. Always phrase your requests in ways that require more than yes or no responses. They should inspire readers to forward names, e-mail addresses, phone numbers, Web sites, or other desired information. In closing, you note whether you will patiently wait for an e-mail response or follow up by phone to discuss reactions to your request.

Don't ever ignore the power of a brief cover note, most often an e-mail. Effective communication does not have to be formal or lengthy. You can first briefly ask for some very specific information and then follow up with more detailed documentation. In fact, people today may respond better at first to a number of quick e-bites, rather than one multiparagraph document. While it is always a good idea to attach resumes to any job-search letter, you do not have to do so with these briefer messages. Eventually, through follow-up efforts, you will send resumes to everyone you contact. Letters of introduction are particularly helpful when you utilize social networking Web sites. They may help you gain critical information or provide entrée to prospective employers of interest.

Letters of Application

A letter of application is a reactive tool used specifically to apply for a posted position. Within this letter, you first state the job title (and number when given), where you saw the posting, and your desire to interview for the position. Later, you support requests for consideration by offering an accurate assessment of your qualifications. These two, or at most three, subsequent paragraphs show readers that you know the field, function, and title in question and that you have thought about what it will take to succeed.

These middle sections are where you very thoroughly share with readers what you learned through inventorying your qualifications and achievements and analyzing your goal-focused competencies and capabilities. This can be done simply by rephrasing your resume's qualification summary. You are the one required to look back, then look forward, and, most important, share your confident, future-focused views. After reviewing these paragraphs, readers must sense that you are worthy of an interview.

Be prepared to reflect knowledge of the job, and use words contained in the announcement. Show readers that you have more than the minimum qualifications. Refer to your attached resume, and expand upon the qualification summary. Again and again, the more you talk the talk, the more likely you will walk the walk, down the path toward job-search and career success.

FACT

Career professionals believe that sending your resume directly to a recruiter's inbox is up to twenty times more effective than posting your resume to a job board. Once you've e-mailed your resume to a recruiter, it is perfectly permissible to follow up via e-mail. According to a Hot-Jobs survey, 53 percent of recruiters say candidates should wait one week before following up.

You should use phrases from your resume that reflect upon past achievements, with a preference for those that project knowledge of the future. Maintain and share your always-improving target vocabulary in letters of application. Use words from the actual job description and from Web sites and articles written about the firm. Through this targeted letter of application, you are applying for a particular job with a specific organization. Give them a clear sense of your focus.

For creative fields, including public relations, advertising, and publishing, you can take more creative approaches, but for others, goal-direct yet formal phrasing will do. Some jobs allow you to take a more humorous approach, while others may require you to illustrate your abilities to create and send formal business communication skills. Know your audience, and keep in mind that you can share creativity in follow-up letters, rather than in first contacts.

Whenever possible, close letters of application with a statement like, "I will call to confirm receipt of this letter and to discuss the next step." You must remember to follow up initial correspondence with phone calls and, if needed, with e-mails, then phone calls again. Do leave voicemail messages if you don't get through when you call. Don't call too often; be persistent, yet not obnoxious.

Later in this chapter, samples illustrate a very user-friendly and quick approach to creating effective letters of application.

Letters of Inquiry

A letter of inquiry is a proactive tool, used to inquire about current opportunities and, most often, to inspire individualized consideration for future ones. In order to gain consideration, you must reinforce the sense of focus represented in your resume. In fact, the more effective you are at revealing your knowledge of the field, the more likely it is you will get an interview. Show reviewers that you have done your homework about the field, function, and firm. Ironically, the last is very much the least important. If readers are impressed with your knowledge of the field and with your abilities to serve within specific functions, you don't need to impress them with your knowledge of their firm. You'll have the opportunity in the interview to show how much you know about the particular organization.

A letter of inquiry is your opportunity to state in very clear terms what field and within what functions you are focusing your search. Ideally, you can cite some commonly used job titles, but they don't have to be specific to any particular organization. Like letters of application, the middle two, or at most three, paragraphs show readers that you have analyzed what it will take to succeed. You support your request for consideration by offering your summary of qualifications.

Address queries like the following:

- Why have you chosen the particular field?
- What does your background have to do with the field and the function you wish to serve?
- What are the key qualities required to serve within the desired day-to-day roles?

Answer these questions proactively, and you will have the opportunity to answer others reactively, via the phone or in person during an interview. Use phrases and vocabulary that are field specific.

ESSENTIAL

Samples appearing later illustrate user-friendly and effective letters of inquiry. Some inquiry and referral notes can be brief and followed by a more detailed letter, but you should always be clear regarding your focus. A very brief, three- or four-sentence expression can close with "a more detailed letter will soon follow" statement, but always include what functions you are interested in.

Some letters of inquiry begin with an "I'm contacting you at the suggestion of" a specific person who is serving as an advocate or network member. A name recognizable to the reader at the very beginning of your correspondence should ensure that it will be thoroughly read and, you hope, that an interview will follow. Close all letters of inquiry with, "I will call to confirm receipt." You might also wish to copy your contact person to generate some behind-the-scenes supportive communication. Don't hesitate to identify the option of "meeting to discuss current opportunities or informally discussing future options."

Networking Requests

Networking involves clearly stating your goals, then asking for specific help from others to attain these goals. These requests can be of persons you know or of those you would like to know. They can follow or be included in letters of introduction to individuals who are at first just names gained via articles, professional association directories, or search engine referrals. As with all communications, the impact will come from follow-up efforts.

Requests for networking assistance should be clear and concise. Not everyone shares a common definition of this term. With a letter, you can seek "information about your career biography," "advice regarding how to gain consideration within your organization," or "referrals to others who can provide information or consideration." When you do research before you actively start your job search, you might focus on the first and third requests. When in job-search mode, you might focus on the second and third.

When communicating with alumni, family, or friends, do not be vague in your requests. If you want the names and e-mail addresses of specific people, ask for them. If you want to know how to break into a specific field or whether the recipient will forward the attached resume to the right person, ask. Regardless of your request, be appreciative in tone and in words. Be sure you say thank you. Then say it again, for good measure.

Follow-Up Letters

Ideally, everyone you contacted would respond promptly and positively. But as you know, job-search undertakings are most often far from ideal. Effective campaigns involve follow-up communication. Patience may be a virtue, but it is not a characteristic of a strategic job search. Your challenge is to figure out what to say next and when to say it.

Your cover letters will broadcast your intent to call and confirm receipt of your resume. Don't expect much out of this exchange. Very few of them will result in any kind of positive response. Most likely, you will leave a message with a receptionist or a voicemail system. Do leave voicemail messages. Identify yourself, state that you sent a cover letter and resume, and express your wish to confirm receipt and, ideally, set up a phone or in-person interview.

You should alternate your communication approaches—phone calls, e-mails, and faxes—and be sensitive to how often you are contacting potential employers. Because most resumes today are e-mailed or faxed, your initial confirmation call can take place within twenty-four hours. The old, "I will call within a week" standard closing phrase is most definitely passé. If next-day calls get through, that's great. If they lead to interviews, wonderful. Most likely, they will yield a polite, "Please be patient." If you talk to an actual person, ask when you should call back. Then follow the suggested time frame. If you were told next week, don't call before that. In general, one contact a week for the first three weeks, then one contact a month after that, is a good rule of thumb.

FACT

Whenever you make a revision in your resume, you have a good reason to send a brief follow-up letter. Whether it's because you've changed your address, added a new course or seminar, or seen another posting on a Web site, after you've updated your resume, send it accompanied by a cover note. Refer quickly to past contacts, yet focus on what is new on the resume.

You can follow calls with brief telegram-style e-mails. A message like the following is appropriate:

"Tried to call today, but could not get through. Understand how busy you are. Just wanted to confirm receipt of resume and cover letter. Can we talk by phone or in person? Thanks."

For the first follow-up contact, you can include another copy of the cover letter and resume. For the following two (maximum) follow-up contacts, you can include just a copy of your resume.

Thank-You Letters

Expressing appreciation is a very effective form of job-search communication. While it may sound trite, you can say thank you at every step along the way. Everyone knows to send a thank-you note after interviews, but too few communicate their gratitude before then. A thanks for confirming receipt of your resume, including an expression of continued interest and a clearly articulated wish for a telephone or a face-to-face interview, is usually the first of these efforts.

A thanks for clarifying status, including an expression of continued interest, with a statement regarding when you might follow up again, is most likely the second. Too often ignored, a thank you for a rejection letter or e-mail is also appropriate. Respond to a "your background does not match" letter or e-mail with an "I remain very interested in your firm, hope at a future date my qualifications might be appropriate for other opportunities" statement. Be careful of tone, but do seek continued consideration as well as some additional focus.

Appreciation should always be expressed to network members and advocates who have referred you to postings or persons. By keeping these individuals informed of your efforts, you inspire their own follow-up efforts. Follow-up calls or e-mails by network members to their contacts requesting special consideration often lead to interviews and speed up an otherwise slow process. In many ways, your follow-up networking letters are as important as those to organizations you wish to work for.

Confirmation, Acceptance, and Declining Letters

While it's usually not legally or logistically required, it is a good idea to confirm most activities and decisions in written form. Whether these expressions are transmitted via electronic means or physically mailed is not important. But it is important that you communicate continually and effectively. The use of e-mails has made this process quicker, easier, and less awkward.

You must call or e-mail a few days before each interview to confirm the time and date and to assist with your preparation for this important series of conversations. When making decisions regarding offers, you must continue to communicate enthusiastically. After you have made a decision, you will accept or decline via a brief note.

These continued communications are good habits to get into and they set the scene for future positive interactions. Preinterview contacts facilitate critical next steps, and post-offer communications impact salary and other discussions. In many cases, they can lead to consideration and offers years from now.

E-mail versus Snail Mail

Those who remember record albums and rotary telephones also remember the job search was different in the olden days. Today, e-mail is the most common and accepted way to send resumes and all follow-up letters. But do not forget that alternating media can diminish the potential for oversaturation and negative consequences and might even give you a competitive advantage.

"Snail mail" is a phrase used for the slow but sure (we think) U.S. Postal Service. At one time, the only persons who delivered resumes, cover letters, and all other correspondence were the men and women in red, white, and blue. Today, we have wearers of the brown (UPS), blue and orange (FedEx), and others who can guarantee delivery in one or two days. Don't ignore the impact of express delivery on specific individuals, particularly those with whom you have spoken over the phone, but remember that e-communication is now the most cost-effective, immediate, and safe form of delivery.

If you think recipients may be concerned about virus-carrying e-mails, copy and paste your resume straight into the text box, and do not identify it as an attachment. Remember to note the title of the job desired and the words "Enclosed resume" in the e-mail subject heading.

E-mailed cover letters can and should be shorter than traditionally mailed cover letters. An e-mail recipient expects correspondence to be brief and to the point. Be sure to note in your subject line something like: Marketing Exec w/10+ years in B2B for Director of Marketing Opening. The body of your message should generate immediate interest by indicating experience and relevant skills. Reference your attached resume. Do not be overly friendly or use any instant messaging abbreviations or smiley-faced emoticons.

You can follow some electronically transmitted letters with hard copies, just to be safe and traditional, but do not depend solely on paper, envelopes, and stamps as your job-search tools. When you do send items by mail, make sure you have the correct postage. Match your resume and cover letter paper, and use large mailing envelopes so you don't have to fold your contents.

Phone and Fax

These communication and transmission techniques are underused but not obsolete. With the preferred method of e-mail, fewer people use the phone and fax as follow-up tools. You are encouraged to use the phone whenever possible and, when the situation warrants, a faxed resume is permissible. While at first awkward for most, phone skills and confidence grow with each call. Do call to confirm receipt of documents, to identify next steps, and to make a clear request for an interview. Leave brief, slow, and clear voicemail messages whenever you call. Don't appear to be a pest, but do be persistent and professional.

After you have left a message or two, e-mail a note. Always briefly and clearly state who you are, when and how your earlier contact was made, and what you would like to happen next. Don't be afraid to state, "I would like to meet with you," or more assertively, "I would appreciate an interview." Also, ask if they would like another copy of your resume to refresh their memory regarding your background. It is okay to provide one with the first two follow-up letters, particularly those that are faxed.

Sample Cover Letters and Follow-Up Letters

The following samples share insights into the job-search efforts of our fictional friends. Through a longitudinal glimpse at these initial contact and follow-up letters, you should be inspired to create or update effective documentation.

To maximize the effectiveness of your resume and correspondence, make your communications personal. Whether you are a soon-to-be or recent college grad, an experienced candidate, or someone seeking a promotion, the content and style of your communication will impact success. Be inspired by the samples that follow, but make sure the documents you use are obviously yours and that they clearly connect to your goals. Your written and spoken voice during your job search must sound like you.

Advertising AE Letter of Application

- This letter of application may be used when applying for a Web posting or a classified advertisement.

- Addressed to actual contact person. Name gained via company Web site, then confirmed by phone.

- Document first uses abbreviated qualification summary from resume to present overall candidacy.

- Second set of bullets paraphrases qualifications in actual ad. These must be changed for each letter of application, depending upon the job and requirements.

- This copy and paste, then change technique can be used when applying for almost any posted job. Make sure the specific qualifications highlighted match the position sought and contain keywords used in the posting and within the field. This is crucial for keyword searches associated with Web-based resume collections.

- In some cases, the specific qualifications may appear before the general ones.

CHRIS SMITH

123 Main Street • Hometown, NY 00000 • (555) 555-1234 • csmith@company.com

August 23, 20–

Jamie Stenson
Account Supervisor
Saatchi and Saatchi
8765 Broadway
New York, NY 14623-0450
FAX (555) 555-5555

Ms. Stenson:

I would like to interview for an Assistant Account Executive position. Relevant courses in Marketing, Finance, and Accounting, as well as independent marketing projects have enabled me to develop practical skills and perspectives. Knowledge of strategic planning, marketing research, budgeting, advertising techniques, and related report-writing and presentation skills have been fine-tuned in varied settings. In general, I offer:

- Marketing research, strategic planning, promotions, customer service, and sales talents nurtured by in-depth and diverse advertising, promotions, and retail internships and employment.
- Technical skills gained via courses including: Principles of Marketing, Marketing Projects and Cases, Psychology of Human Motivation and Emotion, Business Administration, Public Relations Writing, Advertising, Mass Media, Persuasion, and Consumer Behavior.
- Confidence serving on account team and interacting with client colleagues.
- Blend of research, analysis, writing, and presentation talents.
- Proficiency in Word, Excel, PowerPoint, PhotoShop, and Dreamweaver.

Specific qualifications that match those cited on your Web site as required include:

- Marketing research, strategic planning, promotions, customer service, and sales talents nurtured in advertising and promotions internships.
- Blend of quantitative, analytical, and creative problem-solving talents.
- Capacities to conduct and analyze research, and then translate data into persuasive proposals, reports, and graphics.
- Intense curiosity regarding consumer behavior, varied products and industries, and the nature of market segmentation.

I graduated from University of Rochester with dual majors, a minor in Economics, and, most significantly, a Certificate in Management Studies in Marketing. As my resume indicates, I have had a number of related internships with local as well as international firms. I would welcome the chance to discuss my qualifications. I will call to confirm receipt of this fax (originals to follow by mail) and, at your convenience, to arrange a brief meeting.

Sincerely,

Chris Smith

Advertising AE Follow-Up E-mail

CHRIS SMITH
123 Main Street • Hometown, NY 00000 • (555) 555-1234 • csmith@company.com

August 23, 20–

Jane Green
Recruiter
jgrecruiter@company.com

As shared with Jamie Stenson via the attached letter, my post-graduation objective is to begin a career in advertising. It is with focus and enthusiasm that I seek to interview for an account management focused position at Saatchi & Saatchi. After speaking with Ms. Stenson's assistant, Kim, I understand that you coordinate all requests for consideration, and that recent graduates can be considered for internships as well as post-baccalaureate opportunities.

Relevant courses in Marketing, Finance, and Economics, as well as many independent marketing projects, have enabled me to develop practical skills and perspectives. Knowledge of strategic planning, marketing research, budgeting, advertising techniques, and related research, report-writing, and presentation skills have been fine-tuned in varied roles and settings.

As my resume indicates, I have had a number of internships in the past five years. Each has taught me much and nurtured advertising-related skills. I would welcome the chance to discuss my qualifications with you and your Saatchi & Saatchi colleagues as soon as appropriate. I will call to confirm receipt of this e-mail (originals to follow via mail) and, at your convenience, to arrange a telephone or in-person interview.

Trips to New York are easy to arrange. Perhaps we could meet when I am next in the city? I am committed to this field and I will persevere to succeed through job search and beyond. Thank you for your consideration.

Sincerely,

Chris Smith

- E-mail used as initial contact via referral from original communiqué.

- Font as per e-mail setting.

- This follow-up supplements a letter of inquiry for general opportunities within a particular field or a letter of application, in specific application for a posted job.

- The candidate is making first contact with a person whose name has been referred by another.

- E-mail is a quick way to transmit follow-up communiqués.

- Document covers original letter as well as resume. It is copied and pasted into the actual e-mail text box, with other documents sent as attachments.

Letter of Introduction and Networking E-mail

- E-mail introduction sent to initiate networking activities with alumnus.

- Expectations clearly cited.

- Candidate's background only briefly noted.

- Illustrates a letter of introduction and a networking letter, used to gain information and referrals within a particular functional area.

- The candidate is making first contact with a person who might serve as a network member or advocate. Initially, contact was gained through online alumni directory.

- This document seeks specific consideration for a position with the alumnus' firm as well as general referrals.

DANA JOHNSON

123 Main Street • Hometown, NY 00000 • (555) 555-1234 • djohnson@company.com

August 23, 20–

Marty Jones
Account Manager
DDB Needham
mjones@company.com

Mr. Jones:

The advice and support of a University of Rochester alumnus would be much appreciated. My post-graduation objective is to begin a career in advertising. It is with focus and curiosity that I seek to learn about your own career path and, respectfully, request referrals to persons within your firm and other agencies who might grant me an interview.

Through telephone or, if convenient, in-person discussions I would welcome learning about your background to gain insights regarding how I can perhaps enter the field of advertising. Ideally, I would do so as an assistant account executive. Specific suggestions regarding how to network and successfully solicit interviews would be well received.

The attached resume is offered to quickly familiarize you with my background. A more detailed cover letter can follow if you judge my candidacy worthy of consideration by you and your DDB Needham colleagues. As the resume indicates, I have had a number of related internships over the past five years, and my academics have given me strong conceptual foundations upon which I have built field-specific skills. I will call to confirm receipt of this e-mail and, at your convenience, to arrange a phone conversation or a meeting. In advance, thank you for your assistance.

Sincerely,

Dana Johnson

Advertising AE Letter of Inquiry

FRANCIS WILLIAMS

123 Main Street • Hometown, NY 00000 • (555) 555-1234 • fwilliams@company.com

August 23, 20–

Marty Jones
Human Resources Manager
Ogilvy and Mather
123 West 49th Street
New York, NY 14624
FAX (555) 555-5555

Ms. Jones:

I read with great interest your career profile on ZoomInfo.com. If I may be so bold, I would like to interview for an entry-level account management position with O&M. Independent marketing projects, related internships, and relevant courses in Marketing, Finance, and Accounting have enabled me to develop practical skills and hands-on experience in the advertising industry. Knowledge of strategic planning, marketing research, budgeting, advertising techniques, and related report-writing and presentation skills have been fine-tuned in varied settings.

Diverse account management qualifications and capabilities include:

- Marketing research, strategic planning, promotions, customer service, and sales talents nurtured by in-depth and diverse advertising, promotions, and retail internships and employment.
- Technical skills gained via courses including: Principles of Marketing, Marketing Projects and Cases, Psychology of Human Motivation and Emotion, Business Administration, Public Relations Writing, Advertising, Mass Media, Persuasion, and Consumer Behavior.
- Confidence serving on account team and interacting with client colleagues.
- Blend of research, analysis, writing, and presentation talents.
- Knowledge of International Business approaches gained living and working in varied North American, European, and Middle Eastern settings.
- German, French, Dutch, and Farsi fluency, and conversational Spanish capabilities.
- Proficiency in Word, Excel, PowerPoint, PhotoShop, and Dreamweaver.

I graduated from University of Rochester with dual majors, a minor in Economics, and a Certificate in Management Studies in Marketing. As my resume indicates, I have had a number of significant advertising-focused internships. During an interview, I can expand upon internships as well as the above bullets, learn more about the nature of opportunities at Ogilvy & Mather, and support my candidacy for account management-related positions. I will call to follow up this e-mail to see if you will consider an exploratory interview. I will make myself available at your convenience. Thank you.

Sincerely,

Francis Williams

- Times New Roman font and header match resume.

- Recipient was identified on a social networking business site—a good way to network online.

- This illustrates a letter of inquiry for general opportunities within a particular field.

- The candidate is making first contact with a person on his hit list. Initially, contacts are identified via directories or Web sites, then confirmed through phone conversations.

- This document uses the qualification summary as an easy and effective way to present overall qualifications.

- Coverletter–writing doesn't have to be difficult to be effective. Qualifications highlighted must match positions sought and targeted fields.

Advertising AE Thank-You Note

Corey Davis
123 Main Street • Hometown, NY 00000 • (555) 555-1234 • cdavis@company.com

September 17, 20–

Jane Green
Recruiter
Saatchi & Saatchi
jg@company.com

Ms. Green:

I appreciate the opportunity I had to share qualifications for an account assistant position. The more people I meet, and the more I learn from enthusiastic professionals like you, Jamie Stenson, and Bill Burton, the more eager I become to join you and your colleagues on the Saatchi & Saatchi team. I do look forward to hearing soon regarding the outcome of the interview. The writing sample we discussed will be forwarded shortly by e-mail.

Thank you again for your time and consideration. I sincerely hope to begin an achievement-filled career with Saatchi & Saatchi. As a dedicated account assistant, I will contribute to the multifaceted research, analysis, campaign development, and client-relations roles associated with this critical area. It was exciting to see how enthusiastic your colleagues were about their particular accounts, particularly those who have Hershey as a client.

As discussed during the interview, I will strive to personify the blend of creative, quantitative, analytical, and communication talents required to add value to the account team, the client, and the firm.

Sincerely,

Corey Davis

Advertising AE Acceptance E-mail

CHRIS SMITH

123 Main Street • Hometown, NY 00000 • (555) 555-5555 • csmith@company.com

September 27, 20–

Jane Green
Recruiter
Saatchi & Saatchi
jg@company.com

Ms. Green:

It is with great pride that I confirm through this e-mail that I accept the account assistant position. I understand that my immediate supervisor will be Bill Burton and that my starting salary will be $35,000 annually. The start date of October 1st seems ideal, and I will visit your office within the next few days to complete all required forms. I am eager to join the Saatchi & Saatchi team and begin an achievement-filled tenure as an account assistant. Ideally, this will mark the beginning of a long and productive career with the firm.

As we discussed after the offer was extended, I do appreciate your agreeing to a performance and salary review after six months, and another one year after my start date. This will allow me to prove my value and hopefully offset the financial burden of my relocation to the New York City area. Of course, the relocation allowance of $1,500 is most generous and will be used appropriately.

My personal thanks go out to you for your efforts throughout all stages of the consideration and interview process. I will see you soon, when I visit to complete paperwork. If you wish to contact me for any reason, please do so via the phone number or e-mail address above.

Sincerely,

Chris Smith

- This e-mail confirms verbal acceptance of an offer. While not a legal document, it does clarify key points. Some employers continue to send formal offer letters, detailing all aspects of compensation and related maters, but not all maintain this practice. Candidates who don't wish to offend by asking for something in writing can send messages like this one.

- It details issues covered in discussions.

- If any questions are raised regarding the details cited, it's best that this occur immediately following receipt of this note. Then clarifications can be immediately addressed.

- After this note is sent and all is confirmed, thank-you notes and clarification of outcomes should be sent to network members.

Public Relations Letter of Inquiry

- Identifying information notes addresses from which letter is sent.

- Left-justified block text format is e-friendly; can be uploaded to Web sites and copied and pasted into e-mail.

- Illustrates letter of inquiry for opportunities within a particular field.

- Candidate is making first contact with a person on her hit list. Contacts are identified via printed directories, Web sites, or social networking business sites, then confirmed through telephone conversations. This was gained through a professional association membership directory.

- Requests consideration for entry-level or internship options and introduces the concept of an information interview.

- It raises a variety of options that must be addressed during follow-up communication.

JAMIE BROWN

123 Main Street • Hometown, NY 00000 • (555) 555-1234 • jbrown@company.com

April 8, 20–

Marty Jones
ABC PR
234 East 45th Street
New York, NY 00000
Fax (555) 555-5555

Mr. Jones:

How about an honest cover letter as a refreshing alternative? When first asked, "What do you want to do after graduation?" my answer was "I don't know." After introspection and active research, I can now confidently, enthusiastically, and ambitiously answer, "A career in PR." This field will make excellent use of my existing talents and offer the growth and creativity I seek as a business professional. Assets I offer your firm include:

- *Abilities to conduct research on various topics, identify key trends, then present findings in verbal and written reports, promotional materials, feature articles, or press communiqués.*
- *Interest in transforming understanding of behavior and motivation to strategic campaigns, promotional efforts, fundraising events, persuasive publications, and educational activities.*
- *Capacities to use statistical techniques to analyze and present data.*
- *Confidence planning and implementing events independently or in groups, with particular focus on creatively identifying goals, logistics, and details required to succeed.*
- *Experience using Word, Excel, PowerPoint, and Internet applications for academic, creative, and other projects.*

Serving within entry-level or internship capacities, I will achieve my professional and personal goals. I will become an effective event planner and creative writer, a strategist working with clients to develop and implement targeted campaigns, and a peer who will brainstorm with, support, and inspire those around me. I will always be a responsible professional who continues to improve her skills and completes tasks accurately and on time.

I will call to confirm receipt of this letter and accompanying resume and, ideally, arrange telephone or in-person conversations regarding opportunities at ABC. While I am seeking a full-time position, I would welcome consideration for internship or part-time options. Most important, I want to speak with you, a successful professional, about your career, my talents, and about your firm's needs. I'm confident that my dream job can become a reality and I hope this is the first step. I look forward to continued communication and interactions.

Sincerely,
Jamie Brown

Pharmaceutical Sales Letter of Application and Follow-Up

Dana Johnson

123 Main Street • Hometown, New York 00000 • (555) 555-1234 • djohnson@company.com

April 7, 20–

Ms. Marty Jones
District Manager
Pharmaceutical Giant, Inc.
100 San Paso Way
San Francisco, CA 12121
Fax: (555) 555-5555

Ms. Jones:

Thank you for speaking with me the other day. As I have discussed with you and Dr. Smith, my goal is to begin and succeed within a pharmaceutical sales career. Ideally, that career will be with Pharmaceutical Giant. Most critically, I am confident that I can enhance market share of Pharmaceutical Giant products and personify the profile of a physician, patient, and profit-inspired professional. Regular reading of Pharmaceutical Representative Online and other related sites and publications reinforces my goals. It was exciting to see that Pharmaceutical Giant has brands within many of the top profitable categories for the past fiscal year. These include antiulcerants, cholesterol and triglyceride reducers, antidepressants, calcium antagonists, plain antirheumatic non-steroidals, ACE inhibitors, plain cephalosporins and combinations, antipsychotics, non-narcotic analgesics, and oral antidiabetics.

Detailed on the attached resume, contributions to my current employer helped turn 2006 into a successful year despite the economic downturn. Unlike traditional sales positions where the relationship between salesperson and customer ends with the close of a deal, my position requires the establishment of an ongoing relationship, similar to those built between pharmaceutical representatives and physician customers. I am required to convince my customers to turn to me for all their needs, just as a Pharmaceutical Giant representative inspires physicians to prescribe represented medications on a regular basis. In summary, I offer:

- Record of success within direct marketing and information-driven sales roles.
- Confidence nurturing existing relationships and developing new clientele via direct calls using information dissemination strategies.
- Capacity to share knowledge pertaining to pharmaceutical products and protocols.
- Abilities to blend qualitative and communication talents as well as analytical skills to set goals, document impact of sales efforts, and maximize output.

I will call to confirm receipt of this letter and, I sincerely hope, to continue our discussions. Ideally, I will soon have the opportunity to support my qualifications via a formal interview. Also, while eager to apply my talents to opportunities in the Bay area, I would definitely consider relocating for the chance to join Pharmaceutical Giant.

Sincerely,

Dana Johnson

- Detailed introductory paragraph reveals field-focused research.

- Second paragraph highlights most significant experience.

- Closing presentation of qualification summary as it appeared in resumes serves to tie all concepts together.

- This cover letter illustrates a letter of inquiry.

- The candidate is making first formal contact after a telephone conversation, facilitated by a referral from a physician.

- The letter is detailed because the contact encouraged the candidate to include everything he knows, but it keep it to a page. Many pharmaceutical firms ask for supplemental goal sheets. This candidate incorporated some of these concepts in the letter.

- Candidate identifies geographical target, yet raises willingness to relocate.

Investment Banking Template Letter of Inquiry

FRANCIS WILLIAMS

123 Main Street, Apartment 13 • Hometown, NY 00000
(555) 555-1234 • fwilliams@company.com

TO: Contact Name
               Company Name

DATE: February 27, 20–

FAX: (555) 555-5678

SUBJECT: **Analyst Position**

As an Economics major at Harvard, I completed several key economics and statistics courses. In addition, I took undergraduate courses in finance at Boston University. As noted on my resume, I have also served in diverse finance-focused internships. While I have proven that I can excel academically and within internship capacities, I now seek the challenges associated with succeeding as an Analyst at [COMPANY NAME].

Basic qualifications I offer include:

- Knowledge of the industry and economics gained through upper-level and honors courses, as well as substantial internship experience.
- Analytical ability honed by honors microeconomics and fundamental finance courses.
- Ability to work long hours and succeed, demonstrated by academic performance, extensive internship experience in finance industry, and broad cocurricular leadership.

Specifically associated with the responsibilities of an Analyst, I offer:

- Experience completing research projects within demanding, pressure-filled, deadline-driven financial institutions.
- Capacities to quickly understand and examine issues, and identify trends associated with capital formation products and services, including: derivatives, IPOs, Mergers and Acquisitions, Bond Markets, and [FIRM SPECIALTIES HERE].
- Technical skills gained as an intern include: using spreadsheets for sophisticated as well as simple modeling; investigating investment worthiness and profit-and-loss leverages; and presenting findings to critical and analytical colleagues.

Extensive computer skills and exceptional analytical capacities will also help me succeed at [COMPANY NAME]. I will call to confirm receipt of this fax and, I do sincerely hope, to arrange an interview. At present, I have some interview trips to New York City planned. Perhaps I could meet with you during my next visit?

Sincerely,

Francis Williams

Private School Teacher Letter of Application, Inquiry, and Follow-Up

Chris Smith

123 Main Street • Hometown, NY 00000 • (555) 555-1234 • csmith@company.com

March 22, 20–

Marty Jones
Headmaster of the ABC School
2345 School Street
Princeton, NJ 12321
Fax (555) 555-5555

Headmaster Jones:

Commencement signifies a beginning, when I will start new experiences, yet never stop learning. Being a teacher requires self-motivation for ongoing learning and the inspiration of others to do the same. As a teacher at ABC, I will empower students as they progress toward their commencement. Too many students have aversions toward studying languages, exploring theories associated with making and spending money, and examining timeless themes in books not mentioned on talk show television.

Teaching would allow me to use lessons similar to those of my favorite instructors. I can imagine teaching vocabulary in an interactive and engaging manner. I would group students and teach vocabulary for foods by having them make and use picture flash cards. Students would show cards, then ask and respond to questions such as, "Which food do you like best?" I would relate economics to the world of high school students. For example, I could use pizza and wings to explain diminishing returns to scale. The first piece of pizza could be described as the most delicious while the twelfth may perhaps be nauseating. English literature would involve powerful relations and comparisons between different works of literature and society.

A position at ABC will allow me to begin my teaching career, provide intrinsic rewards associated with inspiring students, and provide me the continued learning that I crave. In return, I offer:

- Confidence in tutorial roles, assisting peers with college and secondary courses.
- Sensitivities to ability levels and communication styles of varied learners.
- Desire to teach French language and literature as well as science or economics courses.

My desires to become an effective teacher, mentor, and motivator will drive me as I continue to learn at ABC. I am pleased that Professor Sanders informed you of my candidacy, and I am most eager to discuss my qualifications by phone or in person. Thank you for your consideration.

Sincerely,
Chris Smith

- Illustrates a letter of application as well as a follow-up letter because it is written in response to a referral from a third-party teacher-placement agency.

- It can serve as a personal statement—a document often required of candidates seeking teaching positions.

- This document uses qualification summary adaptation as an easy and effective way to present overall qualifications.

- It also contains sample lesson plan descriptions and expresses great enthusiasm for teaching.

Chapter 8

Resumes as Interview Preparation and Motivation Tools

Somewhere you've read this advice: Use resumes to get interviews, and use interviews to get offers. An even more accurate statement would be: Use your resume to get interviews and use it again during interviews; then you'll definitely get offers. This chapter identifies how to use resumes as both interview preparation and motivation tools.

The Resume, Interview, and You

Never interview without a copy of your resume in your hand, in your heart, and in your head. The interviewer will refer to this document to inspire questions. You can use it to inspire answers as well as attitudes. While it may seem simple and somewhat silly, read the following statement aloud: "as you can see on my resume." Yes, aloud! Listen to yourself saying these seven words. Do so with enthusiasm and confidence. This phrase is the verbal and strategic foundation for planning and maintaining interview communications.

Interview preparation begins with a thorough, job-specific review of your resume. With a job title and job description clearly in mind, develop a list of qualification criteria. Highlight the most relevant experiences on your resume. Identify at least three things on your resume that you must discuss in the interview. Select the bullet points from your qualification summary, experiential accomplishments, or educational achievements that you must cover. This is your general review.

Your resume should be a psychological security blanket, nurturing confidence and diminishing anxiety. Use it as a guide to the key points you should cover in an interview. Your resume is not just for the interviewer; it is a preparation and implementation tool for you. To maximize your interview performance, use your resume to identify and link qualities and accomplishments to the job you are interviewing for. Use the resume during your interview to guide the conversation and ensure that key points were covered.

Your Resume as a Guide for Interview Day

As qualifications criteria were used to review resumes and identify whom to interview, these same qualities are the yardsticks by which all interviewers will measure you. To determine your potential to walk the walk to success within a particular job, your interview talk will be heard and analyzed. Those you interview with will be listening for verbal cues that reveal how strongly you match predetermined criteria. As they listen, they will process what they hear and create an overall impression of your potential to succeed within the specifics of the job.

Focus your thoughts first, and then your statements, on roles and responsibilities of the job. Prospective employers have already identified connections between your resume and their desired and required competencies. All you now need to do is reinforce these resume-linked connections while sharing communication as well as personality style.

Interviews can flow as conversations, but you should figure out ahead of time what key points you want to address. You don't go into academic exams without focusing on specific topics. You don't conduct presentations without some notes or AV tools. Pre-interview resume review activities focus on topics and provide needed visual cues.

It is easy to use this process-oriented knowledge. Before each interview, create a list of qualifications criteria for the position. What specific criteria would be associated with an ideal candidate for the position you will be interviewing for? Identify the basic qualities sought and how one would determine who possesses these traits. Most important, use your resume to create a carefully conceived strategy and list of discussion points.

Preinterview Resume Review Inventory

Before each interview, complete the following exercise on the back of a resume. This will organize your thoughts, identify what last-minute information needs to be collected, and clarify what to highlight during the discussion. Using these notes, you will be focusing the interview into a target-specific conversation. Review your notes beforehand, but avoid using them during the interview.

What, When, and Where

Answer the basic questions first. Briefly note the organization and describe the position you will be interviewing for. If you can do it in, let's say, 100 words, you are ready to move on from this exercise. If you cannot, you have some fact-gathering or thinking to do.

If you have not yet reviewed a detailed job description, request a copy and do so. Then summarize what you have read in your own terms. Describe it as if you were speaking to the fifteen-year-old son or daughter of a close friend. In this way, you will force yourself to simplify and describe actions and outcomes associated with the job in basic behavioral and functional terms.

Define Qualifications

Second, cite three key points that make you qualified for the position in question. Review your resume's qualification summary section, then identify three of those cited or define broader connections that clearly match qualifications for the position you are interviewing for. In general, you are completing the statements, "Thinking about this job, specifically, my three key assets are . . ." or "Thinking about the job, the three key points I want to raise in the interview include . . ." Ideally, these will match some of the phrasing used on the qualifications criteria list you have already created for the job. Each of the three bulleted points should be no more than fifty words.

Illustrate Your Abilities

Third, note three anecdotes that illustrate your capabilities to succeed on the job. Stories should support the three key points cited, linking skills used when taking goal-directed actions and, ultimately, to achieve results or finish a project. Start out by very briefly noting the story. Then, identify actions, results, and tasks that were associated with your accomplishments. Last, cite the key skills used and enhanced as a result of each particular experience. Interviewers are particularly interested in problem situations and how you solved them or participated in the resolution process.

List three questions you would like to ask the interviewer. Ask one question in the first five minutes of the interview and another in the second five minutes so that you can use your interviewer's response in the discussion as it progresses. These initial inquiries should focus on day-to-day job responsibilities and on how performance will be judged. Clarifying and confirming shared expectations early in the conversation will ensure that you raise appropriate issues. Often, the answers you receive inspire immediate re-establishing of key points you wish to discuss later. If three won't do, prepare a list of additional questions to ask during and at the end of the interview session.

While you should definitely prepare for interviews, identifying key points and reviewing typical questions in advance, do not memorize them. Have some anecdotes to share, but don't attempt to deliver previously written soliloquies or word-for-word responses. The oxymoronic phrase "planned spontaneity" describes the best results.

By writing all of the above on the back of your resume, you will have used existing printed text to create new supporting documentation. You will have a handwritten focal point containing well-conceived key points, anecdotes, and employer queries.

Easy Job-Search Conversations

Preparation is how you avoid perspiration. By being prepared, you will skillfully facilitate conversation. Conducting preinterview preparation builds your confidence, provides focus for communication, and enhances outcomes. Too many candidates spend hour after hour researching historical facts and obscure figures associated with an organization, unnecessarily increasing their anxiety. These individuals research companies too much and pay too little attention to their own backgrounds and job descriptions. They don't review resumes, and they limit qualifications criteria analysis to a quick perusal of brief, oversimplified job announcements. Here are some easy-to-follow guidelines for last minute prepping.

Call Ahead

Two or three days before your interview, e-mail or call the employer to confirm your meeting and to request a copy of the job description and a company profile. Offer to stop by to pick up the information or ask if it can be e-mailed or express mailed. Specifically ask this question: Are there questions or issues I should focus on to prepare for our meeting? Imagine how well you can prepare if you receive a list of potential questions or critical issues to examine. You would be surprised how often interviewers will provide this information when asked.

Clarify logistics of the day, particularly for callback interviews, arranged after initial telephone or in-person screening discussions. Know how many people you will be seeing and what to expect of your visit. Don't fear stupid questions, including asking for directions; the more information you have, the smarter you will appear on the day of the interview.

Queries can be made by phone. If you can't get through to the appropriate person(s), leave a voicemail message, followed quickly by an e-mail or faxed note, and then, later in the day, by another call. If you start a few days prior to the interview, you have a greater chance of receiving a response.

Specific Research

Conduct an Internet search or visit a reference librarian, seeking information on the firm and, most important, on general current events articles on the field involved. If possible, enter a few keywords into a general search engine or into search options within the company's Web site. Don't dwell too long on researching the prospective employer. Basic and topical information on the field involved is often much more valuable.

You should be able to discuss industry trends, major players, and what's hot and what's not within the field. While somewhat retro, reference librarians are still competent problem solvers. They thrive on the challenge of locating hard-to-find information under the pressure of a pending deadline. Also, just as a sports fan regularly reads the sports section of the newspaper, don't forget to read the business or related sections of local papers and professional publications.

Online Networking

A Web site such as *www.zoominfo.com* or *www.linkedin.com* can reveal others with the same job title you are interviewing for or the one you desire. If you care to be bold, you might consider e-mailing one of these members to ask for some insight into their position's highlights and challenges. Many people are flattered by this kind of communication, the same way they are flattered to be contacted by a recruiter. This kind of proactive job searching can give you critical knowledge that will set you apart as the candidate of choice.

Timing Is Everything

Arrive approximately twenty minutes early, check in, and, if you haven't already done so, ask if you can review a copy of the job description as well as literature describing the nature of the organization and significant events of the past year. Sit down in a comfortable area and review your resume and cover letter. It's amazing that most job seekers forget this very simple preparation activity. Think about it. What do interviewers review when determining whom to meet? What do they review immediately before and during the interview? Most definitely, the answer is your resume and cover letter.

Bring a favorite photo with you to relieve any stress. It's hard to stay tense when looking at a smiling face of a friend or beloved pet. You cannot help but calm down a bit by glancing at a picture of someone or something that always makes you feel better. Do this discreetly while you are waiting for your interview, *not* during the interview..

Don't forget to review these documents before your interview. Mark critical points or make notes on the back. This one-page personal note sheet can be very effective. Have extra copies of your resume available in case you meet with someone who doesn't have one.

Questions and Answers

Ask two questions within the first ten minutes of the interview, and bring copies of your work to show. Questions should be variations on "What are the qualities you are seeking for this position?" and "What specific expectations in terms of output and outcomes do you have for the person who holds this job?" This will allow you to gain a greater understanding of the position and reflect qualifications later in the interview. The more you learn early in the conversation, the better. Remember, an interview is simply a conversation with a purpose. It is not an adversarial right or wrong or "the interviewer is out to get me" process. Be enthusiastic, optimistic, and inquisitive.

Putting It All Together

Sweaty palms, knotted guts, and beads of sweat are too-frequent physical and psychological symptoms on interview day. If you prepare and have the proper attitude, interviews can be fun. When else is it okay to brag and speak about yourself in positive ways for an hour or two? After creating and reviewing your resume, you should be very appropriately egocentric, focusing on you. You're a great candidate, or you would not have been invited to interview. Enjoy the chance to share your pride in your achievements as well as your personal visions of your future.

Two Key Phrases You Must Think or Say

Interviewers constantly use your resume as a point of reference for forming particular questions. You can and must do the same, by stating things like, "As you can see on my resume," or "As my resume illustrates." Refer interviewers to key experiences or education, and use the phrase specifically in advance of anecdotal discussions. Let the interviewer's eyes focus on specific sections, and don't be surprised if they highlight text or take notes while you speak. This key phrase perks interest and invites magnified attention. Use adaptations, or proceed with a simple, "Again," but do refer to your resume regularly.

In response to questions, do state aloud or allow your internal voice to focus thoughts on the phrase, "Thinking about the job." These four words will inspire you to connect past achievements and related qualities to job-specific requirements. Find creative ways to restate this phrase. Creatively, you might change it to "Thinking about your answers to my questions about the job," or "Thinking about the job description." Or, you might refer to your past answers by stating, "Thinking about job-specific issues I addressed earlier." This is a very effective technique.

Don't practice too much, and don't overanalyze and dissect each role-play or actual interview. You don't want to become stiff or appear too rehearsed. Preparation is meant to relax you and provide stimuli for normal interactions.

You will be amazed at how powerful these two simple phrases can be and how using them in various forms can improve your interview skills. At first, do so via role-play interviews. Have someone ask you typical interview questions, and then respond aloud, as you would in an actual interview. This is perhaps the best way to complete final preparation efforts. While the person asking the questions will be playing the role of interviewer, you will remain yourself and answer as you would in a real interview. Be yourself! Don't be the person you think the interviewer wants you to be. Sincerity during the interview will yield honesty-based relationships as well as the personality and capability required for on-the-job success.

Common Questions and Universal Themes

Almost every job-search resource contains a list of common interview questions. What makes this book unusual is the emphasis it places on using the resume as your foundation for identifying themes to address when answering these and all questions.

Basically, interviewers determine through very special questions and answers whether you have the potential to succeed. Because potential can be a mercurial concept and very difficult to measure, much of the interview process is subjective. No matter how difficult to predict, it is a process that is easy to prepare for. You just have to translate past actions into words and, using appropriate tone, project confidence as well as your knowledge of self and of job-specific qualifications.

Behavioral Interviews

Past behaviors are cited on your resume. Your ability to connect your past to the future and to your desired goal will be the basis upon which your interviewing skills will be judged. In fact, a popular interviewing trend these days is called behavioral interviews. This technique allows interviewers to quantify and objectify a traditionally subjective process. It is based on the principle that states that past behavior is the best predictor of future performance. Moreover, more recent behavior is a better predictor of future performance than older behavior, and trends in behavior are better predictors than isolated incidents.

Interviewers present "what did you do when" scenarios or ask you to identify past incidents when you used certain behaviors to reach a goal. Before the interview, a behavioral interviewer determines the behaviors that are desired. Basically, the interviewer arrives with a pre-established checklist for determining if you have the qualities associated with success in a particular job. Be prepared for this, and don't get rattled by any open-ended questions. Note taking by the interviewer is not unusual, so don't interpret it as negative or positive. Interviewers may seek clarification of or contradiction in your statements by continually probing, so don't become rattled or express frustration.

No matter the style, whether it's conversational, traditional, or behavioral, a review of common questions is extremely helpful. Attempting to memorize answers can do more harm than good, so please use the list to stimulate your thoughts and inspire you to share ideas effectively during interviews. You might ask a friend, family member, or peer to select five and ask them aloud, initiating a role-play interview. Hearing the questions as well as your answers, rather than just thinking about responses, is valuable.

Traditional Interview Questions

To maximize your use of this list, after you review the general as well as behavioral queries, identify a top-five list of questions that relate to a specific job matching your goals. Then conduct a practice session, having a friend or family member ask you these questions. Remember, there are no right answers to particular questions. Responses during an interview must seem well conceived, yet spontaneous. Think of this interaction as a conversation, not an inquisition. It is best to complete this exercise aloud, even if you are doing so alone.

- Why are you interested in this particular field of employment?
- What academic or career achievements are you most proud of?
- Why did you choose your major, and how does it relate to your goals?
- What classes did you find most stimulating, and did they nurture job-connected skills?
- What would you like to be doing in five years?
- What are your greatest strengths and weaknesses?
- How would you describe yourself and how would others describe you?
- How would you characterize career-related success?
- What are your three most significant employment or school-related achievements?
- When did you use persuasive skills or sales talents?
- Why should we hire you?
- What are your long-term career goals?
- How have your academic experiences to date prepared you for a career, and what are your future academic goals?
- What would you do differently with regard to academic or career experiences?
- What was your most difficult decision to date, and how did you go about making it?
- Why did you attend your alma mater?
- What do you think it takes to succeed in the job you are being interviewed for?
- What lessons have you learned from your failures or mistakes?
- What are your geographic preferences, and are you willing to relocate?
- What concerns do you have with regard to this job/academic program and our organization/school?
- How would you describe this opportunity to friends and family members?
- What additional information do you need to determine if this is the right opportunity for you?
- What motivated you to first contact us?

Non-Traditional Interview Questions

Some interviewers like to rattle candidates a bit to see how they think on their feet. They may even want to assess whether you have a sense of humor or how creative you can be. While offbeat questions often seem totally irrelevant, some interviewers feel they gain a better sense of the individual by asking someone what their favorite book was as a child or how their clothes closet is organized at home. There really is no right or wrong answer to these wildcard questions, so just be yourself.

- Who would you want to play you in a movie about your life?
- If you could pick someone from history to have dinner with, who would it be?
- If you won the lottery, what would you do next?
- You become shipwrecked on an island. You have food, water, and fire. What other three things would you want to have with you?
- If you were a super hero, what super powers would you have?

Behavioral Interview Questions

Behavioral questions include the following:

- Describe what happened when you faced problems at work that tested your coping skills. What did you do?
- Give an example of a time when you could not participate in a discussion or could not finish a task because you did not have enough information.
- Give an example of a time when you had to be relatively quick in coming to a decision.
- Tell me about when you used communication skills in order to get an important point across.
- Tell me about a job experience when you had to speak up and tell others what you thought or felt.
- Give me an example of when you felt you were able to motivate coworkers or subordinates.
- Tell me about an occasion when you conformed to a policy even though you did not agree with it.

- Describe a situation in which it was necessary to be very attentive to and vigilant about your environment.
- Give me an example of a time when you used your fact-finding skills to gain information needed to solve a problem; then tell me how you analyzed the information and came to a decision.
- Tell me about an important goal you've set and tell me about your progress toward reaching this goal.
- Describe the most significant written document, report, or presentation you've completed.
- Give me an example of a time when you had to go above and beyond to get a job done.
- Give me an example of a time when you were able to communicate successfully with another person, even when the individual may not have personally liked you.
- Describe a situation in which you were able to read another person effectively and guide your actions by your understanding of his or her individual needs or values.
- Specifically, what did you do in your last job in order to plan effectively and stay organized?
- Describe the most creative work-related project you have completed.
- Give me an example of a time when you had to analyze another person or a situation in order to be effective in guiding your action or decision.
- What did you do in your last job to contribute toward a teamwork environment? Be specific.
- Give an example of a problem you faced on the job and how you solved it.
- Describe a situation when you positively influenced the actions of others in a desired direction.
- Tell me about a situation in the past year when you dealt with a very upset customer or coworker.
- Describe a situation in which others within your organization depended on you.
- Describe your most recent group effort.
- Describe the most challenging person you've interacted with and how you dealt with him or her.

Questions You Can Ask Potential Employers

Questions you might ask potential employers during an employment interview or during a preinterview information conversation include the following:

- How would you describe the job in terms of day-to-day roles and responsibilities?
- What qualities are you seeking in a candidate?
- What type of person would most likely succeed in these roles?
- What kind of performance or production level would exceed your expectations for this position?
- What should I expect of myself over the first few months on the job?
- How will my performance be judged, and by whom?
- Whom should I use as a role model for this position and would it be appropriate to contact this person?
- What characteristics does it take to succeed within this organization and within this position?
- What are the best things about the job and the most challenging requirements of the position?
- Who would have highest expectations of me, or be the one(s) who would be most difficult to impress?
- What is the typical career path and time frame associated with career development?
- How will I be trained, and how can I appropriately seek skills enhancement?
- Who last served in this position, and what is he or she doing now?
- What goals do you have for the person who will serve in this job?
- What project would you expect to be completed first, and what would be involved?

Asking questions of your potential employer reiterates your interest in the open position. It shows you are trying to visualize yourself in this position and determining whether it will be a good fit for you.

Conversations, Not Cross-Examinations

Each interviewer has a personal style, but most interviews can be identified using a few common labels. Many interviews will be conversational or traditional, in which interviewers chat with candidates and ask fairly typical interview questions. Some are behavioral, in which interviewers ask about past achievements, seek details regarding the behaviors and skills that contributed to these undertakings, and ask candidates "what would you do in this situation" questions. Occasionally, particularly for consulting firms, interviews are case studies, in which interviewers ask candidates to analyze specific situational cases and problems; revealing how candidates think on their feet in response to specific analysis-driven cases.

Interviews should not be thought of as simply a series of questions and answers. They are conversations with a common purpose for you and the interviewer. Both use qualification criteria to assess the other's potential to succeed. During the exchange, the more verbally inspired images of success that are sent and received, the more likely an offer will be made.

What You Say

No matter the label used, resumes are tools for you to use during any interview. Interviewers review these documents during your conversation with a particular purpose, so you should do the same. To prepare, review typical questions. Be prepared to expand upon the key points and anecdotes you identified as illustrating qualifications. Bring a resume with you to every interview.

Don't be shy! Talk about your achievements with pride. Interviewers have limited time to get to know the real you. Don't think there are right answers. When asked a technical question, if you don't know the exact answer, talk the interviewer through how you would find the correct information. Don't wait to do so; always ask questions when invited.

Don't overanalyze or dissect your performance after each interview. Decision making is very subjective. The process changes from initial screening through call-back stages and, ultimately, through selection interviews. If your style and strategies remain sincere, no matter the interviewer's style, technique, or temperament, you will find a good fit. If you don't receive an offer, never stop to ask why. Instead, you should, via follow-up contacts, seek consideration for the next available similar opportunity. Remain confident and enthusiastic. Remember to smile and be friendly, yet professional. More often than you think, you can transform someone who rejected you into a strong advocate and network member who might interview you again very soon.

Bring extra resumes with you in case you unexpectedly meet additional interviewers. You might also wish to bring supporting materials to serve as illustrations of your work. Some fields, specifically publishing, public relations, and journalism, require writing samples or portfolios. Be ready to detail what samples you have included and why they demonstrate specific talents.

Ultimately, you will communicate motivations and, most important, qualifications successfully via phone and in-person interviews. Have confidence in your abilities to project qualifications and capabilities. Always check in advance regarding how many people you will be interviewing with and how long the entire process might take. Specifically ask, "Are there any materials you recommend I read prior to my interview?"

What You Wear

Inquire about the appropriate mode of dress. Some situations and organizations are business casual. Neatly pressed slacks, an ironed shirt, and a tie (a sport coat is optional) would be appropriate for men. Slacks or skirt and an ironed shirt or sweater would be appropriate for women. Others are business formal, and suits, ironed shirts, polished shoes, and ties are a must for men, and suits are required for women.

What was once known as casual Friday has become confusing Monday through Friday for contemporary candidates. Old-fashioned rules regarding power suits, colors, and ties may not seem to apply today, but because what you wear may impact what you say and how others perceive your professionalism, in truth, they still do. Your interview image, revealed by your attire, is a projection of common sense rather than fashion sense. It's always recommended that you remain conservative and traditional with the clothing you select for interview days.

FACT

According to a joint survey conducted by the job board Yahoo!, Hot-Jobs, and retailer Banana Republic, the majority of employees wear either business casual or casual outfits to work, indicating that more companies are relaxing office dress codes. As a result, 34 percent of job seekers said on the night before an interview, they spend most of their time deciding what to wear.

Ties can be loosened, jackets removed, and sleeves can be rolled up. It's easy to transform business formal into something more casual, but the opposite is not possible. Unless specifically told otherwise, dress more formally. Suits are always appropriate and required for banking, financial services, consulting, and conservative fields. For other settings, blue blazers, gray or khaki slacks or skirts, crisply ironed shirts, and appropriate neckwear may seem like prep school uniforms, but these basics are always good bets for interviews.

Remember potential red flags. Tone down jewelry, ditch the backpack, temporarily remove nose, eyebrow, or tongue piercings, go easy on perfume or cologne, and wear polished shoes (no flip-flops or backless). Ladies should watch cleavage and hem length, and men should go with long-sleeved shirts rather than short.

After reading this chapter, you are ready to use your resume as an interview preparation and implementation tool. You have learned how to use this document to focus preparation prior to and during these crucial conversations. On interview days, simply looking at your resume should instill confidence and generate effective communication. Resumes contribute to your chances for landing a job well beyond the initial contact stages. Used effectively, they impact all actions and outcomes.

Chapter 9

Resume Review and Critique

You will examine before-and-after reviews that contain insights regarding critical changes. This chapter reveals details that will inspire you to maximize your efforts to create or update great resumes. As you read, and as you see one resume transformed into three, it will be as if you have your own resume coach at your side. This word-for-word review will inspire you to immediate actions.

The Heart and Head of the Resume Coach

Some fans believe a coach can cost a team the game or even the championship ring. Instead of firing the team, owners fire the coach. Amateur and professional sports coaches can and do contribute to wins as well as losses. Decisions they make do impact the outcome of games. As almost all agree, coaches can impact the efforts of teams and individual players, maximizing performance potential and desired outcomes. Resume-writing coaches can do the same.

The job seeker uses both his heart and head while writing a resume. These two different approaches yield different resume-writing and job-search strategies. You've learned how emotional perspectives and hopes must blend with intellectual and strategic thoughts to yield success. Step-by-step strategies inspired you to unite attitudes and actions in order to conduct comprehensive job-search campaigns. Resume-writing and job-search coaches possess and share contradictory yet complementary views as well.

The Heart of the Resume Coach

While appearing optimistic to some, relying too much on heart-driven advice can be detrimental to your career. It is characterized by statements, queries, and often unrealistic hopes that include the following:

- Keep your options open. Do not limit yourself by placing goals on resumes.
- Send out as many multipurpose resumes as possible; respond to almost every posting.
- Even if you don't have any experience, just send out multipurpose resumes and let employers judge your potential to succeed.
- The broader the entries on your resume, the better. You want to appear well rounded.

The Head of the Resume Coach

The head of the resume coach has had to adapt to the philosophies unique to targeted resumes. These views guide you to take active and proactive steps in logical sequence. The related advice and strategies are realistic and logistically sound, yet they are also inspirational. This view is character-ized by statements, queries, and realistic hopes that include the following:

- Focus proactive efforts on three fields and two functional areas within each, but respond reactively and creatively to as many post-ings as you wish, using targeted resumes.
- Complete goal identification, qualifications inventorying, and anal-yses needed to create targeted qualifications summaries for all of your resumes and many letters.
- Be prepared to clearly articulate realistic goals, maintain awareness of qualifications criteria associated with related jobs, and always use field-focused phrasing in documentation, conversations, and interviews.
- Take responsibility for projecting goals as well as qualifications through effective resumes and job-search communication.
- Complete the assessment and research needed to set and share realistic goals and to mirror qualifications via targeted resumes and very focused supplemental documentation.

Both the heads and hearts of resume coaches agree that you should, if possible, create your own resume. While some professional resume writers do create effective documents, especially for very experienced candidates, it is always best to go through the resume-writing steps personally. If you are still dissatisfied, you can bring your resume to a professional for review and critique, but you will benefit from the writing and thought process. The fol-lowing represents a detailed word-for-word, step-by-step critique as it was conducted. Project from past to present and imagine what your interactions would be like if you had access to a qualified resume coach.

FACT

Most people believe that only 20–25 percent of all jobs are posted. Maximum estimates for the posted jobs versus hidden jobs are one-third hidden to two-thirds posted. No matter the numbers, you should never limit your efforts to postings. Proactive moves are the only way to uncover hidden opportunities.

First, you will be privy to the thoughts and actual changes associated with transformation of one last "before" version into an effective multipurpose "after" model. Then you will learn how this one broad resume can become three much more effective targeted versions.

A Few Detailed Reviews

The sample that follows was that of an actual soon-to-be graduate, but the lessons learned from the detailed critiquing are applicable to all resume writers. Recently laid-off workers, soon-to-be and recent college grads, inexperienced workers, experienced executives, midlevel managers, and those seeking basic employment will become educated and motivated by these detailed resume reviews. All job seekers can gain information from the words of the resume coach. Some day soon, your internal voices will echo the knowledge of these concepts and phrases. You will become your own strongest resume coach and, perhaps, support the efforts of others.

Chris Smith

123 Main Street	987 Centre Avenue
Apartment 13	Philadelphia, PA 11111
Hometown, NY 00000	(555) 555-5678
(555) 555-1234	csmith@company.com

EDUCATION

Bachelor of Arts, Political Science, University Of Rochester, Rochester, NY, anticipated May 2008
Dean's List. Completed cluster of three thematically linked courses exploring the natural sciences in physics and astronomy. Completed cluster of three thematically linked courses in Spanish. As member of Student Senate, organized campus activities and worked to ensure a maximal educational experience.

EXPERIENCE

Server, Burgundy Basin Banquet Hall, Pittsford, NY
Greeted customers. Took orders. Maintained accurate records of receipts and gratuities. 2007–Present

Research Assistant for Professor Harry Smart, University Of Rochester, Rochester, NY
Scheduled subjects, conducted interviews, input and analyzed data, and completed library research. Completed comprehensive interview assessing husband-and-wife relationships. Scored, coded, then input data, ensuring easy retrieval and data analysis by graduate students and faculty. Conducted extensive library and Internet research, identifying studies related to husband-and-wife relationships. Spring 2006–Present

Intern/Assistant to the President, The Ardmore GROUP, Ardmore, PA
Reported directly to the president of a multidivisional enterprise that included political consulting, special-interest lobbying, bidding on and awarding state government contracts in health care, social work, and welfare administration. Organized luncheons and various meetings for political operatives and office holders. Conducted research as to what contracts were available for bid and what resources would be necessary to produce that bid. All research with recommendations submitted in written report to the president. Work involved independent trips to the State Capitol and attendance at networking sessions to procure clients. Summer 2007

Assistant to the CFO, Philadelphia Physicians Associates, Philadelphia, PA
Reported directly to Medical Records Supervisor and CFO of regional medical practice. Audited medical records for accuracy. Distributed those records to doctors, attorneys, and insurers. Organized records for depositions. Distributed work to clerical staff. Part time and summers 2005–2006

Coach's Comments, Queries, and Quick Corrections

Here's what the resume coach has to say:

▶ **First, visually this resume is organized and easy to read, yet it lacks something.** The Monaco font is basic, often used as a default setting for e-mails, and it does not really project a professional image.

▶ **Are you looking for jobs in the Philadelphia area?** If yes, then leave both addresses, but do not use as many lines to present this information.

▶ **Do you have a job-search goal?** A general field of interest? Particular functions in mind? It's okay to start with a multipurpose document, but you should use targeted ones for each of those areas you stated. The format, content, and style of this one are not presented effectively for some of those goals. Let's create one general and then a few targeted versions.

▶ **You use two very clear and appropriate headers, but don't you want to tell readers a bit more about some of your educational and practical achievements?** Think about themes you want readers to be aware of as we create a better multipurpose resume and the targeted versions. How would you characterize your education? If you used a multiword headline for education, what would it be? What words best describe the type of education you received? Would the header be different for different targeted resumes?

▶ **You highlighted your degree using bolding and position on the page, but what about the school?** Isn't University of Rochester one of the top schools in the country? Doesn't this school have a unique cluster-oriented curriculum? Shouldn't you proudly highlight the school's name?

▶ **The information under education and experience headers is well written, but it isn't highlighted.** Have you thought of other ways to present both degree and school as well as employer and position?

▶ **The header for experience is also very traditional, but it doesn't allow you to break away from the reverse chronological order rule.** You've blended some very interesting and sophisticated experiences with other less significant experiences. In fact, your first job is a waiter position. What experience themes do you want readers to quickly recognize as you create the better multipurpose resume and targeted versions? How would you characterize your experience? If you used multiword headlines for groupings of experience, what would they be? What are the two most significant and sophisticated experiences? Is there any way to present them more prominently? Would the headers be different for different targeted resumes?

▶ **You highlighted your experience titles using bolding and position on the page, but what about the employer?** Some of the organizational titles might focus the reader's review of descriptions cited.

▶ **Look at all of your academic as well as practical experience.** What are your most significant achievements? What skills and abilities yielded related accomplishments? Can you make a profile containing your greatest assets?

▶ **Okay, let's review a bit.** We're first going to create a better multipurpose resume. Later, we will create targeted resumes for each of your stated goals. These fields include consulting, advertising, and law. Let's not worry about it now, but you will very soon have to review the newly updated multipurpose resume and think about specific qualifications for these fields and what entries to highlight. We'll use order of presentation as well as headlines to highlight the selected skills.

▶ **Now, we will proceed from top to bottom.** Use one line for each address, rather than five. We most likely will need those extra three lines somewhere else. Place bullets in between entries, graphically creating separation for what was on individual lines before.

▶ **Next, we will create a general summary of qualifications.** This will contain four or five bulleted phrases that reveal to readers some of your basic qualities and characteristics. Again, look at all of your academic and employment experiences.

Which are most important? Yes, I agree. Your courses were all research oriented and your research assistant position, political consulting, and medical practice management experience all required strong research, data analysis, writing, and presentation skills. One of your summary statements will reflect this.

Oh, you think of yourself as a good writer. What kind of documents have you written for academic or other purposes? Can you detail how you did so? Do you have samples?

Yes, computer competencies are important. What software can you confidently use? Can you teach others to use these systems? Course titles are often left off resumes, but they can reinforce some of the qualifications statements. For the multipurpose resume, you can list a few general ones, but later, think about including only those related to particular goals.

▶ **Changing your headers to headlines should be relatively easy.** The education headline can now reveal that you've had some liberal arts, science, and political science studies. Better, the headline can reveal that your academics seemed research focused. The experience section can reinforce the same themes. It can show you have had research-driven achievements. Let's think about distinct categories for your research experience, project management, and general business experience.

▶ **For education, using all caps to highlight the name of your school, and presenting it first, followed by city and state, would be effective.** On the next line you can still use bold for the degree. If you have enough room, use bullet points to highlight extracurricular achievements. Let's see if everything fits.

So far, so good. How many semesters did you make the dean's list? What were your overall and major GPAs? Let's not include those, nor enter dean's list if it was for your first semester freshman year.

▶ **Now, let's focus on headlines for experience.** Yes, I agree that the most important experience should go first. The way information now appears you highlight titles and not organizations. We'll use the same format for experience used for education. Make the organizations all caps, followed by city and state. Then, bold the title.

Ideally, describe overall responsibilities under the title and follow with bulleted accomplishments. And the dates can go on the same line as the title, justified to the right margin. In fact, let's justify dates as well as cities and states on the right margin. There, what do you think?

▶ **Yes, I know, we still haven't created headlines nor divided up the experiences by importance and nature of roles.** Okay, the two most important experiences are the research assistant position and the one with the governmental firm. Let's definitely group these two. Yes, add the medical practice management position to this section. The three will appear under a headline that clearly notes the research, writing, and time management skills you possess.

Let's leave off the waiter entry. Yes, it does show that you work hard and contributed to educational expenses. But did you gain significant skills? I know it's hard to take this off when someone advised you to put it on.

If we have room, let's list it at the end of the page. If space permits, it'll stay. If not, it'll go. Okay?

▶ **Let's focus a bit on the actual job descriptions, particularly on the accomplishment bullets.** After we do, we'll revisit the qualification summary to ensure that it reflects the skills used to achieve these outcomes.

Now, are the most significant achievements noted for each position? Is anything missing? Would someone who worked with you in these settings approve? Action phrasing does not require embellishment or deception.

▶ **Okay, the first draft is complete.** Let's play with the font and spacing a bit to fit on one page. Times, Times New Roman, and Bookman Old Style are fine, but Garamond might allow the most to fit. Yes, it does. Oh, we'll play with some of the blank spacing between headlines and entries and between entries. Shrinking it from ten-point to four-point gives you an extra line or two.

▶ **Now that we're close to being finished, let's try something dramatic.** Put education last. Your experience is so strong that it deserves to be more prominent. The fact that courses are in the qualification summary serves the purpose of introducing specific topics. The degree and school don't carry as much weight as your significant work experience.

What do you think? I know every one of your friends lists education first. Do they have strong GPAs and academic honors? Are their majors directly related to targeted goals? Remember, this is your multipurpose document. The targeted ones might have a different order of presentation.

▶ **Will you be uploading this resume to job boards or corporate home pages?** After we're done, you should conduct some Web and library research to focus on the vocabulary and keywords used within your three fields of interest. Consulting, advertising, and law do have their own lexicons, and when your resume is reviewed, they must be identified. No matter whether the keyword scanning is done electronically or visually, by a person or machine, these words and phrases will be—well, as silly as it sounds—key! After your research, we'll transform your multipurpose document into three targeted ones.

▶ **Finally, let's think about all visual and content issues.** I know, it's not that easy. Let's use a collection of questions from a wonderful book. It's weird, but it's best to read and respond aloud. What are your answers to each?

Before-and-After Checklist for Determining Distribution Readiness

The queries on the before-and-after checklist that follows formalize those that would informally or intuitively be asked by a resume coach before drafts are considered final versions. Visually scanning the resume from top to bottom inspires the following questions of both coach and resume writer. What would your answers be for the sample that immediately follows? Is it ready for duplication and distribution? Do you like the before-and-after transformation of this multipurpose document? What about the experience phrasing and bulleted accomplishments? How would you change it into targeted versions?

- Is the identifying information accurate, including your e-mail?
- Is just one address and phone enough? Consider including your cell phone number.
- Is it visually appealing, with information presented in a logical format, and easy to read?
- Can you identify a logical pattern for headline, content, and highlighting techniques?
- Can it be copied and pasted into an e-mail?
- Is the objective brief, and does it use field-specific phrasing?
- Does the summary of qualifications section support the stated objective?
- Does this paragraph or bullet-point listing reveal that you possess the qualifications criteria for target jobs?
- Does this section project to the future as well as reflect upon the past?

- Are most significant goal-related qualifications statements presented first?
- Do special headlines for experience and education project objective-related focus?
- Does the order of appearance effectively portray significance?
- Does the education section present school(s), degree(s), area(s) of concentration, courses, and honors?
- Do courses, papers, and projects appear somewhere?
- Is specialized training presented under a special headline?
- Do headlines project knowledge of targeted fields and draw attention to related achievements?
- Do headlines, quickly reviewed, identify the nature of entries that follow?
- Are all entries described using active and accomplishment-oriented phrasing, including facts and figures?
- Are goal-specific experiences grouped under appropriate headlines, presented in order of significance?
- If entries are simply cited, with no descriptions, are they obviously of less importance than others?
- Are organizations, titles, and dates easy to see, revealing an obvious pattern?
- For space as well as goal-directed purposes, are only the most significant experiences thoroughly described, with most important appearing first?
- If listed by soon-to-be or recent college grad, are leadership roles and achievements cited?
- Are most important headlines presented first, with most significant information appearing under each?
- If your resume is more than one page, is the most important information on the first page, and does the second page have your name and a page number header?
- If you have more than one targeted resume, are objectives for each very clear?
- Did you change order of presentation for each resume and are summaries of qualifications target-specific?

- Can you elaborate upon the resume in a well-crafted cover letter or brief cover note?
- Would readers sense goal-oriented competence and confidence without an accompanying letter?
- Can you use the resume as a clear guide during an interview?
- Are you definitely ready to distribute your resume?

Coach's Final Words on the Multipurpose Resume

▶ **While your responses to the before-and-after checklist were not 100 percent positive, because we're working on a multipurpose document, I think it's ready to go.** What do you think? Yes, you can upload it into your school's resume collection and on-campus recruiting system. You can now begin responding to postings and networking with alumni. But we have to finish those targeted versions if you are to maximize your efforts. Of course, we need to work on cover letters as well.

▶ **Targeted resumes with objectives and qualifications summaries are best.** While you should be proud of yourself and your newly created general resume, it's not quite the best document. You must support your targeted reactive and proactive efforts with clearly focused resumes. No, focus is not bad. It does not limit you. You will be using appropriate resumes and supplemental documents for each field. You can use this wonderful multipurpose version to get the process started, and whenever something unique might arise. Remember, it's your responsibility to share and support goals, not the employer's responsibility to interpret resume content and magically identify goals for you.

Multipurpose Resume After Critiquing

Chris Smith

123 Main Street, Apartment 13 • Hometown, NY 00000 • (555) 555-1234 • csmith@company.com
987 Centre Avenue • Philadelphia, PA 11111 • (555) 555-5678

Qualification Summary

- Confidence conducting detailed research using library and Internet resources.
- Data collection, trend analysis, and writing talents nurtured via practical experiences, as well as academic papers and research projects.
- Confidence in research, writing, editing, proposal development, presentation, event planning, and project management roles.
- Windows, UNIX, HTML, Word, Excel, PowerPoint, PhotoShop, and Internet utilities.
- Skills, interests, and perspectives gained from courses including: Applied Data Analysis, Economics, Debate, Psychology of Business, Arguments in Politics, Political Theory: Politics in the Mass Media, Political Systems, Social Psychology, and Adolescent Psychology.

Research, Writing, and Project Management Accomplishments

UNIVERSITY OF ROCHESTER   Rochester, NY
Research Assistant for Psychology Professor Harry Smart   Spring 2006–Present
- Conducted extensive library and Internet research, identifying studies related to husband-and-wife relationships. Summarized findings and developed detailed listings of citations. Presented findings to weekly faculty-led research team meetings.

THE ARDMORE GROUP   Ardmore, PA
Intern/Assistant to the President   Summer 2007
- Reported directly to the president of a multidivisional enterprise that included political consulting, special-interest lobbying, bidding on and awarding state government contracts in health care, social work, and welfare administration.
- Conducted research regarding contracts available for bidding and what resources would be necessary to produce that bid. All research efforts were transformed into written recommendations submitted in reports to the president. Yielded about one hit per month.
- Work involved independent trips to the State Capitol, attendance at networking sessions and sharing of information with colleagues and supervisor to determine appropriate next steps.

PHILADELPHIA PHYSICIANS ASSOCIATES   Philadelphia, PA
Assistant to the CFO   Part-time and Summers 2005–2006
- Reported directly to Medical Records Supervisor and CFO of regional medical practice.
- Audited medical records for doctors, attorneys, and insurers.
- Organized records for depositions in specialized formats facilitating access by attorneys, arbitrators, and judges addressing specific points of law.

Research-Oriented Studies

UNIVERSITY OF ROCHESTER   Rochester, NY
Bachelor of Arts, Political Science   anticipated May 2008
- As member of Student Senate, effectively interacted with peers, administrators, and others, transforming goals into decisions to implement freshman housing model.

Coach's Internalized and Verbalized Before-and-After Review

This chapter has already revealed a detailed critique, illustrating the transformation from a before draft to a finished after version. Step six of the seven required to create or update resumes involves drafting and critiquing. Questions on the before-and-after checklist reveal for you, with great confidence and closure, whether a resume is ready for distribution.

Resume coaches ask these questions aloud of those creating or updating documents. Silent or spoken answers inspire attitudes needed to stop drafting and start distributing. What would your answers be for the new multipurpose version and, more important, for the targeted versions that follow? For each sample on the pages that follow, see if you can identify obvious and subtle changes made from one resume to the others.

ALERT!

If after you have sent a cover letter or resume you have updated the resume or wish to add additional information, do not hesitate to send follow-up documentation. Refer to earlier communications, yet highlight in your follow-up communiqué all critical new issues and assets on your revised resume.

As you recall, when all responses to the before-and-after checklist are yes, a resume is ready for distribution. If some answers are no, the document can be revised or used until changes are made. While questions asked by coaches, advocates, and others do help, you now have a written script that they might use. In many creative and confidence-building ways, you now have what can be viewed as the very best coach's queries printed on just a few pages. To inspire continued re-evaluation, you might wish to photocopy the before-and-after checklist and post it in a clearly visible location whenever you are creating or updating resumes.

One Multipurpose Resume Equals Three Targeted Resumes

As the resume coach's reactions revealed, targeted resumes will be created to match stated goals. Many job seekers should do the same. One resume cannot do all things for all candidates. The first step to updating and creating resumes involves reviewing samples. This section offers annotated reviews of three resumes created from one. Comments offered by the coach should inspire you when you create one, two, or three targeted resumes.

Coach's Comments for an Advertising Resume

▶ **So, the multipurpose resume is finished.** Oh, you have a new research position. Yes, it's too early to cite many accomplishments, but let's describe it now and you can add more as you progress. Let's add it. No, don't worry about room until we've drafted again. We'll think of some space-saving approaches later.

▶ **Now let's get to the targeted versions.** Have you done your homework? Did you research the fields? Oh, that's okay. We'll start with advertising and then go to the others. Continued research will reveal information and, most significant, key phrases that will be added to updated resumes and supplemental letters. Let's not delay. You need some targeted documents to maximize posting responses as well as self-initiated contacts with prospective employers.

▶ **Now, let's focus on advertising.** Is there a particular job title or functional area of interest? Can you describe it in terms that anyone can understand? Can you describe it using specialized terms? That's good! So, account management is your objective. We'll first create a distinct objective statement, but we might have to blend the objective with a qualification summary to save space.

▶ **Yes, the qualification summary is now the most critical component of your resume.** Targeted versions must reveal that you know your goals and that you know what is required to succeed within these roles. In many ways, the rest of the resume will stay the same. Think about order of presentation, headlines, and specific descriptions.

▶ **Thinking about your newly found knowledge of the field, what are your most significant academic or employment accomplishments?** Have you had directly related experiences that should be highlighted via the qualification summary? The summary must show that you know about this field and that you know about the particular skills you possess that are related to it. In the cover letter you will show more, but the qualification summary must quickly reveal your goals and basic qualifications.

▶ **We do have some space issues, so we must get very creative.** Will you be applying for advertising positions in Philadelphia or just New York? Well, no matter. Let's just use one line for identifying information. You can add the second line to cover letters targeting Philly firms. Also, let's make sure that your course listing is as concise as possible and presents most important classes first.

Coach's Final Words on the Advertising Resume

▶ **Your responses to the short and long list of questions were close to 100 percent positive.** That's great. You should research the field more and constantly improve the qualification summary, but I think it's ready to go. Of course, you must convey much of the knowledge already gained through research in your cover letters as well. With advertising, you can be a bit more creative and add humor to these covering pages. Also, for each firm you can refer to some particular clients and recent awards or sales gains. For this field, the cover letter may be as important as the resume.

▶ **Definitely start sending resumes and cover letters to the many, many firms on your hit list.** Also, network with alums. Learn about their career biographies. Increase knowledge of field-appropriate phrases and terminology. Ask if they can consider you for positions on their client teams, or if they can forward your resumes to someone who can.

▶ **Yes, targeted resumes with objectives and qualification summaries are best, but starting with a headline like the one you used takes the place of an objective statement.** Remember, we had some space issues and this allowed us to save a line or two.

Advertising Targeted Resume After Critiquing

Chris Smith

123 Main Street, Apartment 13 • Hometown, NY 00000 • (555) 555-1234 • csmith@company.com

Advertising Account Management Qualifications

- Curiosity regarding consumer attitudes and behaviors and confidence using data collection, trend analysis, and writing talents to develop client-focused campaign strategies as well as proposals, and to assess campaign effectiveness.
- Experience in roles requiring attitude assessment, brainstorming, persuasive communication, and creation of reports, presentations, and proposals.
- Confidence independently or as a team member developing proposals and presentations, planning events, and completing special projects.
- Interests and perspectives gained from diverse courses including: Psychology of Business and Industry, Applied Data Analysis, Economics, Debate, Arguments in Politics, Politics in the Mass Media, Social Psychology, and Adolescent Psychology.
- Abilities to use Word, Excel, and PowerPoint for quantitative analyses, reports, proposals, presentations, and related campaign support documents.

Political Consulting

THE ARDMORE GROUP   Ardmore, PA
Intern/Assistant to the President   Summer 2007

Reported directly to the president of a multidivisional enterprise that included political consulting, special interest lobbying, bidding on and awarding state government contracts in health care, social work, and welfare administration.

- Conducted research regarding contracts available for bidding and what resources would be necessary to produce that bid. All research efforts were transformed into written recommendations submitted in reports to the president. Yielded about one hit per month.
- Attended networking sessions to procure clients, and sharing of information with colleagues and supervisor to determine appropriate next steps.

Research, Proposal Writing, and Project Management Accomplishments

UNIVERSITY OF ROCHESTER   Rochester, NY
Research Assistant for Psychology Professor Harry Smart   Spring 2006–Present

- Conducted extensive library and Internet research, identifying studies related to husband-and-wife relationships. Summarized findings and developed detailed listings of citations. Presented findings to weekly faculty-led research team meetings.
- Scheduled subjects, conducted interviews, input and analyzed data, and completed library research.

Speech and Hearing Center Research Assistant   Fall 2007–Present

- Identified methodology to be used to measure effectiveness and target criteria impacting therapeutic outcomes.

Liberal Arts Studies

UNIVERSITY OF ROCHESTER   Rochester, NY
Bachelor of Arts, Political Science   anticipated May 2008

▶ **This one is ready to go.** No, focus does not limit you. You will be using different resumes and cover letters for each field. I realize that you don't truly know what you want to do, yet advertising is one of your top choices. This resume clearly reveals your goals. Additional documents and, eventually, interviews will show how much you have learned about advertising and how easy it is for you to speak using field-focused vocabulary.

▶ **Hey, if you can, why don't you sign up for a marketing or advertising course or seminar?** Local chapters of professional associations might offer brief seminars. You don't have to take courses for credit, and they can be offered at a local community college. The more you demonstrate true interest in the field, the more your actions will speak as loudly (or more) than your words on this great resume.

Coach's Comments for a Consulting Resume

▶ **So, now the advertising version is finished. See, it didn't take long to adapt the multipurpose resume to a specific purpose.** In fact, each adaptation should take much less time than the original process, not much longer than thirty to forty-five minutes. The next two probably won't take much more than twenty minutes each.

▶ **Okay, consulting is the next field.** Again, have you done your homework? Did you research this particular field? I understand it's not an easy one for undergrads to enter. Yes, it's that selective, but you don't know if you have what it takes to get an interview if you don't try. Continued research will reveal more information and additional key phrases that will be added to updated resumes and supplemental letters. But let's get the first ones out soon. This field screens candidates and completes initial interviews early.

▶ **Now, let's focus on consulting.** Is there a particular job title or functional area of interest? Yes, each firm does have a variation on the titles used for entry-level opportunities. Some call them Associate Consultants, some use Analysts, and others use Research Analysts. So, instead of an objective statement, we'll use the headline and summary of qualification strategy again. Can you describe what these first post-baccalaureate jobs are all about? What kind of work do

▶ recent grads perform at consulting firms? In fact, can you describe what a consulting firm does? That's good enough, but you cannot stop your research now. It must continue even after you've sent your first group of resumes and cover letters. Follow-up letters can reveal when you've gained additional insights.

▶ **The qualification summary remains the most critical component of this targeted resume.** This section must reveal that you know your goals and what is required to succeed within these research and analytical support roles. Like before, the rest of the resume may stay the same, but you might change order of presentation, headlines, and specific descriptions.

▶ **Now, for the qualification summary, you must project knowledge of self, knowledge of the field, and knowledge of particular job functions.** What are your most significant consulting-related academic or employment accomplishments? Yes, you did work for a consulting firm already. It wasn't exactly a management consulting firm, but it was a consulting firm. Let's include that in the qualification summary and bring that entry as high on the document as we can. Oh, and we'll use a good headline as well.

Order of presentation will be crucial. The first two entries must be impressive. Yes, I agree. You do want to de-emphasize education. In this case it's not your greatest strength. Leave it last on the page, but make sure we highlight specific courses and concepts in the summary.

▶ **The summary must show that you know something about consulting and that you know about the particular skills you possess that are related.** In the cover letter, you will show more, but the qualification summary must reveal your goals and basic qualifications. With a selective field, it may be the most important section of the resume. Because it is read first, if it doesn't grab the attention of the reader, the rest might not be read.

Consulting Targeted Resume After Critiquing

Chris Smith

123 Main Street, Apartment 13 • Hometown, NY 00000 • (555) 555-1234 • csmith@company.com

Management Consulting Qualifications

- Confidence developing proposals and presentations and completing special analytical projects within a consulting firm's deadline-driven and detail-oriented environment.
- Knowledge gained via Economics, Applied Data Analysis, and Psychology of Business courses.
- Experience using economic models, Excel, statistical analyses, and other approaches to quantify data, identify trends, and present findings to colleagues, supervisors, and clients.
- Curiosity regarding strategic planning, profit profiling, industry trending, and competitor analysis.
- Experience in hypothesis testing, brainstorming, and creating reports.
- Abilities to use Word, PowerPoint, and Excel for financial and marketing analyses, reports, presentations, and case documentation.

Consulting Accomplishments

THE ARDMORE GROUP   Ardmore, PA
Intern/Assistant to the President   Summer 2007
Reported directly to president of multidivisional $10 million annual billing enterprise that included political consulting, special-interest lobbying, bidding on and awarding state contracts in health care, social work, and welfare administration.

- Conducted research regarding contracts available for bidding and what resources would be necessary to produce that bid. All research was transformed into written recommendations submitted to the president.
- Involved independent trips to the State Capitol, attendance at networking sessions to procure clients, and sharing of information with colleagues and supervisor to determine appropriate next steps.

Research, Analysis, and Project Management Accomplishments

UNIVERSITY OF ROCHESTER   Rochester, NY
Research Assistant for Psychology Professor Harry Smart   Spring 2006–Present
- Conducted extensive library and Internet research, identifying husband-and-wife relationship studies. Summarized findings and developed listings of citations. Presented findings to weekly faculty-led research team meetings.
- Scheduled subjects, conducted interviews, input and analyzed data, and completed library research.
- Completed comprehensive interviews assessing husband-and-wife relationships.

Speech and Hearing Center Research Assistant   Fall 2007–Present
- Identified methodology to be used to measure effectiveness and target criteria impacting therapeutic outcomes.

PHILADELPHIA PHYSICIANS ASSOCIATES   Philadelphia, PA
Assistant to the CFO   Part-time and Summers 2005–2006
- Audited medical records for accuracy prior to distributing records to doctors, attorneys, and insurers.
- Organized records in formats facilitating ease of access by attorneys, arbitrators, and judges.

Education

UNIVERSITY OF ROCHESTER   Rochester, NY
Bachelor of Arts, Political Science   anticipated May 2008

Coach's Final Words on the Consulting Resume

▶ **Your responses to the questions did reveal some anxiety associated with the selectivity of the field, but they also showed that you think the resume is ready.** You can now begin responding to postings, sending self-initiated contacts to firms, and networking with alumni.

▶ **I believe for this field that networking will be most crucial.** When selectivity is involved, it's often the name of someone stated at the beginning of the cover letter or, better, the fact that this person forwards your documents to the resume screener that impacts success. Use your past consulting employer as a source for referrals. Don't be shy about leveraging his name and his network of colleagues and associates. He can help you identify some smaller entrepreneurial and privately held firms.

▶ **You now need to work on cover letters.** In this case, you must first show that you have the research, analysis, and presentation skills required to effectively fill the roles desired. Read and think about some Harvard Business School case studies and refer to this activity within your correspondence. Pick up and read one of those books on introductory business management. Review some Harvard Business School cases. A liberal arts student like you can very quickly pick up appropriate phrases and concepts applicable to consulting. When you do, quickly update both resume and cover letters. Oh, you can follow up with firms who may have already rejected you. You have nothing to lose.

▶ **While this resume is ready for distribution accompanied by a great letter, you can and should enhance both as your job search progresses.** Continue to read about consulting and network with individuals in the field. Enhance your business-related knowledge and lexicon as you read. Update both documents whenever you wish. Send them anew or again when strategically appropriate.

Coach's Comments for a Paralegal Resume

▶ **This should be the easiest version to complete:** You've done two already, you have some significant experience, and you are sincerely interested in the field.

▶ **Of course, you've thought a great deal about the field already.** Yes, it's a very attainable goal. Many large and a few small firms regularly hire legal researchers and paralegals with academic backgrounds similar to yours. They appreciate the breadth and depth of research skills gained as a liberal arts student, specifically a political science major with a career interest in law. In your case, you also have directly related experience and a strong skill set.

▶ **The qualification summary remains the most critical component of your resume.** This targeted version will reveal that you are seeking a paralegal or legal research position and that you have all of the competence and confidence required to succeed within these roles.

▶ **The qualification summary must effectively reveal your goals and basic qualifications.** To save space, let's use the headline approach again. The words selected for this first headline will clearly state your goals. The bulleted statements that appear next, with the most important first, will summarize what you have to offer. They will serve to preview as well as review all of the qualities and capabilities you possess. No, you cannot use the same as you used for consulting, although some might remain. Think specifically about those experiences and skills that relate to paralegal and legal research.

▶ **A revised order of presentation will make this resume most impressive.** Yes, I agree. You do want to emphasize the law-related experience immediately following the qualification summary. Can you add to the description or accomplishment list? Make sure readers understand how much of this job was law related. The rest of the resume will look very much like the consulting one, except for a new header for education. You are interested in someday applying to law school, right? Many of your courses were taken as an exploration of law, government, and political science topics, correct? So, let's use Pre-Law in the headline. Okay?

▶ **It may seem too quick, but we're done.** It's time again to ask aloud the questions that determine if the resume is distribution-ready.

Paralegal Targeted Resume After Critiquing

Chris Smith

123 Main Street, Apartment 13 • Hometown, NY 00000 • (555) 555-1234 • csmith@company.com

Paralegal and Legal Research Qualifications

- Confidence conducting research using library and Internet resources as well as interview techniques.
- Experience in roles requiring detailed collection and review of documents and creation of reports and indexes.
- Confidence developing proposals and presentations, planning events, and completing special projects.
- Knowledge gained from courses including: Applied Data Analysis, Economics, Debate, Arguments in Politics, Political Theory, Politics in the Mass Media, Political Systems, and Social Psychology.

Legal Research and Litigation Support Accomplishments

PHILADELPHIA PHYSICIANS ASSOCIATES   Philadelphia, PA
Assistant to the CFO   Part-time and Summers 2005–2006
Reported directly to Medical Records Supervisor and CFO of regional medical practice, supporting day-to-day business, law, and insurance-related functions.
- Audited medical records for accuracy prior to distributing records to doctors, attorneys, and insurers.
- Organized indexes and record packets for depositions in specialized formats, facilitating ease of access by attorneys, arbitrators, and judges, and focusing on specific points of law in question.

Research and Project Management Accomplishments

UNIVERSITY OF ROCHESTER   Rochester, NY
Research Assistant for Psychology Professor Harry Smart   Spring 2006–Present
Assisted with study assessing perceptions impacting husband-and-wife relationships.
- Conducted extensive library and Internet research for husband-and-wife relationship studies. Summarized findings and detailed listings of citations. Presented findings to weekly faculty-led research team meetings.
- Scheduled subjects, conducted interviews, input and analyzed data, and completed library research.
Speech and Hearing Center Research Assistant   Fall 2007–Present
Assisted with planning and implementing study assessing effectiveness of speech and language therapy services.
- Scheduled home visits, explained services, helped clients complete assessment questionnaires.

THE ARDMORE GROUP   Ardmore, PA
Intern/Assistant to the President   Summer 2007
Reported directly to president of multidivisional enterprise that included political consulting, special-interest lobbying, bidding on and the awarding of state government contracts in health care, social work, and welfare administration.
- Conducted research regarding contracts available for bidding and resources necessary to produce bids. All research was transformed into written recommendations submitted to the president. Yielded one hit per month.
- Developed and distributed detailed pre-event and post-event documentation and correspondence.

Political Science and Pre-Law Studies

UNIVERSITY OF ROCHESTER   Rochester, NY
Bachelor of Arts, Political Science   anticipated May 2008

Coach's Final Words on the Paralegal Resume

- You should be very proud of this targeted resume. It will easily and effectively support reactive and proactive efforts. You can respond to postings and send this out immediately to firms of interest in New York, Philadelphia, and Washington, D.C.

- But just because the resume is so strong, don't undervalue the potential impact of your cover letter. Within this supporting document share qualifications as well as motivations. Reveal that you know the ideal profile of paralegal candidates and those who serve within these roles. State that you wish to apply to law school only after the appropriate tenure with the firm. If confidentiality allows, within these letters note the firms involved and a summary of some of the cases that were related to your experience with the medical practice.

- Make sure you add the Philadelphia address to the letterhead used for letters targeting firms in your "home city." This will enhance your chances to be invited to interview.

An Actual Resume Success Story

Many of the sample resumes in this book are adaptations of those used by actual job seekers. Ideally, these real-life documents reveal the most effective use of concepts and themes presented within the preceding pages. Most significantly, the final versions presented in this chapter were, in somewhat different forms, used by a successful recent graduate.

This clearly strong, yet typical candidate used all of the varied formats that we examined here. They won him several interviews. He used the resumes in preparation for and during these discussions. He got several offers. Ultimately, this talented individual accepted an offer to work as a paralegal.

This chapter revealed how a draft can become a more powerful finished resume and how one multipurpose resume can, with coaching support, be transformed into targeted versions. You have learned how to be your own resume coach.

Chapter 10

What They Say about Your Resume

We solicited the comments of recruiting and human resources professionals to get an idea of their thoughts on the resumes they review. Their comments were edited for length, not content. The fields represented are diverse—and views are sometimes contradictory— yet some common themes emerge.

Jill Furick

▶ Jill Furick is a human resources manager for the law firm of Ross, Dixon & Bell, LLP.

- A resume only needs to go back ten years.
- Don't put your salary on your resume. Inevitably you will be ruled out because you are too high or your salary is so low we don't think you could have the experience needed.
- I would rather see your computer skills than your personal interests. It doesn't matter to me that you like riding horses or playing basketball: Can you use MS Office?
- Provide references when asked and make sure you have the right information. Nothing is more annoying than trying to track down a person for a reference! After the interview, call each reference and tell them they may get a call from a potential employer.
- Make the HR person's life as easy as possible!
- You can't network sitting on your couch or in front of a computer! Job seekers who think hunting for jobs solely on the Internet frees them from having to network and conduct disciplined, diverse searches are fooling themselves.
- Last but not least, put your resume on the Internet and then get off your rear end and hit the streets! Contact every company you are interested in and hand-deliver, e-mail, or fax a resume. Don't expect an interview, but you never know whom you will run into!

William C. Belknap

▶ William Belknap is a cofounder and partner in the firm Performance Leadership. He has been working with resumes for more than thirty years.

- Over the years, studies have shown a typical resume reader only gives your resume a ten- to eighteen-second scan during her first reading. It is critical to structure your resume to attract her eye to your accomplishments and your expertise. How?
- Let's start at the top. We call this your "positioning statement." It should communicate to the reader your level, functional area,

and experience. In the old days some people would put their job objective here. Today it should simply read "Experienced Human Resources Executive" or "Experienced Software Developer." It is the first line after your name and address. The next line right under your function and level is the positioning statement. It explains what distinguishes you. The two lines together might look like this:

Experienced Human Resources Executive

With 20 years of experience in the Health Care industry focusing on executive compensation, recruiting, and training

- The next section should be an executive summary of your expertise and your key results, not the dated "summary section" which told people you "leaped tall buildings with a single bound" and which no one believed! Instead, the executive summary should be a place that allows the reader to see all the good stuff about you during her ten-second scan. If done right, it will get your resume into the "A" pile for a more thorough reading later.
- The expertise section should be just a few bullets saying what you are really good at in just a few words. Examples:

Union Negotiator

C++

Designing Sales Compensation

They should contain no hyperbole like "world class negotiator."

- The results section should be just four or five of your best accomplishments. Example:

Launched three new products in one year. All three gained market share over our competitors.

- Hiring managers are only interested in what you can do for them. They want your resume to answer the questions "How many home runs will you hit for me, and how many bases will you steal?"

So let's talk about what a hard-hitting accomplishment bullet should look like. Every accomplishment bullet must have a punch line with a quantifiable result. Using the accomplishment above: "launched three new products in one year." If we had stopped here there would be no punch line, so adding "all three gained market share over the competition" tells the reader these were successful launches.

When you use a strong punch line you avoid having to use hyperbole. When I see a resume with "successfully this and successfully that," I am immediately suspicious. Your punch lines are the proof of your success, not your hyperbole.

- Your resume has to be laid out well (lots of white space), in a bulleted format, with short sentences and no spelling or grammatical errors.

Joshua D. Shapiro

▶ Joshua Shapiro is the deputy speaker of the Pennsylvania House of Representatives. He served as chief of staff for U.S. Congressman Joseph M. Hoeffel.

In my capacity as chief of staff to a United States congressman, it was typical for me to receive upwards of 350 resumes for a single vacancy on the staff. It was impossible to read each one thoroughly. A resume must stand out—it must grab my attention at first glance. To do this, the successful applicant should:

- Use catchy headings that stand out and tell the reader what you've done. A resume from a typical college grad should have about five to seven headings, including schooling, internships, work experience, etc.
- Think brevity, brevity, and brevity. It is not necessary to tell your whole life story on your resume—leave something for the cover letter and the interview.
- Keep it to one page.

- Put one thing on your resume that is unique. I once interviewed someone (who was just as qualified on paper as lots of other applicants) because he listed on his resume that he "has a proclivity for tea." Seems strange, but it was enough to get my attention and grant him an interview to give him the opportunity to prove himself. It worked. He got the job.
- Remember, the resume is just to get you a seat at the table; your interview and references are also important in my business.
- Remain positive. Keep an open mind. Relax. Be yourself. Be unique.

Stephanie Chiesi Reh

▶ Stephanie Chiesi Reh is a senior HR generalist at Hand Held Products (a Welch Allyn Affiliate).

- Tailor your resume to the position description as much as possible. Many candidates apply for several positions at several different companies and submit the same resume for each. When preparing to apply for a position, you should first verify that you have the experience and qualifications necessary to perform the job. If you do not meet the advertised criteria, your chances of being selected are slim, because you are competing against the most qualified candidates. Recruiters are looking for the best resume that most closely resembles the job specification.
- I often receive cover letters or phone calls from candidates who attempt to amplify their resume by providing me with extra information because, "you can't put everything on your resume." I disagree. Unless a recruiter is convinced by your resume that you may be a good fit, he or she will not read your cover letter. Cover letters are best kept brief, including only pertinent information such as salary and relocation requirements, and where you saw the position advertised (particularly important if it is an employee or colleague referral). All other information should somehow appear in the resume itself.

- Paper resumes are, for the most part, a thing of the past. Therefore, format and length are much less important than relevant, thorough, well-written content. It takes time and considerable attention to detail, but it will be worth your effort.
- Customizing your resume shows the potential employer that you want a particular job, not just any job.

Jonathan Bujno

▶ Jonathan Bujno is a senior clinical recruiter with the Clinical Resource Network.

- The resume, like the diary or journal, is an examination of one's life. However, the resume, unlike the diary or journal, is used as a tool to lead you to employment, success, and money. Perhaps this is why writing a resume is such a difficult process. One thinks, "If this is no good, there's no way I'm going to get interviewed. There's no way I'm going to get that job." To me, there is a fair amount of truth to this. Initially, resumes are relied upon to screen candidates in or screen them out. It is often impossible to screen every candidate by phone, and managers will rely on the resume to represent skills and accomplishments. You may be the most qualified for the position; however, if your resume is a poor representation of your background, you may not be considered for the position. Therefore, you must take a careful approach to resume writing to ensure that you accurately portray potential.
- Writing a resume can be a lot easier than most people make it. The problem is, people tend to update their resume when they are in a bind—like after being laid off or terminated. It's hard to remember what you did on the job for the last four years. It's even harder to write a good resume when you're in a rush. Here are a few tips: If your Human Resources Department gives you a job description when you're hired, keep it and file it somewhere. Also, buy a notebook and take it to work with you. Each time you do something new or accomplish something on the job, write it down. Updating your resume will now be much easier. Instead of trying to

remember what it is you did, you can calmly refer to these resources and piece together your resume. Also, include examples of work-related initiative. Your resume shouldn't read like a corporate job description. Make sure you include a few lines that show why you are better suited than the other applicants.

- Your resume will be used as an interviewing tool. A good recruiter will probe everything you put on there. Know it well and be careful of inconsistent information. Also, we're seeing an increasing amount of formal background checks being done. Criminal and financial histories, references, employment history, education confirmation are now, more than ever, being checked by professionals—and they don't miss much.

- Regarding format, keep it simple—simple fonts, simple paper, simple color, and simple bulleted facts that are relevant to the position you are applying for. Design your own resume rather than using the standard MS Office template. This will help your resume stand out. Include a summary of professional objectives, education, experience, and technical skills. From there, you may add (to name a few): certifications, publications, accreditations, community organizations, and additional education. Use common sense when considering the length of the resume. Don't be wordy and ramble, but don't cut yourself short either.

- Proofread and when you think it's perfect, give it to someone else and let them look it over. Finally, we all know references will be available upon request, so you don't need to include that.

- Preparing your resume doesn't have to be a frustrating experience if you don't want it to be. By being a bit more proactive and following a few easy steps, you'll be ready to seize that next opportunity—stress-free!

Danilo Minnick

▶ Danilo Minnick is the director of volunteer services and student recruitment at Literacy Partners, Inc. He formerly served as senior recruiter for the Peace Corps Regional Office and is a retired Peace Corps volunteer who worked in The Gambia.

I view tons of resumes—not only volunteer applicants but also for staff positions. Believe me, I have gotten good at recognizing poor versus well-constructed documents. It really is the most important element of one's job search, and along with a professional cover letter, the first step to "selling" yourself with the hope of being called for an interview. The essential basics and extra frills that do get my attention include:

- One page, especially for "newbies" (students or inexperienced workers). Of course, midcareer professionals or execs can go beyond that, but when a twenty-something submits three pages, I wonder if they're full of themselves.
- Bold and bullets recommended (no underlines or abbreviations except for the U.S. states).
- No salary or personal information.
- Identification includes name, address, phone, and e-mail, centered on the page.
- Education and training are musts, even if just listing high school or certificates.
- When describing job responsibilities, use action words and accomplishments.
- Use bullets or concise three- to four-line paragraphs; a big block of type takes too long to browse quickly.
- Use a "Professional History" or related subheading to summarize many jobs. Through this section, expand upon qualifications that don't quite belong as detailed descriptions under the core employment listing.
- Use concise, consistent, dynamic phrasing that stresses result and accomplishments.
- Include a targeted or generalized skills summary.
- Avoid pronouns, use proper verb tenses, and check many times for spelling and mistakes. For example, if an applicant isn't represented professionally, the Peace Corps asks for a revised resume since all documents are shared with the host representatives before they decide whom they want to work in their countries.
- Don't ever lie.

Mark A. Indovina

▶ Mark Indovina is chief technology officer at Vivace Semiconductor Inc.

- To me, your resume is your personal sales brochure or data sheet published to highlight work history and qualifications.
- Once submitted for consideration, your resume is used as the road map that guides discussions during a phonescreen or face-to-face interview.
- I am against the prevailing attitude that resumes should be as short as possible. How can a single page of text adequately describe the accomplishments of a career individual? I expect an individual with more than five years of experience to have a two- to three-page resume (particularly true for technical fields).
- My fundamental resume "law" is very simple: Be detailed, but factual (honest!!!) with items documented on your resume. As I noted earlier, the resume is the data sheet used during any discussions with the candidate. Expect to be asked detailed questions about the statements you make on your resume. On too many occasions when interviewing a student, questions about classes taken were answered with "I don't remember." These meetings are cut short and, obviously, the candidate didn't get the offer.
- These days I would expect face-to-face interviews for technical positions to be held in a group setting with the candidate as the center of attention. This can be very intimidating, but I find the process to be an excellent barometer of how well the candidate blends into the group.
- Infrequently, but regularly, throughout the meeting you might be asked to stand up and solve simple problems at a white board. If so, don't hesitate to ask questions if you're confused. I would also be prepared to be "chatty" (those doing the interview are nervous too!); the astute candidate will also know when to shut up.

Linda Matias

▶ Linda Matias is the president of CareerStrides, a nationally Certified Resume Writer (CRW), and the former president of the National Resume Writers' Association.

- Statistics indicate that the majority of hiring managers glance at resumes instead of reading them fully. It's hard to blame them, since most receive hundreds of resumes for every open position. With this statistic in mind, use bullet points sparingly—to bring attention to your most notable accomplishments. If the whole document is bulleted, it is difficult for the reader to know what is important and quickly grasp your achievements. It's best to include responsibilities in paragraph form and only use bullets for special highlights.
- When developing your resume give thought to the person who will be reading it. What are his or her immediate concerns? How will you be able to solve that person's problems?
- Since the resume serves only as a synopsis of your accomplishments, you won't be able to include everything you've ever done. However, it is important that you identify all your achievements and then take great care in determining which ones you will include.
- Chances are, if your current manager was impressed by a specific accomplishment, your next employer may also be impressed. Therefore consider including the observations made by your current/previous manager.
- If you send a resume that lacks focus, the hiring manager will assume that you are unfocused and ready to accept any job that comes along. In the meantime, your competition is submitting focused resumes that speak to what the organization is looking for. Who do you think will be the one called in for an interview?
- It's okay if you have more than one focus. Most job seekers do. However, if you fall into this category, this means that you will need more than one resume. There really isn't any way around this. If you want to get noticed, the resumes you are submitting have to home in on what the hiring organization is looking for.

Nancy D. Miller

▶ Nancy D. Miller is CEO/executive director of CEO VISIONS: Services for the Blind and Visually Impaired.

I am most impressed with resumes that are:

- Neat, twelve- to fourteen-point type (ten-point is too small).
- Clearly organized, simple to read, not in color so that copying is easier.
- Chronological with dates of employment starting from most recent.
- No more than two pages (preferably one); includes talents, hobbies, specialties.
- Neat and typo-free and without whiteout.

I am most impressed with resumes that include:

- Computer or software expertise.
- Languages spoken and/or written other than English.
- For recent grads, part-time and/or volunteer work statements that specify which jobs were paid.
- Education, with university, date, and degree received.

Because a cover letter is as important as a resume:

- Write to me and refer specifically to the job I am advertising or that you are conducting a general search.
- It should be personalized.
- Let your personality show through without being cutesy.

Barry Goldman

▶ Barry Goldman is part of the recruiting team at Lawrence Livermore National Laboratory.

While the first half of my career was as a recruiter, the latter part has been administering internships—including placing students in projects at an R&D facility. I have more than thirty years of experience in Human Resources, ranging from recruitment, staff relations, compensation, and education. Past employers include McGraw-Hill, Stauffer Chemical, Exxon, and Westinghouse. The following are my thoughts on the topic of resumes:

- A resume is not intended to get you a job. It is intended to get you in the door to be interviewed. As a result, resumes should be targeted to the specific opening for which you are applying. The initial reviewers of a resume may very well be just screeners without any technical expertise. The resume will be reviewed against established criteria for the posting. Therefore, use the same wording as the ad—otherwise, a nontechnical person might not recognize your match and screen you out instead of in!

- There are many kinds of resumes or formats for resumes. Determine the format that is appropriate for the application. Keep in mind there are also differences in resumes that will be hand-submitted or included with a cover letter versus one that may be sent electronically.

- Every word on a resume should have meaning. If it doesn't, omit it.

- While not about resumes, it's okay if you're able to interview with others based on family and contacts of friends. Remember, if you are offered the job, it is not usually because of whom you know but your skills and what you are bringing to the job.

- If you are applying in response to an ad, use the language from the ad. If applying as a cold call, it is even more important to research the company. Check out their home page. Maybe there is a search engine that will allow you to research your interests in line with company programs. Check out their organizational chart and job postings. Postings will give you a flavor for their needs and types of openings.

- The more you can identify project or employee names that can be referenced on your application, the more you will increase your chances of being successful by getting it to the attention of the right people.

- As a past recruiter, a thank-you letter after an interview is advised—anything to keep visibility on your name and availability and highlight your differences from the other applicants. Managers also like this form of follow-through as they would like to see this characteristic in their employees.

- It is important to effectively convey your message in your statement of interest or cover letter. The following tips will help you organize your thoughts:

  1. When writing a statement of interest, talking about what turned you on to a particular interest or field will not strengthen your chances of being considered or called into an interview.
  2. Likewise, discussing what you hope to get out of an internship will also not increase your chances of being considered.
  3. Talk about what you are interested in, what skills and abilities that you can contribute. This is why any company may be willing to pay you to work for them.

Barbara Cohen Farber

▶ Barbara Cohen Farber is the executive director of administrative staffing for Lloyd Staffing, a national search firm. In her twenty-year career, she has successfully placed nearly 5,000 job seekers into administrative office service opportunities.

I see more than 350 resumes a week. I home in quickly on the facts I need to make a judgment call. Keep information focused. If you are seeking support from a staffing service recruiter, follow a few simple guidelines.

- Go basic with your paper and formatting. No graphics, no weird fonts, and stick with white, ivory, or cream paper.
- Be mindful of spelling. Spell check can't distinguish if the text should be *is* or *it* and that won't show as a typo. Watch sentence structure and tense. No first person.
- Bullets help to make the facts stand out. Where did you work, from when to when, and what did you do?
- Don't assume a title explains your responsibilities.
- What did you do at your last job that will be applicable at the company you are applying to?
- Try to stay on one page; two pages only if your experience is substantial.

- Avoid photos. Stay away from personal hobbies or interests. Let this info get uncovered in your interview; don't waste space on your resume.
- Make it look pleasing to the eye. Keep format consistent.
- List computer skill proficiencies, include all software expertise.

A resume is a screening tool used by hiring companies to determine who will make the cut for the interview. If I give advice to a candidate it is based on my experience of what works or what doesn't. As someone in the staffing and search industry, I encourage candidates to take the recruiter's recommendation since it is likely they know how best to present your qualifications to prospective employers.

Alan Soane

▶ Alan Soane is a recruiting specialist for Xerox.

As a recruiting professional who has reviewed thousands of resumes, I am continually asked what I look for in a resume or what are considered best practices as far as format, content, and length. To the usual chagrin of the asker, my response is there is no best or magic template for all resumes. Each individual resume should clearly answer the questions that intended audiences carry as a filter and lens.

- A good resume will prompt the intended reviewer to fully read the document by being attractive, informative, and concise. A common perception of a resume is that it gets your foot in the door, the means of gaining an interview where you will actually have the opportunity to sell yourself. Although this is still true to an extent, with the advent of the Internet, e-mail, and commercial job boards, a resume has never had to stand on its own more than the present day. The information age has enabled job openings to be communicated to larger and larger pools of job seekers, which is a positive, but it has also buried recruiting, HR, and management professionals in an avalanche of resumes.

- Thoughtful presentation of your relevant experience, skills, and personal attributes against the position for which you are applying is the best course to take.

Jennifer Gage

▶ Jennifer Gage is manager of employee relations at Transmation, Inc.

- Your resume is your introduction to a potential employer—your marketing tool. It should be an accurate representation of who you are and what you have accomplished.
- If there are clerical errors, overuse of clichés, lots of style, and no substance—the reader will most likely make some unflattering assumptions.
- There are no hard, fast rules for resume length, but if you have more than a one-page resume, make sure it is full of valuable information.
- Most recruiters see hundreds of resumes per day—you may only have thirty to sixty seconds for your resume to make an impression before it is filed away somewhere, never to be seen again.
- It is important to highlight your unique contributions in your resume. The resume should not simply be a laundry list of your job duties.
- Include action-result statements, or statements that detail an action that you took and the resulting benefit to your organization. If possible, quantify these results (percentage of time saved, cost reduction, etc.). These statements show that you did more than come to work and do your job—you contributed to the bottom line profitability of the organization.
- It is important to remember that, in most cases, the resume is simply your ticket in the metaphorical door. However, if you don't make it through, you'll never have a chance at the job. A resume will get you the interview—an interview will get you the job.

Joyce A. Ponserella

▶ Joyce A. Ponserella is the medical officer recruiter for Navy Officer Programs.

- A resume that includes a college or university address as well as a home address is wonderful. Phone numbers are a must for both locations, and anyone who doesn't have or use e-mail is nuts. It's the quickest and easiest—not to mention cheapest—way to reach someone.
- Since the programs I recruit for are highly competitive, it is important to know the applicant's GPA, particularly in their major, but also overall.
- Experience is a very important area as well. However, if your experience doesn't relate to the area you want to work in, why bother with it. For example: Major: Biology; GPA: none listed. Course Highlights: Ecology, Genetics, Endocrinology, Microbiology. Experience: Customer Service Assistant, Enterprise Rent-A-Car. This is fine if you are looking for a job in the car rental business, but useless if you are applying for most everything else. Also, if I have to draw my own conclusions about GPA, I will assume you weren't proud of it, and therefore I am not interested in you for my organization.
- In another example: Majors: Neuroscience, Psychology; GPA: 3.67 overall. Psychology: 3.82, Neuroscience: 3.49. Experience: Summer 2001, Harvard Medical School Summer Undergraduate Research Program doing full-time research in Alzheimer's disease research unit; Summer of 2000, Burke Rehabilitation Hospital, Intern in Traumatic Brain Injury unit, assisting staff with patient care and day-to-day evaluation of patients. This individual has really given me some useful information. I know exactly what this person can do for my organization.

Mac Ismail, PE

▶ Mac Ismail, PE, is president and chief operating officer for Urbitran Group.

- I rarely give consideration to the resume. To me, the interview is much more important. When I do look at the page, I note the name and where the candidate lives—we have offices all over and I'm looking for a location fit. I also look for keywords relating to the type of engineering performed.

- I also look at the name of the school that the candidate graduated from and the types of activities that the person was or is involved with (i.e., sports, extracurricular events, etc.). This is very important to me because it shows that the person is a team player and has leadership ability.

- I get concerned if I see a twenty-year career with jumps every two years because I wonder why there has been so much moving; however, on a candidate with just a few years of experience, I understand the need to make strategic moves quickly and early on for growth. I'm turned off by too much information and lengthy resumes. I think something should be left for discussion. For me, the one-on-one is paramount. Someone may be a great engineer, but terrible at writing resumes. I also look at the names of the firms where the candidate has worked. That tells me something about skills and capabilities. The resume for me is just a formality.

Dave Bassi

▶ Dave Bassi is the recruiting manager for the State of Wyoming Department of Corrections.

Are there three sides of a fence? If so, I've been on all of them! Initially, I was a college student, trying desperately to compose the perfect resume that would land me a job that paid far more than I was worth! Later, I was employed as a career counselor for six years. This involved instructing job seekers on the art of marketing themselves to prospective employers through the use of the various resume formats. Currently, I am a recruiting manager who reviews anywhere from thirty to fifty resumes each month.

Consciously, or maybe subconsciously, I look at each resume and critique them from all locations on the "fence." What is the applicant trying to tell me (or sell me)? What parts of the resume were good? What parts were not so good? Finally, how can this applicant help me? Much of resume writing is common sense (with a little showmanship thrown in for good measure). All I can do is try to relate some of my experiences from each side of the fence:

- A good resume won't guarantee you a job. However, a bad resume will guarantee you won't get the job you want! The goal of the resume is to get you an interview. A poorly written resume decreases your chances of being invited to interview and increases chances of receiving dreaded rejection letters!

- When writing your resume, be truthful. Sometimes, you may feel the need to embellish qualifications to make you appear more competitive in a tight job market. Don't do it!

- Put your most marketable assets toward the top of your resume.

- Always have a current resume handy.

- Read the job announcement carefully. Read the job specs, compare against your assets, decide to apply, and reflect your analysis of assets versus requirements.

- Edit your resume for form and content. Ensure the layout is eye-catching yet uncluttered.

- Think like the employer. Put yourself in the place of the person doing the hiring. Would you rather read about someone's exciting work accomplishments and scholastic achievements, or would you rather read about his or her interest in bug collecting? Target your resume contents to the needs of the employer—don't list inconsequential niceties that you're happy to see in print.

- Tell me what you want in a cover letter, and show me in your resume why I should give you what you want: an interview and a job.

- If you send me a resume by e-mail, that does not excuse you from your obligation to write a cover letter.

- Find out my name! If you want to apply to my agency, call to find out who gets the application.

- Your resume is only one tool in your job-search arsenal, albeit a very important tool. Rarely, if ever, has an applicant been hired solely on the basis of a resume. But until someone comes along with a better way for applicants to get noticed, you better have a good product at your disposal.

Jennifer R. Jenkins

▶ Jennifer R. Jenkins is the college recruiter at the May Institute.

I am a college recruiter for a very special place; therefore, my main focus is on soon-to-be and recent college grads seeking to work with special needs clients and patients. With this target group in mind, my views on resumes include:

- One of the recommendations I often make (to this population of job seekers) is to live their resume rather than just writing it. I encourage students to create their resumes by exposing themselves to a variety of experiences such as volunteer work, internships, and/or co-ops. If they are able to gain experience throughout college, they are literally building a resume.

- When I am working with a soon-to-be graduate who has not had these types of experiences, they tend to have a very basic resume. In many cases, this tells me very little about who they are, their post-college focus, or their areas of strength.

- I realize that many college students have cumbersome schedules and don't want to jeopardize their school grades by getting in over their heads. However, I worked in college admissions for many years prior to Human Resources, and I was impressed with the number of students who combined their work-study job with their area of study. For example, Psychology students often sought out Admissions jobs, which allowed them the opportunity to build on their counseling and people skills.

- Another option is to do an internship/co-op during the summer months. These may even be paid positions. The May Institute, a non-profit human service agency, hires a number of college students during the summer months, as well as throughout the school year. These opportunities offer great hands-on experience, exposure to the field, flexible schedules, and an income!

Lindsay R. Greene

▶ Lindsay R. Greene is the fund development specialist for United Way of the Texas Gulf Coast.

Here are my thoughts on resumes and job searching:

- There are several styles of resumes. Some are more formal than others. Choose the style that best fits you. Your resume is the first impression an interviewer has of you.
- The two most important factors on a resume are accuracy/attention to detail (no typos!) and conciseness. Keep it to the point. Complete sentences are not necessary; bullets are much easier to read.
- Keep your resume limited to one page unless you have a Ph.D.
- Have someone else review your resume for typos and ask them if your resume is easy to read. After looking at your document for several hours, it is often hard to see your own errors.
- Your resume should quickly tell the interviewer if you are a good candidate for the open position through your skills and job experience.
- Include any volunteer and civic activities you are involved in locally. These additional experiences show that you are a well-rounded individual and may display additional skills you possess that are not necessarily evident from your past work experience.
- Your cover letter—and please do write a cover letter—should expand on these skills and experiences. Your resume will not get you hired for a job, so therefore, the main goal of your resume and cover letter should be to get an interview. Once you get your foot in the door, you can impress the interviewer with your charming personality and knowledge. Your goal will then change to being hired for the open position.
- During the interview, you can refer to your resume and will often be asked to explain or expand on something on your resume. Be prepared for this.
- If possible, relate the skills learned from past positions to the current job opening. Do some research on the company you have an interview with and refer to this research as necessary.

- I am always impressed when the person I am interviewing has done their "homework." The Internet is very helpful today for this sort of information. Use it!
- Write a thank-you note to everyone who interviewed you.

Common Thoughts

This chapter provided insights into the thoughts of recruiters and others who review resumes, determine whom to interview, and actually conduct interviews. Some common themes arose among the diverse views of professionals from varied industries and employment fields, including the following:

- Tailor your resumes to job descriptions, and customize your resume and cover letters to match specific jobs. Use keywords specific to fields and functions and wording that appeared in the announcement. Omit information not relevant to your stated goal, or to the position you are applying for. When possible, include specific skills, including computer competencies.
- Note accomplishments that are target specific, addressing "so what" issues that are raised during screening as well as interviews. Inform readers what past accomplishments have to do with the specific job. Allow focused achievement presentations to enhance the possibility that your resume is placed in the "yes" pile.
- The resume is as important as the cover letter and vice versa. Customize both and show that you understand and that you can appropriately use field-specific concepts and words. Be detailed and factual.
- Be prepared to use your resume as an interview tool and be ready, when asked, to expand upon entries. The resume should be used by both employers and candidates during interviews.
- Use a format that allows easy accessibility to you; include home phone, cell phone, and e-mail address.
- The idea that one resume can fit all needs is crazy. Create target-specific versions as needed.

- Use bold and bullets, as well as special headings and order of impor-tance to highlight.
- Gain focus and share focus. Remember, focus, focus, focus is the key!

Every recruiter has different preferences, but these tips give you some insight into how they view resumes. This perspective is useful in crafting your resume so that it carries the message you want it to and appeals to human resources professionals.

PART 2

Sample Resumes

Chapter 11

Sample Designs

This chapter contains fifteen common resume formats and designs. Look each one over carefully and experiment with combining different formats to get the results you feel best match the image you wish to convey.

Chris Smith

123 Main Street • Hometown, NY 00000 • (555) 555-1234 • csmith@company.com

Consulting Qualifications

- Specialized knowledge of e-business models and techniques related to market segmentation.
- Skills gained conducting real and academic focused case analyses related to Wal-Mart and Dell Computers and projects investigating marketing and distribution strategies.
- Capacities to research, analyze data, identify trends, and create proposals, plans, and documents.
- Word, Excel, PowerPoint, InDesign, Netscape, Explorer, and Internet talents.
- German and English fluency and conversational French and Swedish talents.

Economics, Business, and Mathematics Studies and Honors

2004–2008   UNIVERSITY OF ROCHESTER, Rochester, NY
Bachelor of Arts, Economics, with Mathematics Minor, anticipated May 2008
Economics GPA of 4.0 and **Overall** GPA of 3.92 and **Mathematics** GPA of 3.91
- John Dows Mairs Economics Prize for a Junior achieving the best in the field
- Golden Key Honour Society and Omicron Delta Epsilon Economics Honor Society
- Courses at Uppsala University, Uppsala, Sweden, Fall 2006

2004–2008   WILLIAM E. SIMON SCHOOL OF BUSINESS ADMINISTRATION, Rochester, NY
Management Studies Certificate, with Marketing Track, May 2008
- Simon Scholar tuition scholarship applied to future enrollment at Simon School

Selected Business, Economics, and Mathematics Courses

Financial Accounting, Statistics, Principles of Economics, Intermediate Micro- and Macroeconomics, Economic Growth in America, Economic Thinking, Teaching Assistant for Microeconomics, Probability and Statistical Inference, Advanced Microeconomics, Econometrics, Marketing, Economics of the Organization, International Organizations.

Research and Policy Analysis Experience

2007   EUROPEAN PARLIAMENT, Brussels, Belgium
Intern: Supported efforts of German SPD delegation and 35 MEPs. Performed competitive analysis of German parties impacting federal elections of 2007. Also, researched and wrote paper on topic of emissions trading from environmental, economic, and industrial standpoints.

Business, Strategic Planning, and Quantitative Experience

SAATCHI & SAATCHI ROWLAND, Rochester, NY
Summer 2007   **Freelance Media Assistant:** Assisted media team with DuPont 2007 and 2008 media planning.
Winter 2006   **Account Management and Media Intern:** Assisted with customer profiling and competitive ad spending runs for DuPont Teflon.
Summer 2006   **Account Management and Media Intern:** Performed product research and customer profiling, interviews with sales representatives to construct marketing plans for various Bausch & Lomb products, such as ReNu, Purevision, and Ocuvite.

Chris Smith

123 Main Street • Hometown, NY 00000 • (555) 555-1234 • csmith@company.com

CONSULTING QUALIFICATIONS

- Specialized knowledge of e-business models and techniques related to market segmentation.
- Skills gained conducting real and academic focused case analyses related to Wal-Mart and Dell Computers and projects investigating marketing and distribution strategies.
- Capacities to research, analyze data, identify trends, and create proposals, plans, and documents.
- Word, Excel, PowerPoint, InDesign, Netscape, Explorer, and Internet talents.
- German and English fluency and conversational French and Swedish talents.

ECONOMICS, BUSINESS, AND MATH STUDIES AND HONORS

UNIVERSITY OF ROCHESTER   ROCHESTER, NY
Bachelor of Arts, Economics with a Mathematics Minor   **anticipated May 2008**
- Economics GPA of 4.0 and Overall GPA of 3.92, and Mathematics GPA of 3.91
- Recipient of John Dows Mairs Economics Prize for a Junior achieving the best in the field
- Golden Key International Honour Society and Omicron Delta Epsilon Economics Honor Society

WILLIAM E. SIMON SCHOOL OF BUSINESS ADMINISTRATION   ROCHESTER, NY
Management Studies Certificate, with Marketing Track   **anticipated May 2008**
- Courses include: Financial Accounting, Statistics, Principles of Economics, Intermediate Micro- and Macroeconomics, Economic Growth in America, Economic Thinking, Probability and Statistical Inference, Econometrics, Marketing, and International Organizations
- Recipient of Simon Scholar tuition scholarship applied to future enrollment at Simon School

BUSINESS, STRATEGIC PLANNING, AND POLICY ANALYSIS EXPERIENCE

EUROPEAN PARLIAMENT   BRUSSELS, BELGIUM
Intern   **2007**
Supported efforts of German SPD delegation and 35 MEPs. Performed competitive analysis of German parties impacting federal elections of 2007. Also, researched and wrote paper on topic of emissions trading from environmental, economic, and industrial standpoints.

SAATCHI & SAATCHI ROWLAND   ROCHESTER, NY
Freelance Media Assistant   **Summer 2007**
Assisted media team with DuPont 2007 and 2008 media planning.

Account Management and Media Intern   **Winter 2006**
Assisted with customer profiling and competitive ad spending runs for DuPont Teflon.

Account Management and Media Intern   **Summer 2006**
Performed product research and customer profiling, as well as talking with sales representatives and constructing marketing plans for various Bausch & Lomb products, such as ReNu, Purevision, and Ocuvite. Expanded knowledge of marketing, strategic planning, account management, and client relations. Nurtured project management, writing, communication, and team skills.

Chris Smith

123 Main Street • Hometown, NY 00000 • (555) 555-1234 • csmith@company.com

CONSULTING QUALIFICATIONS

- Specialized knowledge of e-business models and techniques related to market segmentation.
- Skills gained conducting real and academic focused case analyses related to Wal-Mart and Dell Computers and projects investigating marketing and distribution strategies.
- Capacities to research, analyze data, identify trends, and create proposals, plans, and documents.
- Word, Excel, PowerPoint, InDesign, Netscape, Explorer, and Internet talents.
- German and English fluency and conversational French and Swedish talents.

ECONOMICS, BUSINESS, AND MATH STUDIES AND HONORS

UNIVERSITY OF ROCHESTER   Rochester, NY
Bachelor of Arts, Economics, with **Mathematics** minor   anticipated May 2008
Economics GPA of 4.0, **Overall** GPA of 3.92, and **Mathematics** GPA of 3.91

- Recipient of John Dows Mairs Economics Prize for a Junior achieving the best in the field.
- Golden Key International Honour Society and Omicron Delta Epsilon Economics Honor Society.

WILLIAM E. SIMON SCHOOL OF BUSINESS ADMINISTRATION   Rochester, NY
Management Studies Certificate, with Marketing Track   anticipated May 2008

- Courses include: Financial Accounting, Statistics, Principles of Economics, Intermediate Micro- and Macroeconomics, Economic Growth in America, Economic Thinking, Probability and Statistical Inference, Advanced Microeconomics, Econometrics, Marketing, and International Organizations.
- Recipient of Simon Scholar tuition scholarship applied to future enrollment at Simon School.

RESEARCH AND POLICY ANALYSIS EXPERIENCE

EUROPEAN PARLIAMENT   Brussels, Belgium
Intern   2007

- Supported efforts of German SPD delegation and 35 MEPs and performed competitive analysis of German parties impacting federal elections of 2007.
- Also, researched and wrote paper on topic of emissions trading from environmental, economic, and industrial standpoints.

BUSINESS, STRATEGIC PLANNING, AND QUANTITATIVE EXPERIENCE

SAATCHI & SAATCHI ROWLAND   Rochester, NY
Freelance Media Assistant   Summer 2007
Account Management and Media Intern   Winter 2006
Account Management and Media Intern   Summer 2006

- Assisted media team with DuPont 2007 and 2008 media planning.
- Assisted with customer profiling and competitive ad spending runs for DuPont Teflon.
- Performed product research and customer profiling, and interviews with sales representatives to construct marketing plans for various Bausch & Lomb products, such as ReNu, Purevision, and Ocuvite. Expanded knowledge of marketing, strategic planning, account management, and client relations.

Left Margin Timeline, Side Headers, Indented Copy, with Paragraph Descriptions

Chris Smith

123 Main Street • Hometown, NY 00000 • (555) 555-1234 • csmith@company.com

QUALIFICATIONS

- Specialized knowledge of e-business models and techniques related to market segmentation.
- Skills gained conducting real and academic focused case analyses related to Wal-Mart and Dell Computers and projects investigating marketing and distribution strategies.
- Capacities to research, analyze data, identify trends, and create proposals, plans, and documents.
- Word, Excel, PowerPoint, InDesign, Netscape, Explorer, and Internet talents.
- German and English fluency and conversational French and Swedish talents.

EDUCATION

2004–2008   UNIVERSITY OF ROCHESTER, Rochester, NY
Bachelor of Arts, Economics, anticipated May 2008
Economics GPA of 4.0 and **Overall** GPA of 3.92
Minors: **Mathematics**, with a current GPA of 3.91
- John Dows Mairs Economics Prize for Junior achieving the best in the field
- Golden Key Honour Society and Omicron Delta Epsilon Economics Honor Society
- Courses at Uppsala University, Uppsala, Sweden, Fall 2006

2004–2008   WILLIAM E. SIMON SCHOOL OF BUSINESS ADMINISTRATION, Rochester, NY
Management Studies Certificate, with Marketing Track, anticipated May 2008
- Courses include: Financial Accounting, Statistics, Principles of Economics, Intermediate Micro- and Macroeconomics, Economic Growth in America, Economic Thinking, Probability and Statistical Inference, Econometrics, Marketing, Economics of the Organization, International Organizations
- Simon Scholar tuition scholarship applied to future enrollment at Simon School

EXPERIENCE

2007   EUROPEAN PARLIAMENT, Brussels, Belgium
Intern: Supported efforts of German SPD delegation and 35 MEPs. Performed competitive analysis of German parties impacting federal elections of 2007. Also, researched and wrote paper on topic of emissions trading from environmental, economic, and industrial standpoints.

SAATCHI & SAATCHI ROWLAND, Rochester, NY
Summer 2007   **Freelance Media Assistant:** Assisted media team with DuPont 2007 and 2008 media planning.
Winter 2006   **Account Management and Media Intern:** Assisted with customer profiling and competitive ad spending runs for DuPont Teflon.
Summer 2006   **Account Management and Media Intern:** Performed product research, customer profiling, and interviews with sales representatives to construct marketing plans for various Bausch & Lomb products, such as ReNu, Purevision, and Ocuvite.

CHRIS SMITH

123 Main Street • Hometown, NY 00000 • (555) 555-1234 • csmith@company.com

BUSINESS, ECONOMICS, AND LIBERAL ARTS STUDIES

UNIVERSITY OF ROCHESTER ROCHESTER, NY
Bachelor of Arts, Economics **anticipated May 2008**
- Economics GPA of 4.0 and Overall GPA of 3.92
- Minor: **Mathematics**, with a current Mathematics GPA of 3.91
- John Dows Mairs Economics Prize for a Junior achieving the best in the field
- Golden Key International Honour Society and Omicron Delta Epsilon Economics Honor Society
- Completed courses at Uppsala University, Uppsala, Sweden, Fall 2006

WILLIAM E. SIMON SCHOOL OF BUSINESS ADMINISTRATION ROCHESTER, NY
Management Studies Certificate, with Marketing Track **anticipated May 2008**
- Completed Financial Accounting, Statistics, Principles of Economics, Intermediate Micro- and Macroeconomics, Economic Growth in America, Economic Thinking, Probability and Statistical Inference, Advanced Microeconomics, Econometrics, and Marketing
- Recipient of Simon Scholar tuition scholarship applied to future enrollment at Simon School

BUSINESS AND POLICY ANALYSIS EXPERIENCE

EUROPEAN PARLIAMENT BRUSSELS, BELGIUM
Intern **2007**
- Supported efforts of German SPD delegation and 35 MEPs. Followed daily Parliamentary procedures and performed analysis of German parties impacting federal elections of 2007
- Also, researched and wrote paper on topic of emissions trading from environmental, economic, and industrial standpoints

SAATCHI & SAATCHI ROWLAND ROCHESTER, NY
Freelance Media Assistant **Summer 2007**
Account Management and Media Intern **Winter 2006**
Account Management and Media Intern **Summer 2006**
- Assisted media team with DuPont 2007 and 2008 media planning
- Assisted with customer profiling and competitive ad spending runs for DuPont Teflon
- Performed product research, customer profiling, and interviews with sales representatives, creating marketing plans for Bausch & Lomb products, such as ReNu, Purevision, and Ocuvite

CONSULTING QUALIFICATIONS

- Specialized knowledge of e-business models and techniques related to market segmentation
- Skills gained conducting real and academic focused case analyses related to Wal-Mart and Dell Computers and projects investigating marketing and distribution strategies
- Capacities to research, analyze data, identify trends, and create proposals, plans, and documents
- Word, Excel, PowerPoint, InDesign, Netscape, Explorer, and Internet talents
- German and English fluency and conversational French and Swedish talents

Jamie Brown

123 Main St. • Hometown, MN 00000 • (555) 555-1234 • jbrown@company.com

EXPERIENCE

June 2006
to Present

RBC Capital Markets (formerly Dain Rauscher Wessels), Minneapolis, MN
Analyst, Investment Banking, Healthcare Group
One of fifteen investment banking professionals serving life sciences companies worldwide. Advise clients on M&A candidates and perform strategic analysis; conduct due diligence; determine valuation parameters; evaluate pro formas; and identify potential acquirers/ targets. Assist in the execution of equity, debt, and private placement offering process.

Identify potential clients; develop presentations; participate in introductory meetings; evaluate company, analyze sector- and market-related issues affecting a transaction. Manage documentation; support Equity Research, Capital Markets, and Sales & Trading; and assist in transaction committee approval process. Perform company valuation including discounted cash flow analyses, comparable company analyses, and precedent transaction analyses. Develop financial models to analyze mergers, equity, debt, and private placement offerings. Assist Research Analysts and advise Investment Bankers on technology and product assessment, applying industry knowledge gained via education and professional experiences.

Summer 2005

Vaccinex Inc., Rochester, NY
Research Intern, Cellular and Molecular Immunology Department
Worked in a team with twenty professionals including summer interns, research associates, Ph.D. candidates, and Senior Scientists. Reported to the Director of Research & Development.

Summer 2004

University of Rochester Medical Center, Rochester, NY
Laboratory Assistant, Department of Pharmacology and Physiology Peracchia Lab
Worked in a laboratory with eight staff members including Ph.D. candidates, postdoctoral candidates, and the Principal Investigator. Developed cell colonies and oocytes for gap junction experiments.

Summers 2002
and 2003

Harvard Medical School, Brookline, MA
Department of Epidemiology Research Assistant
Supported three Principal Investigators and a Ph.D. candidate in the collection and organization of Physician and Nurse interviews and medical literature.

EDUCATION

2002–2006

University of Rochester, Rochester, NY
Bachelor of Science in Chemical Engineering, May 2006
Emphasis on Life Sciences systems; including courses in Biochemical Engineering, Biotechnology, Biochemistry, Clinical Diagnostics, Reactor Design, Separation Processes, and Organic Chemistry.

2002–2006

William E. Simon School of Business Administration, Rochester, NY
Management Studies Certificate, with Finance and Accounting Track, May 2006
Earned certificate for completion of courses in Financial Markets, Financial Accounting, Marketing Management, Economics, Computer Programming, and Statistics.

Jamie Brown

123 Main St. • Hometown, MN 00000 • (555) 555-1234 • jbrown@company.com

INVESTMENT BANKING EXPERIENCE

RBC Capital Markets (formerly Dain Rauscher Wessels)   **Minneapolis, MN**

Analyst, Investment Banking, Healthcare Group   June 2006–Present

- One of fifteen investment banking professionals serving life sciences companies worldwide.
- Advise clients on M&A candidates and perform strategic analysis; conduct due diligence; determine valuation parameters; evaluate pro formas; and identify potential acquirers/targets.
- Assist in the execution of equity, debt, and private placement offering process.
- Identify potential clients; develop presentations; participate in introductory meetings; evaluate company, analyze sector- and market-related issues affecting a transaction.
- Manage documentation; support Equity Research, Capital Markets, and Sales & Trading; and assist in transaction committee approval process.
- Perform company valuation including discounted cash flow analyses, comparable company analyses, and precedent transaction analyses.
- Develop financial models to analyze mergers, equity, debt, and private placement offerings.
- Assist Research Analysts and advise Investment Bankers on technology and product assessment, applying industry knowledge gained via education and professional experiences.

RESEARCH EXPERIENCE

Vaccinex Inc.   **Rochester, NY**

Research Intern, Cellular and Molecular Immunology Department   Summer 2005

- Worked in a team with twenty professionals including summer interns, research associates, Ph.D. candidates, and Senior Scientists. Reported to the Director of Research & Development.

University of Rochester Medical Center   **Rochester, NY**

Laboratory Assistant, Department of Pharmacology and Physiology Peracchia Lab   Summer 2004

- Worked in a laboratory with eight staff including Ph.D. candidates, postdoctoral candidates, and Principal Investigator.

Harvard Medical School   **Brookline, MA**

Department of Epidemiology Research Assistant   Summers 2002 and 2003

- Supported three Principal Investigators and a Ph.D. candidate with collection of interviews and literature.

BUSINESS AND ENGINEERING STUDIES

William E. Simon School of Business Administration   **Rochester, NY**

Management Studies Certificate with Finance and Accounting Track   May 2006

- Earned certificate for completion of courses in Financial Markets, Financial Accounting, Marketing Management, Economics, Computer Programming, and Statistics.

University of Rochester   **Rochester, NY**

Bachelor of Science in Chemical Engineering   May 2006

Jamie Brown

123 Main St. • Hometown, MN 00000 • (555) 555-1234 • jbrown@company.com

BUSINESS AND FINANCE EXPERIENCE

June 2006–
Present

RBC Capital Markets (formerly Dain Rauscher Wessels), Minneapolis, MN
Analyst, Investment Banking, Healthcare Group
- One of fifteen investment banking professionals serving life sciences companies.
- Advise clients on M&A candidates and perform strategic analysis; conduct due diligence; determine valuation parameters; evaluate pro formas; and identify potential acquirers/targets.
- Assist in the execution of equity, debt, and private placement offering process.
- Identify potential clients; develop presentations; participate in introductory meetings; evaluate company, analyze sector- and market-related issues affecting a transaction.
- Manage documentation; support Equity Research, Capital Markets, and Sales & Trading; and assist in transaction committee approval process.
- Perform company valuation including discounted cash flow analyses, comparable company analyses, and precedent transaction analyses.
- Develop models to analyze mergers, equity, debt, and private placement offerings.
- Assist Research Analysts and advise Investment Bankers on technology and product assessment, applying industry knowledge gained via education and experience.

RESEARCH EXPERIENCE

Summer 2005

Vaccinex Inc., Rochester, NY
Research Intern, Cellular and Molecular Immunology Department

Summer 2004

University of Rochester Medical Center, Rochester, NY
Laboratory Assistant, Department of Pharmacology and Physiology Peracchia Lab

Summers 2002
and 2003

Harvard Medical School, Brookline, MA
Department of Epidemiology Research Assistant

BUSINESS AND ENGINEERING STUDIES

2002–2006

William E. Simon School of Business Administration, Rochester, NY
Management Studies Certificate, May 2006
- Certificate for completion of courses in Financial Markets, Financial Accounting, Marketing Management, Economics, Computer Programming, and Statistics.

2002–2006

University of Rochester, Rochester, NY
Bachelor of Science in Chemical Engineering, May 2006
- Emphasis on Life Sciences systems; including courses in Biochemical Engineering, Biotechnology, Biochemistry, Clinical Diagnostics, Reactor Design, Separation Processes, and Organic Chemistry.

Jamie Brown

123 Main St. • Hometown, MN 00000 • (555) 555-1234 • jbrown@company.com

INVESTMENT BANKING QUALIFICATIONS

- Comprehensive Analyst experience within major regional bank.
- Confidence within research, analysis, due diligence, and deal support capacities, gained within experiences in Corporate Finance, M&A, Corporate Credit, Private Equity, and Sales and Trading areas.
- Specialized knowledge of health care, biotechnology, and pharmaceutical deals.

BUSINESS AND FINANCE EXPERIENCE

June 2006–
Present

RBC Capital Markets (formerly Dain Rauscher Wessels), Minneapolis, MN
Analyst, Investment Banking, Healthcare Group

- Advise clients on M&A candidates and perform strategic analysis; conduct due diligence; determine valuation; evaluate pro formas; and identify potential acquirers/targets.
- Assist in the execution of equity, debt, and private placement offering process.
- Identify potential clients; develop presentations; participate in introductory meetings; evaluate company, analyze sector- and market-related issues affecting a transaction.
- Manage documentation; support Equity Research, Capital Markets, and Sales & Trading; and assist in transaction committee approval process.
- Perform company valuation including discounted cash flow analyses, comparable company analyses, and precedent transaction analyses.
- Develop financial models to analyze mergers, equity, debt, and private placement offerings.
- Assist Analysts and advise Investment Bankers on technology and product assessment, applying industry knowledge gained via education and professional experiences.

RESEARCH EXPERIENCE

Summer 2005

Vaccinex Inc., Rochester, NY
Research Intern, Cellular and Molecular Immunology Department

Summer 2004

University of Rochester Medical Center, Rochester, NY
Laboratory Assistant, Department of Pharmacology and Physiology Peracchia Lab

Summers 2002
and 2003

Harvard Medical School, Brookline, MA
Department of Epidemiology Research Assistant

BUSINESS AND ENGINEERING STUDIES

2002–2006

University of Rochester, Rochester, NY
Management Studies Certificate for courses in Financial Markets, Financial Accounting, Economics, Computer Programming, and Statistics, May 2006
Bachelor of Science in Chemical Engineering, May 2006

Jamie Brown

123 Main St. • Hometown, MN 00000 • (555) 555-1234 • jbrown@company.com

education

WILLIAM E. SIMON SCHOOL OF BUSINESS ADMINISTRATION ROCHESTER, NY
Management Studies Certificate *May 2006*
- Earn certificate for completion of courses taught by College and Simon School faculty.
- Emphasis on Finance and Accounting; including courses in Financial Markets, Financial Accounting, Marketing Management, Economics, Computer Programming, and Statistics.

UNIVERSITY OF ROCHESTER ROCHESTER, NY
Bachelor of Science in Chemical Engineering *May 2006*

experience

RBC CAPITAL MARKETS (FORMERLY DAIN RAUSCHER WESSELS) MINNEAPOLIS, MN
Analyst, Investment Banking, Healthcare Group *June 2006 to Present*
- One of fifteen investment banking professionals serving life sciences companies worldwide.
- Advise clients on M&A candidates and perform strategic analysis; conduct due diligence; determine valuation parameters; evaluate pro formas; and identify potential acquirers/targets.
- Assist in the execution of equity, debt, and private placement offering process.
- Identify potential clients; develop presentations; participate in introductory meetings; evaluate company, analyze sector- and market-related issues affecting a transaction.
- Manage documentation; support Equity Research, Capital Markets, and Sales & Trading; and assist in transaction committee approval process.
- Perform company valuation including discounted cash flow analyses, comparable company analyses, and precedent transaction analyses.
- Develop financial models to analyze mergers, equity, debt, and private placement offerings.
- Assist Research Analysts and advise Investment Bankers on technology and product assessment, applying industry knowledge gained via education and professional experiences.

VACCINEX INC. ROCHESTER, NY
Research Intern, Cellular and Molecular Immunology Department *Summer 2005*

UNIVERSITY OF ROCHESTER MEDICAL CENTER ROCHESTER, NY
Lab Assistant, Department of Pharmacology and Physiology Peracchia Lab *Summer 2004*

HARVARD MEDICAL SCHOOL BROOKLINE, MA
Department of Epidemiology Research Assistant *Summers 2002 and 2003*

qualifications

- Unique blend of business and science studies as well as investment banking experience.
- Knowledge of investment banking, healthcare, biotechnology, and pharmaceutical industries.
- Confidence applying scientific method as well as financial analytical models to test hypotheses and support qualitative thinking with quantitative methodologies.

DANA JOHNSON

123 Main Street ■ Hometown, New York 00000 ■ 555.555.1234 ■ djohnson@company.com

OBJECTIVE

Pharmaceutical sales representative position.

QUALIFICATIONS

- Experience building and maintaining relationships with physicians, surgeons, and nurses.
- Ability to interface with individuals at all levels of health care organization.
- Results oriented and ready to implement marketing strategies that meet and exceed goals.
- Adept at processing and conveying complex terminology via written and verbal communication.
- Timely and assertive follow-up skills to handle inquiries and reinforce existing relationships.

MARKETING AND COMMUNICATION ACHIEVEMENTS

Albert Einstein Hospital   **New York, NY**
Assistant Director of Public Relations   *May 1999–Present*
Function as PR account representative for Medical Center and 750-bed Hospital. Develop and maintain relationships with physicians, surgeons, and nurses. Generate publicity for urology, orthopedics, neurology, neurosurgery, blood/marrow transplant, emergency medicine, dermatology, radiology, anesthesiology, and otolaryngology. Proactively and effectively pitch stories to news media. Serve as spokesperson and liaison to local/national news media, on-call 24/7 as needed. Write news releases and speeches. Assist news crews and direct press briefings. Develop text for brochures, fundraising pieces, and Web sites. Write op-ed pieces and letters to the editor. Direct, write, produce, and edit videos. Develop and implement strategic publicity plans.

New Jersey Corn Cooperative   **New Brunswick, NJ**
Communications Manager   *June 1995–December 1998*
Directed all aspects of corporate communications/public relations for 600-member cooperative. Managed production of monthly member newsletter, quarterly employee newsletter, and annual report. Served as spokesperson and liaison to local and national news media. Wrote news releases, pitched stories, created print ads/brochures, and assisted with speech writing. Directed public relations events at fairs, schools, and festivals. Performed all in-house photography.

Princeton Vineyards & Winery   **Princeton, NJ**
Sales Representative   *Summers 1992 and 1993*
Served as tasting room sales representative and tour guide for 30,000-gallon winery. Managed all tasting room operations and represented winery at festivals and other events.

EDUCATION

New York University   **New York, NY**
Bachelor of Science, Communication   *May 1995*

DANA JOHNSON

123 MAIN STREET ■ HOMETOWN, NEW YORK 00000 ■ 555.555.1234 ■ DJOHNSON@COMPANY.COM

PHARMACEUTICAL SALES QUALIFICATIONS

- Comprehensive knowledge of health industry, ability to cultivate client relationships, industry contacts, goal-driven personality, and commitment to long-term profitability and productivity.
- Experience building and maintaining relationships with physicians, surgeons, and nurses.
- Ability to interface with individuals at all levels of health care organization.
- Adept at processing and conveying complex medical terminology via written and verbal communication.

ACHIEVEMENTS

- Increased number of proactive media hits by an average of 15 percent annually in designated clinical areas.
- Ninety-nine percent of proactive pitches are broadcast or printed by at least one media outlet.
- Assumed major responsibility planning, coordinating, and directing patient remotes for Children's Miracle Network Telethon from 1999 through 2007; events that raise nearly $2 million annually for hospital.
- PR department landed 2,400 media hits in 2007; 2,200 in 2006; 1,300 in 2005; compared to 1,000 in 2004 and 800 in 2003.
- As a result of proactive media pitch on free skin cancer screening, over 1,000 patients were screened annually, detecting numerous deadly melanomas, basal cell carcinomas, and squamous cell carcinomas.

HEALTHCARE AND MARKETING EXPERIENCE

ALBERT EINSTEIN HOSPITAL   NEW YORK, NY
Assistant Director of Public Relations   **May 1999–Present**

- Function as PR account representative for Medical Center and Hospital.
- Develop and maintain relationships with physicians, surgeons, and nurses.
- Generate publicity for urology, orthopedics, neurology, neurosurgery, blood/marrow transplant, emergency medicine, dermatology, radiology, anesthesiology, and otolaryngology.
- Serve as spokesperson and liaison to local/national news media, on-call 24/7 as needed. Write news releases and speeches.
- Develop text for brochures, fundraising pieces, and Web sites, and write op-ed pieces and letters to the editor.
- Direct, write, produce, and edit videos.

NEW JERSEY CORN COOPERATIVE   NEW BRUNSWICK, NJ
Communications Manager   **June 1995–December 1998**

- Established new department and directed all corporate communications/public relations for 600-member cooperative.
- Managed production of monthly member newsletter, quarterly employee newsletter, and annual report.
- Served as spokesperson and liaison to local and national news media.
- Wrote news releases, pitched stories, created print ads, and assisted with speech writing.

EDUCATION

NEW YORK UNIVERSITY   NEW YORK, NY
Bachelor of Science, Communication   **May 1995**

DANA JOHNSON

123 MAIN STREET • HOMETOWN, NEW YORK 00000 • 555.555.1234 • DJOHNSON@COMPANY.COM

PHARMACEUTICAL SALES QUALIFICATIONS

- Experience building and maintaining relationships with physicians, surgeons, and nurses.
- Ability to interface with individuals at all levels of health care organization.
- Results-oriented and ready to implement marketing strategies that meet and exceed goals.
- Adept at processing and conveying complex terminology via written and verbal communication.
- Timely and assertive follow-up skills to handle inquiries and reinforce existing relationships.

MARKETING AND COMMUNICATION ACHIEVEMENTS

Albert Einstein Hospital, New York, NY
Assistant Director of Public Relations, May 1999–Present
Function as PR account representative for Medical Center and 750-bed Hospital. Develop and maintain relationships with physicians, surgeons, and nurses. Generate publicity for urology, orthopedics, neurology, neurosurgery, blood/marrow transplant, emergency medicine, dermatology, radiology, anesthesiology, and otolaryngology. Proactively and effectively pitch stories to news media. Serve as spokesperson and liaison to local/national news media, on-call 24/7 as needed. Write news releases and speeches. Assist news crews and direct press briefings. Develop text for brochures, fundraising pieces, and Web sites. Write op-ed pieces and letters to the editor. Direct, write, produce, and edit videos. Develop and implement strategic publicity plans.

New Jersey Corn Cooperative, New Brunswick, NJ
Communications Manager, June 1995–December 2000
Directed all aspects of corporate communications/public relations for 600-member cooperative. Managed production of monthly member newsletter, quarterly employee newsletter, and annual report. Served as spokesperson and liaison to local and national news media. Wrote news releases, pitched stories, created print ads/brochures, and assisted with speech writing. Directed public relations events at fairs, schools, and festivals. Performed all in-house photography.

Princeton Vineyards & Winery, Princeton, NJ
Sales Representative, Summers 1992 and 1993
Served as tasting room sales representative and tour guide for 30,000-gallon winery. Managed all tasting room operations and represented winery at festivals and other events.

EDUCATION

New York University, New York, NY
Bachelor of Science, Communication, May 1995

DANA JOHNSON

123 Main Street • Hometown, New York 00000 • 555.555.1234 • djohnson@company.com

PHARMACEUTICAL SALES QUALIFICATIONS

- Experience building and maintaining relationships with physicians, surgeons, and nurses.
- Ability to interface with individuals at all levels of health care organization.
- Results-oriented and ready to implement marketing strategies that meet and exceed goals.
- Adept at processing and conveying complex terminology via written and verbal communication.
- Timely and assertive follow-up skills to handle inquiries and reinforce existing relationships.

MARKETING AND COMMUNICATION ACHIEVEMENTS

1999–Present   ALBERT EINSTEIN HOSPITAL, New York, NY
Assistant Director of Public Relations
- Function as PR account representative for Medical Center and Hospital.
- Develop and maintain relationships with physicians, surgeons, and nurses.
- Generate publicity for urology, orthopedics, neurology, neurosurgery, blood/ marrow transplant, emergency medicine, dermatology, radiology, anesthesiology, and otolaryngology.
- Proactively and effectively pitch stories to news media.
- Serve as spokesperson and liaison to local/national news media, on-call 24/7 as needed. Write news releases and speeches.
- Assist news crews and direct press briefings.
- Develop text for brochures, fundraising pieces, and Web sites.
- Write op-ed pieces and letters to the editor.
- Direct, write, produce, and edit videos.

1995–2000   NEW JERSEY CORN COOPERATIVE, New Brunswick, NJ
Communications Manager
- Directed all communications/public relations for 600-member cooperative.
- Managed production of monthly member newsletter, quarterly employee newsletter, and annual report. Served as spokesperson and liaison to local and national news media.
- Wrote news releases, pitched stories, created print ads/brochures, and assisted with speech writing.
- Directed public relations events at fairs, schools, and festivals.
- Performed all in-house photography.

Summers 1992 and 1993   PRINCETON VINEYARDS & WINERY, Princeton, NJ
Sales Representative

EDUCATION   NEW YORK UNIVERSITY, New York, NY
Bachelor of Science, Communication, May 1995

DANA JOHNSON

123 MAIN STREET • HOMETOWN, NEW YORK 00000 • 555.555.1234 • DJOHNSON@COMPANY.COM

PHARMACEUTICAL SALES QUALIFICATIONS

- Experience building and maintaining relationships with physicians, surgeons, and nurses.
- Ability to interface with individuals at all levels of health care organization.
- Results-oriented and ready to implement marketing strategies that meet and exceed goals.
- Adept at processing and conveying complex terminology via written and verbal communication.
- Timely and assertive follow-up skills to handle inquiries and reinforce existing relationships.

MARKETING AND COMMUNICATION ACHIEVEMENTS

Albert Einstein Hospital, New York, NY
Assistant Director of Public Relations, May 1999–Present
Function as PR account representative for Medical Center and 750-bed Hospital. Develop and maintain relationships with physicians, surgeons, and nurses. Generate publicity for urology, orthopedics, neurology, neurosurgery, blood/marrow transplant, emergency medicine, dermatology, radiology, anesthesiology, and otolaryngology. Proactively and effectively pitch stories to news media. Serve as spokesperson and liaison to local/national news media, on-call 24/7 as needed. Write news releases and speeches. Assist news crews and direct press briefings. Develop text for brochures, fundraising pieces, and Web sites. Write op-ed pieces and letters to the editor. Direct, write, produce, and edit videos. Develop and implement strategic publicity plans.

New Jersey Corn Cooperative, New Brunswick, NJ
Communications Manager, June 1995–December 2000
Directed all aspects of corporate communications/public relations for 600-member cooperative. Managed production of monthly member newsletter, quarterly employee newsletter, and annual report. Served as spokesperson and liaison to local and national news media. Wrote news releases, pitched stories, created print ads/brochures, and assisted with speech writing. Directed public relations events at fairs, schools, and festivals. Performed all in-house photography.

Princeton Vineyards & Winery, Princeton, NJ
Sales Representative, Summers 1992 and 1993
Served as tasting room sales representative and tour guide for 30,000-gallon winery. Managed all tasting room operations and represented winery at festivals and other events.

EDUCATION

New York University, New York, NY
Bachelor of Science, Communication, May 1995

Chapter 12

Sample Resumes

If imitation is the sincerest form of flattery, it is also the best resume-writing and job-search strategy. Sample resumes give you a great place to start, whether you're writing your resume from scratch or making your existing resume more effective.

Getting Started

In Chapter 9, you reviewed and analyzed several sample resumes. The following samples represent varied career fields, yet they possess characteristics common to all great resumes. Don't limit your review to resumes that match your goals. Find one or two that do, and then investigate a few more that strike you as particularly appealing.

Font sizes and word counts were reduced slightly to allow sample resumes to fit on the illustration pages. When creating your resume, feel free to write as much as will fit while maintaining a visually appealing document. Most resumes created on 8½" x 11" pages will contain more copy and lines than the samples.

Keep those pens, highlighters, and sticky notes handy! You'll make the best progress, and get the most out of your reviews, if you take notes as you go. Circle elements you think are particularly effective. Query the elements that don't work for you. Later, as you start writing your own first draft, you'll use these gut reactions to make your own resume as powerful as possible.

Also keep track of words, phrases, designs, and details you find appealing. When looking at elements, consider how well these reflect who you are. If you pride yourself on being professional and slightly conservative, don't worry about adding lots of flash and style to your resume. Likewise, if you want to convey an attitude of being creative and edgy, don't structure your resume to look overwhelmingly professional and dry.

CHRIS SMITH

123 Main Street • Hometown, MT 00000 • (555) 555-5555 • csmith@company.com

ACCOUNTING EXPERIENCE AND ACHIEVEMENTS

ROSS PECOE, INC., Billings, MT
Senior Accountant, 2003–Present
Oversee all accounting and payroll functions for a $20 million publicly held company that develops, manufactures, and markets proprietary X-ray systems.

- Assist controller in preparing financial statements and SEC reports.
- Prepare budgets and projections and monthly budget-to-actual reports and distribute to managers.
- Review work of staff accountant and approve journal transactions for data entry.
- Manage accounting duties of a venture-capital-funded start-up spin-off organization, Beta Technologies, including financial reporting and coordinating annual audit with external auditors.
- Interact with systems and payroll services professionals regarding problems and solutions.
- Assisted with analyzing implications, making final decisions, and completion of consolidation of three European subsidiaries.

Accountant, 2001–2003
- Assisted with monthly closings and financial reporting.
- Worked directly with controller to prepare primary and secondary public stock offerings.
- Implemented Solomon general ledger accounting package.
- Installed and set up modules, developed procedures for new system, and trained staff.

STEADFAST CORPORATION, Cheny Creek, MT
Staff Accountant, 1999–2001
- Monitored cash and accounts receivable for venture-capital-funded software development firm.
- Assisted in general ledger close, including foreign currency translation of foreign subsidiaries.
- Trained new employees to administer the accounts payable and order entry functions.

GRADUATE AND UNDERGRADUATE ACCOUNTING STUDIES

BRONTE COLLEGE, Newcastle, MT
Master of Science in Accountancy, Expected Completion May 2009

CARROLL COLLEGE, Helena, MT
Bachelor of Arts, Business Management, Accounting/Finance emphasis, June 1999

TECHNICAL ACCOUNTING SKILLS AND COMPETENCIES

- Skills associated with progressively responsible internal auditing, managerial accounting, budgeting, and financial analysis roles.
- Capacities to use and teach others Excel and QuickBooks.
- Experience interacting with external auditors, internal financial colleagues, as well as financial managers and senior executives.
- Capacities to draft, edit, and finalize detailed financial reports.
- Specialized knowledge of due diligence and risk analysis associated with venture capital funding and initial private offerings.

CHRIS SMITH

123 Main Street • Hometown, VA 00000 • (555) 555-1234 • Cell (555) 555-5678

csmith@company.com

QUALIFICATIONS

- Over 12 years of progressive sales and sales management responsibilities leading to current position as National Account Manager
- Experience developing and implementing marketing strategies, overseeing sales professionals, and developing effective sales relationships with direct users and resellers of personal computers and mainframes, as well as peripheral equipment, customer service contacts, and computer consulting services
- Capacities to hire, train, and motivate sales colleagues and to create reports identifying key profit areas and potential markets

ACHIEVEMENTS

- Progressive achievements within management and direct sales roles, directly contributing to expanded profits and sales
- A career averaging consistent percentage increases year after year, contributing to millions of dollars in sales and profits
- Capacities to generate continued sales growth within an industry where competitors increased annually and market required sensitivities to pricing and service

SALES ACCOMPLISHMENTS

STARBUCK COMPUTERS INC., Richmond, VA

2002 to Present
National Account Manager

Develop and implement national sales strategy for computer and peripheral manufacturer, consultant, and support-service provider. Initiated, built, and nurtured relationships with several Richmond-based *Fortune* 500 corporations including Ackler Industrial, the Carnulton Group, Hanlon and Associates, and Polamin Company. Oversaw resale accounts as well as direct-user accounts. Involves identification and analysis of potential business applications within target accounts and cultivation of key business relationships with senior management to facilitate sales.

- Average performance over five-year period was 125%.
- Grew Starbuck profits 200% over 5 years to $15M amidst decreasing unit pricing, increasing sales goals, and enhanced competition.
- Completed all five years in the top 12% of the National Account Channel as Golden Star Award winner.
- Created new revenue streams resulting in an estimated $30M in Starbuck sales and $40M in new services for the company.
- Regularly report sales results and status of strategies to senior marketing executives and CEO.

CHRIS SMITH
Page Two

STARBUCK COMPUTERS INC., Richmond, VA

1999 to 2002 *Dealer Account Executive*

As team leader and dealer liaison, oversaw completion of relationship building, bidding, delivery, and all sales efforts required to market Starbuck products and services through dealer locations.

- Initiated cooperative sales strategy with reseller business owners.
- Designed marketing promotions and directed reseller's sales efforts into business and education accounts.
- Average performance over six year period was 110% and recognized by Golden Star Club Awards.
- Grew sales by 400% to $20M.
- Oversaw training and completed performance reviews of 10–15 Sales Representatives.

1997 to 1999 *Corporate Chain Account Sales Representative*

Provided administrative and technical sales support to Richmond corporate chain account locations, including Power Electronics, Computer Corral, and Circonne Computer.

- Regularly called upon accounts to maximize knowledge of retail personnel, address concerns, and promote in-store visibility.
- Developed marketing promotions and trained store personnel.
- Tracked individual store sales and profit data to determine efficient coverage schedule and recognize particular achievements.

Summers and Part-time 1995 to 1997 *Customer Support Representative*

- Resolved customer issues including invoicing discrepancies, shipping errors, and upgrades for hardware.

EDUCATION

1993 to 1997 UNIVERSITY OF TEXAS AT DALLAS, Dallas, TX
B.A., Communications and Political Science, May 1997

Administrative Assistant

DANA JOHNSON

123 Main Street • Hometown, NY 00000 • (555) 555-6509 • djohnson@company.com

Administrative Qualifications

- Skills and perspectives gained through progressively responsible administrative roles.
- Abilities to prioritize tasks and complete tasks accurately and on time in deadline-sensitive settings.
- Professionalism required to address concerns of patients and clients while maintaining office efficiency and following standardized procedures and policies.
- Flexibility required to transform instructions and feedback of diverse supervisors into projects completed independently and thoroughly.
- Capacities to use, support, and train others to use Word, Excel, Access, and PowerPoint.

Administrative and Office Management Experience and Achievements

LOYALTY INVESTMENTS, Albany, NY
Administrative Assistant, 2003–Present
- Provide administrative support for new business development group; assist CFO with special projects.
- Ensure smooth workflow; facilitate effectiveness of 14 sales consultants.
- Direct incoming calls; initiate new client application process; maintain applicant record database.
- Aid in streamlining application process.
- Assist in design and implementation of computer automation system.

JENNINGS HOSPITAL, Washington, D.C.
Radiation Therapy Department Secretary, 2001–2003
- Answered phones, scheduled appointments, greeted patients and visitors, and prepared and filed charts.
- Typed and printed invoices and requisitions.
- Supervised inventory and general office organization.
- Served as liaison between physicians, staff, and patients.

Additional Business Experience

GROVER FINANCE, Buffalo, NY
Telemarketing Sales Representative, Summers and Part-time 1998–2001
- Secured new business using customer inquiries and mass-mailing responses; provided product line information to prospective clients. Initiated loan application and qualifying processes.
- Maintained daily call records and monthly sales breakdown.
- Acquired comprehensive product-line knowledge and ability to quickly assess customer needs and assemble appropriate financial packages.

Education

HOFSTRA UNIVERSITY, Hempstead, NY
Bachelor of Arts, English, Concentration: Business 2001
- Dean's List 2 of 4 eligible semesters and overall GPA 3.3

TRIBORO JUNIOR COLLEGE, Denver, CO
Associate of Arts, Business, 1999–2001

Francis Williams

123 Main Street • Hometown, New Jersey 00000 • (555) 555-1234 • fwilliams@company.com

OBJECTIVE

Senior Admissions and Enrollment Management Position.

ADMISSIONS ACHIEVEMENTS

2004 to Present **Seton Hall University Office of Undergraduate Admissions**, South Orange, NJ

Senior Assistant Director of Admissions—Director of International Recruitment and Admission

- Develop, implement, and assess the annual recruitment plans for international admissions.
- Assist with the coordination of the international student orientation programs.
- Develop new international recruitment publications and coordinate the mailing calendar.
- Coordinate international application review and foreign credit evaluation for 1,100 applicants annually.
- Manage all need-based and merit-based scholarship programs for international students.
- Conduct regular training sessions for counseling staff on issues regarding international admissions.
- Plan and execute international travel including alumni events and student interviews.
- Update and revise the University's undergraduate international admissions Web site.

2002 to 2004 **Seton Hall University Office of Undergraduate Admissions,** South Orange, NJ

Assistant Director of Admissions—Director of Transfer Recruitment and Admission

- Developed, implemented, and assessed the annual recruitment plans for transfer admissions.
- Created and coordinated the transfer open house and orientation programs.
- Developed new transfer publications and coordinated the transfer mailing calendar.
- Automated the transfer program to track potential applicants straight through conversion.
- Developed and maintained articulation agreements with several two-year institutions.
- Coordinated the training of all counseling staff on issues regarding transfer admissions.
- Created and updated a transfer reference manual to accurately reflect changing guidelines.

2000 to 2002 **Rutgers, the State University of New Jersey, Office of Admissions,** New Brunswick, NJ

Admissions Counselor

- Coordinated the student ambassador program and supervised its 65 volunteers.
- Developed an overnight hosting program for campus events administered by the Admissions Office.
- Assisted with international application review and credential evaluation.
- Organized several phone-a-thons to assist Admissions with its recruitment activities.
- Managed a significant travel region for domestic recruitment.
- Conducted on-campus interviews and large group information sessions.

EDUCATION

Rutgers, the State University of New Jersey, New Brunswick, NJ

Bachelor of Arts, Economics, with International Relations Minor, 2000

University of North London, United Kingdom

Overseas studies program involving economics, history, and culture courses, 1997

Francis Williams
Page Two

PROFESSIONAL MEMBERSHIPS

- National Association of College Admissions Counselors (NACAC)
- New Jersey Association for College Admissions Counselors (NJACAC)

Advertising Account Executive

Jamie Brown

123 Main Street • Hometown, NY 00000 • (555) 555-1234 • jbrown@company.com
987 Centre Avenue • Apartment 13 • New York, NY 10001 • (555) 555-5678

ADVERTISING ACCOUNT MANAGEMENT QUALIFICATIONS

- Marketing research, strategic planning, promotions, customer service, and sales talents nurtured by in-depth and diverse advertising, promotions, and retail internships and employment.
- Skills gained via courses including: Principles of Marketing, Marketing Projects and Cases, Psychology of Human Motivation, Public Relations Writing, Advertising, and Consumer Behavior.
- Blend of research, analysis, writing, and presentation talents.
- German, French, Dutch, and Farsi fluency, and conversational Spanish capabilities.
- UNIX, HTML, Excel, PowerPoint, PhotoShop, Netscape.

ADVERTISING, MARKETING, AND FINANCE EXPERIENCE

DAYS ADVERTISING, INC., Pittsford, NY
Intern/Assistant to an Account Manager: Assisted with design of television and radio ads and proposals for varied clients, including Wegmans and Bausch & Lomb. Developed customer database. Summer 2006

ADEFFECTS, Rochester, NY
Intern/Assistant to an Account Manager: Researched and developed promotional materials for retail, manufacturing, and restaurant clients. Gained knowledge of small business marketing. Suggested changes in advertising materials, consumer outreach strategies, and marketing literature. May 2005–July 2006

THE FINANCIAL GROUP, INC. DISCOUNT BROKERAGE FIRM, Pittsford, NY
Intern/Assistant to Operations Manager, January–May 2006

PEARLE VISION CENTER, Pittsford, NY
Sales Representative: Assisted customers and ordered inventory targeting upscale market. Summer 2006

IT HAPPENS, Antwerp, Belgium
Marketing Intern: Determined target markets and developed advertisement budget for concert and enter-tainment agency. Collected and analyzed financial and marketing data. Conducted market surveys to deter-mine market penetration. Assisted graphic artists with ads, posters, and brochures. Summer 2003

BUSINESS, ECONOMICS, AND LANGUAGE STUDIES

UNIVERSITY OF ROCHESTER, Rochester, NY
Bachelor of Arts, French, with a major GPA of 3.5, May 2007
Bachelor of Arts, Psychology, May 2007
Minor: **Economics**

WILLIAM E. SIMON GRADUATE SCHOOL OF BUSINESS ADMINISTRATION, Rochester, NY
Management Studies Certificate, Marketing and Finance/Accounting Tracks, May 2007.

HOBART AND WILLIAM SMITH COLLEGES, Geneva, NY
Completed varied Economics and Liberal Arts Courses prior to transferring, 2003–2004.

Advertising Media Planner

JAMIE BROWN

123 Main Street • Hometown, PA 00000 • (555) 555-1234 • jbrown@company.com

MEDIA PLANNING QUALIFICATIONS AND ACHIEVEMENTS

- Area of expertise is advertising media planning, with special knowledge of television and magazine options.
- Ability to project and elicit client enthusiasm and drive using a quantitative yet common sense approach.
- Adept at analyzing client needs, demographics, pricing and account team strategies, and then developing appropriate courses of action to yield desired results.
- Seven years advertising media planning experience; handling accounts with up to $7 million annual budgets.
- Strong service and interpersonal skills with clients, colleagues, and media sales professionals.
- Proven supervisory skills, effectively training staff in new concepts and procedures, monitoring performance, and maximizing output.
- Expertise associated with use of Word, Excel, Access, and PowerPoint for development of plans, proposals, budgets, financial analyses and projections, as well as presentations.

MEDIA PLANNING EXPERIENCE

THE MERCER MEDIA GROUP   Philadelphia, PA
Senior Media Planner   1997 to Present

- Direct all phases of media planning services for national accounts, primarily based in Eastern Region.
- Plan media and placement for five of the firm's largest clients, with annual media budgets ranging from $1 million to $7 million, and total media budgets in excess of $15 million.
- Oversee efforts of two Media Coordinators, a Media Assistant, and two support professionals.
- Created Excel and Access systems to track media plans and purchases, client quarterly sales, and profits.
- Regularly interact with account services colleagues and with clients to address queries, determine commitment to existing plans, and redirect plans as needed.

Account Supervisor and Media Coordinator   1995 to 1997

- Trained, guided, and directed staff of five while monitoring ad placement system.
- Assisted in creation of advertising campaigns and acted as liaison between client, agency, and media vendors, including selection, budget, and advertisement placement.

MERTON KASS & HOWE   Philadelphia, PA
Advertising and Public Relations Internship   Summers and Part-time 1993 to 1995

- Conducted market research, wrote press releases, produced traffic reports, worked media events, and assisted with advertising production.

EDUCATION

RUTGERS UNIVERSITY AT CAMDEN   Camden, NJ
B.A. in Mass Communication, with a minor in English   1995

PROFESSIONAL AFFILIATION

The Advertising Club of Pennsylvania

Dana Johnson

123 Main Street • Hometown, VA 00000 • (555) 555-1234 • djohnson@company.com

MEDIA SALES AND PRODUCTION ACHIEVEMENTS

WCVT-TV (Channel 3)   Wise, VA
Senior Sales Account Executive   1999–Present
- Established and maintained national corporate accounts as well as regional and local accounts
- Interacted with national NBC Sales, regularly identifying and leveraging new packages based on demographics and ratings
- Utilized production experience to establish and grow Advertising for All strategy targeting regional and local revenues, primarily generated from independently owned retailers and service providers
- Developed relationships with regional ad agencies, specifically media planners, to establish client-focused team approach
- Accounted for over $2 million in new clients revenues over four-year period, and average annual revenues of $500,000
- Initiated and developed marketing strategies and target grid for the second ranked TV station in fifth largest market for effective sales programs/promotions

Sales Account Executive   1998–1999
Sold time and production support to potential clients
- Assisted with establishment of all media and production plans, proposals, and budgets submitted to potential and existing clients
- Implemented existing local, regional, and national strategies and media sales programs
- Increased sales and production revenues

Associate Director/Stage Manager   1997–1998
- Production Department Stage Manager for Noon, Five O'Clock, and News at Ten newscasts, all public affairs programs, editorials, and news cut-ins
- Assembled sets and operated chyron machine

VNBC-TV (Channel 8)   Charlottesville, VA
Assistant to the Advertising Manager for "Good Morning Charlottesville"   1995–1997
- Prepared statistical analyses of advertising lineage for use in assessing competitive ranking
- Provided resource contact and encouragement to Sales Staff

VNBC-TV (Channel 8)   Charlottesville, VA
Production Intern   1993–1995 Part-time and Summers
- Wrote hard news and feature stories, scheduled/interviewed guests
- Researched materials and packaged tapes for production
- Operated teleprompter

Dana Johnson
Page Two

WNUV-TV (Channel 62)	Charlottesville. VA
University of Virginia Campus Cable Television and Radio Station Producer	1992–1995

- Responsible for researching materials for mini documentary
- Scheduled and interviewed guests for round-table discussions
- Wrote and edited scripts and edited master tape

University of Virginia Campus Cable Television Production Assistant	1991–1992

- Performed as camera technician, stage manager, and teleprompter operator
- Assembled lighting and audio equipment

EDUCATION

UNIVERSITY OF VIRGINIA	Charlottesville, VA
B.A., Economics, with Afro-American Studies minor, magna cum laude	1995

PROFESSIONAL AFFILIATIONS

National Association of Media Workers
National Association of Broadcast Journalists

QUALIFICATION SUMMARY

- Record of success sourcing new accounts and building sales of existing accounts
- Abilities to translate demographic and rating statistics into projections of potential revenues for clients and media buyers
- Confidence interacting with clients, media buyers, national corporate representatives, and network media sales executives
- Capacity to use production experience to entice first-time television advertisers to purchase time and production services

Francis Williams

123 Main Street • Apartment 13 • Hometown, NY 00000 • (555) 555-1234
fwilliams@company.com

APPLICATIONS PROGRAMMING EXPERIENCE

BENTLEY LIFE INSURANCE, New York, NY

2003–Present **Programmer Analyst/Senior Programmer**

Supervised junior programmers on varied System Projects.
- Actively participated in projects involving e-Commerce, CRM, BI, or ERP functions.
- Developed, maintained, and supported Sales Illustration Systems in C.
- Wrote "Illustration Software Installation" routine in INSTALIT software.
- Designed file transfer process for Mainframe to PC using NDM software.
- Hands-on experience with PC hardware, Windows, IBM, Novell Software, Emulation Software (Rumba, Extra, etc.), Dial-In Software (SimPC, XTalk, etc.), and have understanding of LAN technologies.
- Developed an Executive Information System on the mainframe using COBOL 2.

MEDWARE CORPORATION, New York, NY

2000–2003 **Senior Programmer—Patient Scheduling System**

Served as senior member of programming and testing team for software company specializing in health care industry.
- Designed and implemented system enhancements and new products.

1998–2000 **Programmer/Analyst**
- Developed online message system for members of the programming group.
- Instituted utilities that aided detection and repairs of client bugs.

SHADOW ASSOCIATES, Hartford, CT

Summers 1996, **Co-op Computer Programmer**
1997
- Developed and maintained program that monitored product availability and inventory for branch sites, displaying new product releases, and accessing updated information daily.

GRADUATE AND UNDERGRADUATE ENGINEERING EDUCATION

NEW YORK UNIVERSITY, New York, NY
MS Electrical Engineering, Software and Networks emphases, 2000
BS Engineering, 1998

QUALIFICATIONS

- Knowledge of C, COBOL, SQL Server 2000/2005, Web Services, Visual Basic, JavaScript, Assembly, C++ Cajon, Pascal, LISP, IBM, PL/I, Prolog, AION Databases: SQL/DS, Oracle
- Effective design, resource allocation, and status evaluation skills associated with large projects that shaped production testing and data collection processes.
- Proficient designing and implementing program enhancements, including an online message system, database repair/troubleshooting utilities, and release system to update clients.

Corey Davis

123 Main Street • Hometown, NJ 00000 • (555) 555-1234 • cdavis@company.com

PROFESSIONAL PROFILE

- Over seven years in Architecture and Facility Management-related industries with emphasis in Computer Design Base, Education, and Communication.
- Skilled in three-dimensional CADD modeling and rendering.
- Particular ability to visualize in three dimensions and utilize computer software for design, budgeting, estimating, and project management activities.

PROFESSIONAL ARCHITECTURE EXPERIENCE

Computer Design Software, Inc. East Brunswick, NJ
2001–Present *Architect*

Provide industry consultation and implementation expertise in architecture and Facilities Management for firm developing, distributing, and providing user support for specialized software used by architects, contractors, and property managers.

- Assisted with development and testing of Computer-Aided Design and Database software
- Provided demonstration and technical support for pre- and post-sales activity
- Acted as subject matter expert for future software enhancements and requirements
- Served in leadership roles for various joint studies teaming with IBM and other major corporations in the evaluation of CDB software for architecture

Hanna, Olin and Sherman Architecture Philadelphia, PA
1995–2001 *Architect*

Participated in conceptual design, design development, and construction documentation of architecture and landscape design.

- Created exploration, analytical, and presentation models materially and on computers for residential and commercial projects
- Fabricated sculptural wood and bronze detail elements installed in varied projects
- Projects included private residences, multifamily units, and professional offices

City of Philadelphia Philadelphia, PA
1993–1995 *Building Inspector*

PROFESSIONAL REGISTRATIONS

Licensed Architect, State of New Jersey Certificate 2344888

EDUCATION

University of Pennsylvania Philadelphia, PA
Master of Architecture 1993

Massachusetts Institute of Technology Cambridge, MA
Bachelor of Science, Architecture 1991

Art Instructor

CHRIS SMITH

123 Main Street ■ Hometown, IN 00000 ■ (555) 555-1234 ■ csmith@company.com

AREAS OF INSTRUCTIONAL EXPERTISE

- Eclectic experience teaching studio art, art appreciation, and art history within elementary and secondary public schools.
- Experience teaching studio art, crafts, and mixed media as private instructor and as director of special recreation program.
- Confidence developing group curriculum and exercises for students of varied ability levels, from beginner to expert.
- Expertise associated with media including: oils, acrylics, water colors, ceramics, and airbrush.
- Experience supervising student teachers, developing district-wide curricula, and advocating for funding.
- Capacities to translate passion into effective learning plans, utilizing varied modalities and instructional techniques.

SCHOOL-BASED INSTRUCTION

GARY REGIONAL SCHOOL DISTRICT   GARY, IN
Secondary Art Instructor   **1995–Present**

- Developed new and updated existing curriculum regularly for Studio Art, Art History, and Art Appreciation courses.
- Studio Art focused on composition, color, and conceptual problem solving, requiring completion of projects using varied media, including: charcoal, pen and ink, acrylics, and airbrush.
- Inventoried, ordered, and controlled budget of approximately $10,000 annually.
- Implemented curriculum with classes for gifted art students, including a district-wide art competition and scholarship in 1998.

Elementary Art Instructor   **1991–1997**

- Visited school sites on a regular basis, implementing a creativity-focused curriculum.
- Teamed with teachers to incorporate art projects and related lessons into existing units.

STUDIO AND RECREATION-BASED INSTRUCTION

ART DUDE STUDIOS   GARY, IN
Private Art Instruction   **2001–Present**

- Planned and implemented private instruction focusing on talented teens and adults.
- Addressed specific portfolio development needs of students seeking admissions and scholarships to art schools.

GARY PARKS AND RECREATIONAL ASSOCIATION   GARY, IN
Summer Art Institute Director   **Summers 1993–2003**

- Created and facilitated arts and crafts activity programs offered at six sites throughout the city.
- Media included sewing, weaving, knitting, sculpting, clay, jewelry, painting, and drawing.
- Successfully hired, trained, and directed fifteen Arts Aides to supervise each site.

EDUCATION AND CERTIFICATIONS

INDIANA UNIVERSITY   BLOOMINGTON, IN
State of Indiana Secondary Education Certification in Art   **1991**
Bachelor of Fine Arts in Studio Art, *cum laude*   **1989**
State of Indiana Elementary Education Certification   **1989**

Corey Davis

123 Main Street • Hometown, Illinois 00000 • 555-555-1234 • cdavis@company.com

OBJECTIVE

Banking loan officer, branch management, or training position.

QUALIFICATIONS

- Outstanding record of achieving sales goals as Branch Manager; successfully conducting residential and commercial mortgage acquisition and personal and commercial loan transactions and marketing programs.
- Extensive experience developing commercial lending packages for private clientele, including financial restructuring, REFI, equipment financing; coordinating activities with COMIDA, GCIDA, IBDC, and ESCDC, and attorneys, appraisers, title companies, and governments.
- Capacity to train, supervise, and motivate others to achieve maximum performance.
- Experience in branch management, business development, and as commercial lending officer and training officer.
- Comprehensive knowledge of Cook County consumer, industrial, and commercial clientele.
- Expertise to develop marketing strategies and collateral, internal management programs, and professional business plans through utilization of Word, Excel, and PowerPoint.
- Successfully developed and implemented marketing strategies and collateral material.

BRANCH, LOAN, AND TRAINING ACHIEVEMENTS

BIG BANK OF ILLINOIS, Chicago, IL
Branch Manager/Commercial Business Development Officer, 1994–1999
- Co-Managed District Officer Call Program to retain, expand, and track commercial customer base.
- Instituted Branch Neighborhood Equity Call Program, which enhanced sales of Home Equity and first and second mortgage products 33% over a six-month period.
- Designed and managed District Product Development Program which included development of H.E.L.O.C., Home Equity Loans, residential mortgage products (2-Year Fixed ARM, 5-Year Fixed ARM), Business Installment Loan (BIL), and marketing collateral.
- Served as one of two Chicago Area Sales Trainers, supervising professional sales training program for twenty-three-branch network which included Train-the-Trainer, market identification and definition, needs analysis, program development, implementation, results assessment, and follow-up responsibilities.

UNIVERSITY SAVINGS AND LOAN ASSOCIATION, Evanston, IL
Branch Manager/Mortgage Development Specialist, 1985–1994
- Developed Branch Neighborhood Equity Call Program to introduce and expand Home Equity Programs, resulting in a 16% increase in Lines and Loans in first month.
- Designed and managed Branch Product Development and Customer Information and Sales incentives.

SECOND CITY SAVINGS BANK, Chicago, IL
Branch Manager/IRA Specialist, 1975–1985
- Designed brochures for IRA marketing program and instituted model for customer focus groups.
- Co-designed and managed new IRA marketing strategies through Customer/Client Focus Groups.
- Managed overall loan operations of third-largest branch, with transactions averaging over $10 million per year.

Corey Davis
Page Two

FINANCIAL SERVICES ACHIEVEMENTS

ILLINI LOANS FINANCIAL ASSOCIATES, Chicago, IL
Owner, Part-time 1995–Present
- Integrated all management, marketing, and client services efforts, including: insurance, commercial mortgage/equipment financing, coordinating SBA programs, factoring, lines of credit, Letters of Credit, warehousing, floor plans, leasing.
- Successfully placed loans for businesses of varied sizes and individuals with diverse scenarios; ranging from $5,000 LOC to $25 million development of fruit processing factory.
- Utilized knowledge of cash flow, capital formation, marketing analysis, and lending procedures, marketing skills to successfully address client needs and resolve issues.
- Originated, processed, and coordinated all closing activities related to residential mortgage/home equity loans. Established working relationships with attorneys, appraisers, borrowers, and title companies.

CONSULTING ACHIEVEMENTS

UNITED WAY OF GREATER COOK COUNTY, Chicago, IL
Office Manager/United Airlines, January–September 2005
Area-Wide Interim Director/Cook and Area Counties, January–September 2005
- Served within Train-the-Trainer capacities, training selected individuals to perform United Way presentations, track results, and input payroll deduction data.
- Implemented IT Systems for input format and follow-up procedures.
- Scheduled and performed group presentations.
- Organized and facilitated board meetings and "Cabinet" meetings for both United Airlines, Cook, and neighboring counties.
- Established formal 3-Year Business Plan for each county to increase overall total annual contributions.
- Served as Business Development Officer.

PROFESSIONAL DEVELOPMENT AND EDUCATION

- Illinois Credit School; AIB/IFE courses in credit, insurance of accounts, mortgage, consumer and commercial lending principles, real estate law; Chicago Association of Agents and Brokers; Illinois State Certified Instructor/Sales; State of Illinois Notary Public
- University of Chicago, Bachelor of Science, 1975

JAMIE BROWN

123 Main Street • Hometown, MD 00000 • (555) 555-1234 • jbrown@company.com

BANKING QUALIFICATIONS

- Experience in customer service-focused teller roles, completing personal and commercial banking transactions.
- Confidence training and motivating teller colleagues.
- Specialized accounting courses supported by business curriculum.
- Knowledge of Excel, Word, PowerPoint, and CS Professional Suite, as well as tax and Internet applications.

BUSINESS, FINANCE, AND ACCOUNTING EDUCATION

UNIVERSITY OF MARYLAND, University Park, MD
Bachelor of Science in Business Administration, with Finance and Accounting emphases, anticipated May 2008
- Overall GPA: 3.7 and Finance and Accounting GPA: 3.7 (out of 4.0) and Dean's Honor Roll All Semesters
- Beta Gamma Sigma Business Honor Society President and Member
- Phi Kappa Phi Honor Society, Accounting Society, and Delta Sigma Pi Business Fraternity

SELECTED FINANCE, ACCOUNTING, AND BUSINESS COURSES

Money, Credit and Banking, Introduction to Marketing, Tax Accounting, Advanced Accounting, Intermediate Accounting, Auditing, Strategic Management, Cost Accounting, Financial Management, and Operations Management

BANKING AND ACCOUNTING EXPERIENCE

BANK OF MARYLAND, College Park, MD
Teller, Part-time 2005–Present
Process account transactions, reconcile and deposit daily funds. Inform customers of bank products, refer public to designated personnel, provide account status data, and handle busy phone. Orient, train, supervise, and delegate tasks for new hires. Assisted with planning and implementing extended hours customer service strategies.

GORDON, ODOM & DAVIS, INC., Baltimore, MD
Accounting Intern, Spring 2007 and Fall 2007
Completed compilations, reviews, audits, and tax returns for individual and corporate clients. Created financial schedules and reports using Excel spreadsheet programs.

TRADER PUBLICATIONS, San Diego, CA
Accounting Assistant, Summer 2007
Compiled daily reports for magazine and advertising revenues. Completed Accounts Receivable and Payable efforts.

LEGAL AID SOCIETY, San Diego, CA
Bookkeeping Volunteer, Summer 2006

LAW RELATED EXPERIENCE

SULLIVAN, DELAFIELD, ET AL, San Diego, CA
Legal Assistant, Summer 2007–Present

Francis Williams

123 Main Street, Apartment 13 • Hometown, CA 00000 • (555) 555-1234 • fwilliams@company.com

Bilingual Japanese-English Qualifications

- Bilingual Japanese-English talents gained working and studying in Japan and via comprehensive academics.
- Research, data and trend analysis, report writing, and presentation skills targeting bilingual audiences.
- Abilities to teach and tutor English as a Second Language to students of varied ages, ability levels.

Bilingual Experience and Achievements

2005–Present JAPAN EXTERNAL TRADE ORGANIZATION, San Francisco, CA
Analyst
- Conduct research for Information Alliance Technology Program, identifying and examining potential U.S.-Japanese high-tech firm linkages.
- Assist with annual and monthly Japan-U.S. and Japan-California publications.
- Established and oversaw all efforts associated with monthly topical seminars addressing Japan-U.S. commerce issues and featuring internationally recognized speakers.
- Serve as translator, transcribe documents, write correspondence, and complete projects.

2002–2005 ASIAN MARKETING RESEARCH, Belmont, CA and Tokyo, JAPAN
Bilingual English-Japanese Telephone Researcher
- Conducted surveys regarding views of Japanese executives on airline services, advertising options, computer hardware and services, and other topics.

Part-time 2001–2005 INTERNATIONAL INSTITUTE OF JAPAN, Tokyo, JAPAN
English Instructor for Non-English Speakers
- Taught high school and college students basic and advanced English conversation skills.

Summers 2003–2005 ASIAN MARKETING COMMUNICATION RESEARCH, Belmont, CA
Bilingual English-Japanese Telephone Researcher

1999–2005 INDEPENDENT LANGUAGE INSTRUCTION, Yokohama and Tokyo, JAPAN
English Tutor

Bilingual Education and Specialized Training

UNIVERSITY OF ARIZONA, Tucson, AZ
Graduate Coursework in Teaching English as a Second Language, 1998–2000

UNIVERSITY OF THE PACIFIC, Stockton, CA
Bachelor of Arts, Japanese, January 1999

UNIVERSITY OF CALIFORNIA SANTA CRUZ, Santa Cruz, CA
Intense Japanese Language Program, Summer 1997

KEIO UNIVERSITY, Tokyo, JAPAN
Completed Japanese Language Courses, 1997–1999

(Note: Resume in Japanese appears on reverse side.)

DANA JOHNSON

123 Main Street • Hometown, MN 00000 • (555) 555-1234 • djohnson@company.com

BOOKKEEPING QUALIFICATIONS

- Over 12 years of bookkeeping experience within progressively responsible roles.
- Experience overseeing comprehensive bookkeeping, including supervision of clerks and support staff.
- Capacities to address organizational finance related issues as well as those of individuals.
- Skills to develop financial data and summary findings on monthly, quarterly, and annual basis.
- Expertise associated with use of QuickBooks, Excel, TurboTax, and other financial software.

BOOKKEEPING EXPERIENCE

ASSOCIATES, INC.   EDEN PRAIRIE, MN
Senior Bookkeeper   **1999–Present**

- Oversee bookkeeping for mortgage and home equity loan firm, specializing in addressing first home purchases, debt consolidation, educational payment needs of clients from diverse financial backgrounds.
- Generate and present general ledger and investors' monthly reports for firm that generates over $10 million in mortgage and loan portfolios annually.
- Oversee A/R and A/P staff to ensure accuracy of accounts.
- Monitor efforts of third-party payroll services, checking accuracy of scheduled payments.
- Personally manage multiple accounts for major investor, real estate developer with commercial and residential properties in several states.
- Effectively interact with all finance savvy senior managers, specifically reporting to CFO.
- Support annual auditing and tax efforts of CPA firm.

MORNINGSIDE CO.   HOPKINS, MN
Bookkeeper   **1995–1999**

- Supervised general ledger through trial balance, as well as A/P, payroll, and payroll tax returns for construction and home improvement firm with annual revenues in excess of $2 million.
- Converted bookkeeping procedures from written documents to in-house computer system.
- Coordinated department's work flow, supervising A/R and A/P Clerks.

Accounts Receivable Clerk   **1994–1995**

THE DARNELL BANK   EDEN PRAIRIE, MN
Teller   **1990–1994**

EXCELSIOR CORP.   MANKATO, MN
Administrative Assistant   **1987–1990**

EDUCATION

SOUTHWEST STATE UNIVERSITY   MARSHALL, MN
Accounting and General Business Courses   **1990–1994**

FRANCIS WILLIAMS

123 Main Street, Apartment 13 • Hometown, CA 00000 • (555) 555-1234 • fwilliams@company.com

BUDGET ANALYSIS AND FINANCE ACHIEVEMENTS

2001–Present	Golden Life Insurance Company	Los Angeles, CA

Budget Analyst

- Balance $1.3 billion budget using internally developed and regularly revised software
- Reconcile accounts on ISA/ABC system to other financial systems
- Assist management in budget preparation
- Conduct training classes on the financial system for upper-level management
- Prepare comparison of expense to budget reports for executives on demand and on weekly, monthly, and quarterly basis
- Submit accounts and IRS filing for the Political Action Committee
- Generate financial analysis and reporting projects using Focus Report Writing and Excel, including macro programming, and MS Word
- Contribute annually to budget development and strategic planning processes

1995–2001	The Pacific Group	Los Angeles, CA

Auditing Analyst

- Prepared contract proposals and illustrative cost calculations
- Constructed Actuarial Valuation and analyzed actuarial gains and losses
- Independently generated regular reports for 40 individual clients and oversaw development of reports for 60 corporate clients
- Determined the minimum and maximum contribution allowable by law for the IRS
- Assured accuracy of comprehensive financial information database

1992–1995 *Accounting Technician*

- Maintained and reported on financial records and created financial statements associated with money market mutual fund for 60 corporate clients
- Balanced Trial Balance and generated journal entries
- Maintained, compared, and reconciled the fund on three computer systems
- Assisted system analysts in preparation and implementation of new computer system

FINANCE AND BUSINESS EDUCATION

	University of Washington	Seattle, WA
1992	*Bachelor of Science Degree in Finance*	

QUALIFICATION SUMMARY

- Competencies required to track and balance a $1.3 billion budget
- Record of developing, utilizing, and training others to use proprietary software and internalized systems for budget monitoring purposes
- Capacities to support executive decision making on budgeting
- Experience as regular contributor to groups making strategic financial plans
- Creativity associated with generating and explaining financial reports

COREY DAVIS

123 Main Street • Hometown, CO 00000 • (555) 555-1234 • cdavis@company.com

CASE MANAGEMENT AND ADVOCACY EXPERIENCE

THE WOMEN'S SAFE PLACE   GOLDEN, CO
Director of Case Management Services and Legal Advocate   *1995–Present*
- Provide counseling and referral services for residents of shelter for abused women and their children.
- Train and regularly interact with 24-hour hotline volunteers, supporting telephone crisis counseling and authorizing admission of residents on an emergency basis and for long-term transition periods.
- Conduct individual and group orientations, take case histories, and facilitate counseling sessions.
- Assist women completing Temporary Restraining Orders and serve as liaison with legal counsel.
- Provide expert testimony during domestic violence legal cases and report outcomes to staff.
- Assist with public relations and fundraising and regularly contribute to grant writing activities.

FAMILY SERVICES OF DENVER   DENVER, CO
Social Worker   *1990–1995*
- Provided services for clients and families with medical, psychological, housing, and financial needs.
- Supervised agency volunteers and graduate student interns.
- Worked collaboratively with various community agencies to provide needed services.
- Conducted in-service training offered staff and those from other agencies.

GREATER GOLDEN SCHOOL DISTRICT   GOLDEN, CO
Case Manager   *1985–1990*
- Served within counseling and referral roles for at-risk students and their families.
- Coordinated outreach, intake, and referrals for those with financial, educational, and medical issues.
- Maintained detailed case records and statistics for reports distributed to district and state officials.

LIVINGSTON HIGH SCHOOL   GOLDEN, CO
School/Family Counselor   *1981–1985*
- Provided individual counseling related to scheduling, college applications, and behavioral issues.
- Coordinated parent-teacher conferences and conducted family conferences and counseling sessions.

SOCIAL WORK AND COUNSELOR TRAINING

COLORADO STATE UNIVERSITY   FORT COLLINS, CO
Master of Arts, Social Work   *1985*
Master of Arts, School Counseling   *1981*
Bachelor of Arts, Sociology, with a minor in Education   *1980*
COLORADO COMMUNITY COLLEGE   DENVER, CO
Associate of Arts, Sociology   *1978*

CREDENTIALS, LICENSURE, AND AFFILIATIONS

- State of Colorado Licensed Social Worker and State of Colorado Counseling Certification
- American Association of Social Workers and State of Colorado Association of Social Workers

Certified Public Accountant

CHRIS SMITH, CPA

123 Main Street • Hometown, TX 00000 • (555) 555-1234 • csmith@company.com

ACCOUNTING QUALIFICATIONS

- Comprehensive experience in public and private accounting roles.
- Background in varied industries and specialized knowledge of engineering and oil and gas areas.
- Skills gained via audit, tax services, supervisory, and training accomplishments.
- Specialized accounting degree supported by general business curriculum and updated by ongoing professional development.
- Knowledge of Excel, Creative Solutions, Lacerte Tax Program, QuickBooks, Word, Access, and FileMaker Pro.

ACCOUNTING EXPERIENCE

MASTERMIND ENGINEERING, Houston, TX   1997 to Present
Accounting Manager: Complete SEC Reporting and Disclosure forms. Manage general ledger closing and maintenance. Supervise and review all accounting and finance areas. Administrate 401(k) pension plan. Implement accounting, payroll, and manufacturing software. Report directly to CFO, providing financial data and analytical reports to maximize profits and support managerial decisions. Hire, train, evaluate, and supervise accounting, bookkeeping, and analyst professionals.

DUNPHY & REILLY, INC., Houston, TX   1993 to 1997
Senior Internal Auditor: Conducted operational and financial audits of manufacturing subsidiaries. Designed and implemented audit programs to test the efficiency of all aspects of accounting controls. Recommended changes and improvements to corporate and divisional management. Trained and supervised staff auditors in all aspects of the audit engagement. Involved with corporate management in areas of acquisition and corporate development.

CHURCHILL NORTH, Houston, TX   1987 to 1993
Supervising Senior Accountant: Supervised, planned, and budgeted audit engagements. Oversaw and completed checks of audit reports, financial statements, and tax filings. Recruited, trained, supervised, and evaluated staff accountants. Gained experience from client assignments, including those in oil and gas, manufacturing, real estate, and nonprofit arenas. Proficient training use of spreadsheet packages. 1989 to 1993.
Senior Accountant: Served as liaison between Supervisor, Staff Accountants, and clients. Assisted with preparation of financial statements, tax filings, and audit reports. 1987 to 1989.

GORDON, ODOM & DAVIS, INC., Austin, TX   1985 to 1987
Staff Accountant: Completed compilations, reviews, audits, and tax returns for individual and corporate clients. Created financial schedules and reports using Excel and Supercalc spreadsheet programs. Passed Audit, Law, and Theory portions of CPA exam at first sitting.

ACCOUNTING EDUCATION

UNIVERSITY OF TEXAS, Austin, TX
Bachelor of Science, Accountancy, May 1985

Jamie Brown

123 Main Street ■ Hometown, OR 00000 ■ (555) 555-1234 ■ jbrown@company.com

Professional Profile

- Over a decade of positions as pastry chef, bakery manager, and related roles in varied venues.
- Thorough knowledge in the preparation of an extensive assortment of baked goods, including pastries, cookies, puddings, muffins, breads, and specialties.
- Creative talents to develop attractive thematic customer- and event-inspired presentations.
- Experience addressing needs and budgets of restaurant, catering, and retail bakery.
- Competencies to organize production and personnel to maximize use of space and finances.
- Recipient of numerous culinary awards for superior creations inspired by passion for excellence.

Pastry Chef Achievements

THE BEVENSHIRE HOTEL, Eugene, OR
Pastry Chef and Bakery Manager, 2004–Present
- Plan and prepare desserts on a daily basis for restaurant patrons.
- Oversee all operations of retail bakery, and prepare desserts and breads for catered functions.

DELTA PINES BAKERY & CAFE, Corvallis, OR
Pastry Chef, 2001–2004
- Prepared an extensive assortment of desserts, rotating on a weekly basis, including cakes, cookies, cobblers, puddings, tarts, special-order desserts, and wedding cakes.
- Created breakfast pastries and breads for lunch specials.

THE PLUMROSE RESTAURANT, Corvallis, OR
Pastry Chef, 1999–2001
- Planned and executed monthly menu which included six desserts, two sorbets, two ice cream dishes, and two fresh breads daily for lunch and dinner.
- Ordered all bakery and dairy supplies and prepared desserts for retail store and special orders.

THE WILLARD HOTEL, Boston, MA
Assistant Pastry Chef, 1995–1999
- Worked with executive pastry chef, monitoring baking, mixing, and finishing of cakes, pastries, and a full range of bakery products on an as-needed basis.
- Completed special orders for banquets, catered functions, and hotel restaurant.

LE HOTEL DE VIVRE, Bangor, ME
Pastry Cook, 1993–1995

Culinary and Pastry Training

AMERICAN PASTRY ARTS CENTER, Medford, MA
Course in Chocolates and Candy, 1993–1995

GOURMET INSTITUTE OF AMERICA, Boston, MA
Associate of Culinary Arts, with Certificates in Food Services and Catering Management, 1993

Chris Smith

123 Main Street • Hometown, NY 00000 • (555) 555-1234 • csmith@company.com

Chemical and Environmental Engineering Qualifications

- Strong problem-solving skills acquired via engineering curriculum, including varied special projects.
- Capacities to plan, implement, and report on the findings of individual or group projects.
- Confidence within engineering and science-focused settings, transforming instructions into detail-focused and accurately completed projects and reports.
- Academic and professional interest in energy efficiency, environmental issues, and quality assurance.
- Familiarity with Mathematica, MathCAD, Visual Basic, Excel, Word, and Lotus Notes.

Chemical Engineering Education

UNIVERSITY OF PENNSYLVANIA, Philadelphia, PA
Bachelor of Science in Chemical Engineering, minor in Environmental Engineering, with a cumulative GPA of 3.6, December 2006

Engineering Courses and Design Projects

Organic Chemistry, Quantum Chemistry, Atmospheric Chemistry, Physical Geology, Environmental Geology, Energy Resources & Utilities, Physics, Engineering Mechanics, Calculus, Multi-Dimensional Calculus, Differential Equations, Chemical Process Analysis, Thermodynamics, Chemical Reactor Design, Fluid Dynamics, Heat & Mass Transfer, Separation Processes, Process Control, Process Design

- **Steam heating system:** In group, designed steam heating system from a centralized power plant to a block of four buildings. Enhanced capacities to work in groups and apply concepts of fluid mechanics. Presented plan in written report. Spring 2005
- **Solar box cooker:** In group, designed and tested two solar box cooker prototypes. Refined capabilities to design, troubleshoot, and test prototype, assessing the most efficient of two designs. Fall 2006
- **Geothermal heating system:** In group, developed paper design for residential home geothermal heating system. Fall 2006
- **Catalytic disproportionation process:** With partner, completed flow sheet design for a catalytic disproportionation process, identifying areas of potential energy savings. Presented findings in written report. Fall 2005

Engineering Experience

PENNSYLVANIA ENERGY RESEARCH AND DEVELOPMENT AUTHORITY, Harrisburg, PA
Energy Resources Division Intern, Summer 2006
- Examined petroleum and natural gas industry to determine appropriate allocation of funds to regional studies and projects.
- Visited various energy source sites including a wind plant, solar collection site, natural gas drilling site, and a biofuel plant.
- Collected, analyzed, and reported on results of survey of potential Appalachian natural gas supply.

Chris Smith **Page Two**

Collegiate Awards and Activities

- University of Pennsylvania Benjamin Franklin and Moore School of Engineering Scholarship
- National Merit Scholarship
- Social Chair of University of Pennsylvania Chapter of the American Institute of Chemical Engineers

Employment

H. L. GAGE SALES INC., Albany, NY
Office Assistant, Summer 2002–2005

UNIVERSITY OF ROCHESTER FITNESS CENTER, Rochester, NY
Student Supervisor/Fitness Instructor, 2003–2006

EAST GREENBUSH HEALTH & FITNESS, East Greenbush, NY
Fitness Instructor, Summer 2002–2005

Dana Johnson
123 Main Street • Hometown, NJ 00000 • (555) 555-1234

Field Hockey Coaching Profile
- Successful coaching experience at high school, collegiate, and U.S. Olympic Developmental levels.
- Capabilities gained as Division III Head Coach and Division I Assistant Coach.
- Skills to plan practices, recruit, assess talent, enhance individual and team performance, and raise funds.
- Desire to utilize teaching techniques in practice and game situations.
- Abilities to develop popular and profitable camp programs.

Coaching Experience

U.S. Futures Program—New Jersey and Delaware
2005–Present   2007 and 2006 Head Coach and 2005 Assistant Coach

United States Olympic Sports Festival, Minneapolis, MN and Los Angeles, CA
2003–2007   2007 Head Coach and 2005 Assistant Coach

University of Delaware, Newark, DE
2003–Present   Assistant Field Hockey Coach and Assistant Field Hockey Camp Director
2007 Record: 14 wins and 4 losses; and 2006 Record: 12 wins and 6 losses

USA Olympic Developmental Camp
2003–Present   Coaching Staff D, C, and B Levels

Bentley College, Waltham, MA
1999–2003   Head Field Hockey Coach
2003 NCAA Division III Northeast Regional Champions, 2002 NCAA Final Four, and 2001 NCAA Division III Regional Finals

Waltham Academy, Waltham, MA
1999–2003   Varsity Field Hockey Coach
2003 Central Mass Division I Champions and Massachusetts State Semi-Finals and 1987 Central Mass District III Quarterfinals and Wachusett League Champion

Education

University of Delaware, Newark, DE
2005   M.A. in Sport Sciences

Springfield College, Springfield, MA
1995–1999   B.S. *cum laude* in Health, Physical Education, and Recreation
Member of 1999 and 1998 USA Field Hockey Squad, Outstanding College Athletes of America 1999, Captain, 1998–1999, and Member, 1995–1998, Field Hockey Team

Teaching Experience

Waltham Public Schools, Waltham, MA
1999–2001   Physical Education Instructor
1998–1999   Student Teacher

Chris Smith

123 Main Street • Hometown, NY 00000 • (555) 555-1234 • csmith@company.com

EDUCATION, COCURRICULARS, AND HONORS

ALLENDALE COLUMBIA SCHOOL, Rochester, New York
Senior Year, 2005–2006
- Yearbook Editor-in-Chief
- Upper School Chorus
- Pittsford Crew Club Varsity Crew Team Member
- Varsity Swimming Team Member and Captain

Junior Year, 2004–2005
- Yearbook Sports/Special Events Editor
- Explorers Post Program in Psychology
- Upper School Chorus
- Cum laude Society and High Honor Roll
- Varsity Swimming Team Member and Captain and Varsity Crew Team Member
- Della Simpson Book Award for Excellence in English and History
- Student Life Committee Class Representative

Sophomore Year, 2003–2004
- Co-chair Holiday Bazaar—raised $1,500 for Strong Children's Hospital
- Pittsford Crew and Varsity Swimming Team Member
- High Honor Roll
- Upper School Chorus
- Sophomore Class Forum Speaker

THE SANTA CATALINA SCHOOL, Monterey, California
Freshman Year, 2002–2003
- Gold Cord Honor Roll and Top 10% of class
- Varsity Swimming Team Member
- Amnesty International
- Lower School Volunteer Aide
- Co-chair St. Patrick's Day Dance

THE MABEL BARRON SCHOOL, Stockton, California
2nd through 8th Grade, 1995–2003
- Student Council President, 2003; Council Secretary, 2002; Council Treasurer, 2001; and PTSA Student Member, 1998–2002
- Amy Lina Award Winner, 2003

EMPLOYMENT

HARLEY SCHOOL, Pittsford, New York
Day Camp Counselor, Summers 2005 and 2003
- Planned and led activities and games for 5- and 6-year-old campers

Youth Swim Instructor, Part-time 2003–Present
- Prepared lessons, taught basic breathing and strokes, and motivated 6- to 9-year-old students

EDDIE BAUER, Victor, New York
Sales Associate, Summer 2004

HARRO EAST ATHLETIC CLUB, Rochester, New York
Lifeguard, Summer 2003

Chris Smith

Page Two

ATHLETICS ACHIEVEMENTS

ALLENDALE COLUMBIA SCHOOL, Pittsford, New York

Pittsford Crew, 2005–Present

- Pittsford Crew, Founded Fall 2003, William C. Warren Boathouse, constructed 2004 by donations, team fundraisers, and community support
- Compete in Western New York area regattas, Tail of the Fish, Cascadilla Invitational, New York State Scholastic Rowing Championships
- Port Side, Stroke, Club 4 New York State Scholastic Rowing Championship Gold Medal Winner
- Northeast Rowing Camp, Raymond, Maine, summer 2005; worked with Yale University and University of Miami coaches focused on rowing posture, connection, and slide control
- 8:19, 2k erg score
- 21.15.77 5k erg score

Varsity Swimming Team Member, 2003–Present

- Section Five Athletic League, Male Season
- 500, 200, freestyle; 100 breaststroke
- School record, 400 freestyle relay, 200 medley relay, 200 freestyle relay

Captain, 2004–2005, 2005–2006

- Organized team activities dinners, served as liaison between team and coach, helped organize fundraisers for Florida training trip

THE SANTA CATALINA SCHOOL, Monterey, California

Varsity Swimming, 2002–2003

- 500, 200, freestyle; 100 breaststroke
- 3rd place, 100 breaststroke, league championships

TIGER AQUATICS, Stockton, California

USS Swim Club Team Member, 1995–2002

- Age group, year-round swim club
- Traveled throughout California for competitions

PERSONAL PROFILE

Resident of Hanover, New Hampshire. Lived in Washington, D.C.; Princeton, New Jersey; Stockton, California; and Rochester, New York.
Traveled to Spain, France, and Italy. Enjoy reading, politics, sports, and music.

College Internship Resume

Corey Davis
123 Main Street • Hometown, NY 00000 • cdavis@company.com
987 Centre Avenue • Homeville, NJ 10001 • (555) 555-1234

OBJECTIVE

Summer Internship in biotechnology or biomedical engineering, utilizing and expanding upon:
- Knowledge of and experience using basic physics and chemistry laboratory techniques and procedures.
- Skills gained from research project on the ethics of the human genome project.
- Abilities to conduct library research and document lab research efforts in detailed or summary notes.
- Experience with: spectrometer, oscilloscope, super conducting materials, and varied lab equipment.
- Word, Excel, Publisher, Mathematica, Works, Quicken, Medline, C++, UNIX, FTP, and Internet skills.

BIOMEDICAL ENGINEERING AND SECONDARY EDUCATION

UNIVERSITY OF ROCHESTER, Rochester, NY

B.S. Biomedical Engineering, with concentration in Mechanical Engineering   **Expected May 2009**
- Overall GPA: 3.58/4.0; Engineering GPA: 3.72/4.0; and Dean's List 3 Semesters.

COLUMBIA HIGH SCHOOL, Maplewood, NJ

High School Diploma, with Honors   **June 2005**
- Graduated in top 10% with an overall GPA of 3.8/4.0, and 2200 SAT score.
- Varsity Track and Field Team Member and Letter Recipient.

BIOMEDICAL ENGINEERING COURSES

Introduction to Biomedical Engineering, Introduction to Computer Programming, Engineering Mechanics I, Statistics, Engineering Thermodynamics, Principles of Biology, Chemistry, and Physics

COLLEGIATE AWARDS AND ACTIVITIES

- Bausch & Lomb Scholarship for Science and Rush Rhees Scholarship for Secondary Achievement.
- Biomedical Engineering Society Member and Blood Drive Committee Chair.
- Men's Varsity Indoor/Outdoor Track and Field Team Member.

TECHNICAL AND MEDICAL EXPERIENCE

UNIVERSITY OF ROCHESTER MEDICAL CENTER, Rochester, NY   **2004–2005**
E.G. Miner Library Computer Assistant: Address Windows and Macintosh software and hardware issues.

TOWN OF SOUTH ORANGE, South Orange, NJ   **2002–2004**
Emergency Medical Technician: Licensed to practice emergency medicine at the ambulatory level.

EMPLOYMENT

ACE HARDWARE, South Orange, NJ   **2002–2006**
Sales Associate

FRANCIS WILLIAMS

123 Main Street • Hometown, PA 00000 • (555) 555-1234 • fwilliams@company.com

PROFESSIONAL PROFILE

- Instructional expertise at law school and undergraduate levels.
- Instruction and Research interests: Business Administration, Legal Studies, Criminal Law and Procedures, Supreme Court Rulings, Legal Trends and History.
- Research, writing, and presentation skills nurtured as author, lecturer, teacher, clerk debater, and mediator.

TEACHING AND LEGAL EXPERIENCE

DREXEL UNIVERSITY, Philadelphia, PA

Professor, 2003–Present

- Teach undergraduates Criminal Law, Criminal Procedures, Crime in America, and Business Law.
- Stimulate class involvement through use of case studies, mock trials, and law-school simulation.
- Annually serve as Freshman Advisor to diverse students and Faculty Advisor to Pre-Law Majors.

UNIVERSITY OF PENNSYLVANIA SCHOOL OF LAW, Philadelphia, PA

Adjunct Professor, 2003–Present

- Teach Criminal Procedures to First-Year Students enrolled in the Evening Studies Program.

DICKINSON COLLEGE AND DICKINSON SCHOOL OF LAW, Carlisle, PA

Assistant Professor, 2000–2003

- Taught undergraduate courses in Business Administration and Law, including: Criminal Law, Crime in America; Courts and Criminal Law; Criminal Procedures; Crime in America; and The Courts.
- Taught First-Year Law Students Criminal Procedures and Juvenile Procedures.

JOHN CARROLL UNIVERSITY, University Heights, OH

Adjunct Professor, 1997–2000

- Taught Legal Writing, Criminal Procedures, and Legal Reasoning to First-Year Students.

SUPREME COURT OF THE STATE OF OHIO, Columbus, OH

Clerk to the Honorable Justice Stanford Harvard, 1995–1997

SELECTED WRITINGS

- *Many Mondays in October: Supreme Court Trends in Criminal Rulings,* Law Texts Publishers, 2005
- *Undergraduate Studies of Criminal Procedures,* Law Texts Publishers, 2003

PROFESSIONAL, GRADUATE, AND UNDERGRADUATE STUDIES

JOHN CARROLL UNIVERSITY, University Heights, OH

Juris Doctor Degree 5th in a Class of 300, with Highest Honors, 1995

- Editor Law Review, 1997–1998; Law Review Staff, 1996–1997; and T.A. for Criminal Procedures, 1996–1998

CASE WESTERN RESERVE UNIVERSITY, Cleveland, OH

Master of Arts in Business Administration, with Honors, 1992

Bachelor of Science in Criminal Justice, *summa cum laude,* 1990

JAMIE BROWN

123 Main Street · Hometown, AR 00000 · (555) 555-4432 · jbrown@company.com

OBJECTIVE

Computer Programmer

PROFESSIONAL EXPERIENCE

2004–Present   PUBLIC AUTHORITY FOR CIVIL INFORMATION, Little Rock, AR
Technical Manager
- Performed and directed software coding, testing, and debugging for online and batch processes.
- Maintained over 300 assembler modules and developed 75.
- Formulated screen manager program, using Assembler and Natural languages, to trace input and output to the VTAM buffer.
- Developed program to monitor complete security control blocks, using Assembler and Natural.

1996–2004   STATE OF ARKANSAS, Fayetteville, AR
Systems Programmer
- Initiated start-up and implemented operations.
- Designed and managed implementation of a network providing the legal community with a direct line to Supreme Court cases.
- Developed a system that catalogued entire library's inventory.
- Used C++ to create a registration system for a university registrar.

EDUCATION AND PROFESSIONAL DEVELOPMENT

ARKANSAS TECH UNIVERSITY, Russellville City, AR
Completed varied programming courses, 1996–Present

UNIVERSITY OF ARKANSAS AT PINE BLUFF, Pine Bluff, AR
Bachelor of Science, Mathematics and Computer Science, 1996

CODING AND COMPUTER SCIENCE COURSES

Advanced IBM 370 Assembler, SNA Fundamentals, MVS/ESA Architecture, Natural 2 Programming Language, MVS/XA Concepts and Facilities, MVS/XA Job Control Language, MVS/XA Using Utility Programs, MVS/XA Using and Creating Procedures

OPERATING SYSTEMS, LANGUAGES, AND SOFTWARE

Windows 2000, UNIX, C++, Java, Visual Basic, Assembler, Oracle, SQL Server 2000

Counseling Psychologist

Dana Johnson, Psy.D.

123 Main Street • Hometown, FL 00000 • (555) 555-1212 • djohnson@company.com

PROFESSIONAL PROFILE

Bilingual English-Spanish psychologist who has served youth and adult populations within agency, clinical, and school settings. Experienced individual and group therapist within community programs offering services to clients from diverse socioeconomic and psychosocial backgrounds. Assessment, training, and referral professional; school counselor; and teacher of English as a Second Language.

QUALIFICATIONS, CLIENTELE, AND THERAPEUTIC STRATEGIES

Eclectic graduate and undergraduate studies focusing on family dynamics, rationale, emotive, and behavioral strategies. Background in family therapy, general psychotherapy, and assessment and treatment of behavioral and deficit disorders. Skilled developing and implementing treatment plans in social service and educational arenas. Experience coordinating service networks and collaborating with health-service professionals. Completed case management training with the Department of Social Services.

DOCTORAL, MASTERS, AND UNDERGRADUATE STUDIES

Nova University, Fort Lauderdale, FL
Psy.D., Counseling Psychology, 2000
MA, Counseling Psychology, with Community Clinical Concentration, 1997

Barry University, Miami Shores, Florida
BA, with Developmental Psychology and Human Development dual majors, cum laude, 1988

CLINICAL EXPERIENCE

2001–Present	**Mental Health Services of Ft. Lauderdale,** Ft. Lauderdale, FL *Counseling Psychologist:* Facilitate individual and group counseling for clients diagnosed with varied neurotic, psychotic, developmental, and behavioral disorders. Collaborate with health-service professionals to develop treatment plans for emotionally disturbed adolescents. Assist clients in developing survival skills to aid transition from residential to independent living. Coordinate service networks for academic, psychological, and social assistance.
1999–2001	**Tyler Adoption Agency,** Miami Beach, FL *Counselor:* Served as assessment, recruitment, and referral specialist. Traveled to community sites and executed presentations to recruit prospective parents for minority children. Conducted testing and home studies of prospective parents to determine eligibility. Followed up for evaluation purposes 3 months, 6 months, 1 year, and 2 years post-adoption. Served as referral source to private and public mental health services as needed.
1995–1999	**Dade County, Department of Social Services,** Miami Beach, FL *Bilingual Case Worker:* Assessed client needs, developed treatment plans, and managed cases. Communicated with court officials. Served as child advocate for court proceedings.

Dana Johnson, Psy.D.
Page Two

MULTICULTURAL SCHOOL COUNSELING AND TEACHING EXPERIENCE

1992–1995   **American School of Barcelona, Spain**
International Primary School Counselor: Administered psychological and educational testing for students ranging from prekindergarten to 5th grades. Counseled students, families, and teachers. Designed remedial and therapeutic plans. Led group activities for self-image enhancement and behavior modification. Worked with teachers on preventive strategies for social and disciplinary problems.

1989–1992   **Institute of America,** Madrid, Spain
Guidance Counselor and English as a Second Language Instructor: Counseled students and families for clientele ranging from prekindergarten to 12th grade. Administered psychological and educational testing. Designed complete record-keeping system for all students. Implemented behavior modification programs. Administered achievement, vocational, and college prep tests. Made policy on admissions and discipline. Worked with teachers on individual educational and behavioral programs. Taught English as a Second Language to students in grades 3–6.

Credit Analyst

Corey Davis
123 Main Street • Hometown, OH 00000 • (555) 555-1234 • cdavis@company.com

CREDIT ANALYSIS AND FINANCE QUALIFICATIONS

- More than 10 years experience in retail banking and commercial lending.
- Specialized expertise associated with credit and financial analysis and use of modeling and regression analysis to assess risk and project rates.
- Proficient analyzing financial statements, assessing risk, and evaluating credit worthiness.
- Experience using Excel, Lotus Notes, and internal systems for analyses and creating supporting illustrations for credit reports and presentations to colleagues and board.
- Experience using Dutch fluency and German conversation skills in business contexts.
- Naturalized U.S. Citizen.

FINANCE, ACCOUNTING, AND BUSINESS DEGREES

THE OHIO STATE UNIVERSITY GRADUATE SCHOOL OF MANAGEMENT, Columbus, OH
Master of Business Administration, with Finance Concentration, May 2003
- Completed Executive MBA Program with Honors, for Finance and Overall GPAs of 4.0.
- Courses included: International Finance, Money and Capital Markets, Investment, Corporate Finance, Corporate Financial Reporting, and Global Macroeconomics.

THE OHIO STATE UNIVERSITY, Columbus, OH
Bachelor of Science, Business Administration, with Accounting Concentration, 1995

BANKING AND CREDIT ANALYSIS ACCOMPLISHMENTS

WISTERIA BANK, Grace City, OH
Senior Credit Analyst, 2003–Present
- Oversee efforts of 8 Analysts working on commercial and personal lending teams.
- Review all documentation and recommendations before final determinations are rendered.
- Calculate and track positive and negative yield statistics, reporting findings to management.

Commercial Loan Credit Analyst, 2000–2003
- As member of lending team, analyzed and evaluated financial statements.
- Developed pro forma statements and cash flow projections.
- Documented findings; prepared independent recommendations on advisability of granting credits for corporate lenders.

Senior Personal Banker, 1997–2000
- Monitored overdraft reports, reviewed and executed consumer loans, supervised vault area, audited tellers, and provided customer service.

Personal Banker, 1995–1997
- Established and serviced professional clientele accounts. Expedited investments in treasury bills, repurchase agreements, CDs, retirement accounts, and discount brokerage for bank clients. Assisted branch corporate lender weekly on a revolving commercial loan.

Chris Smith

123 Main Street • Hometown, CO 00000 • (555) 555-5555 • Cell (555) 555-9999

DAY CARE QUALIFICATIONS AND COMPETENCIES

- Over 9 years of experience within home and school settings, teaching and caring for children aged 2 months to 7 years.
- Commitment to needs of infants, preschoolers, and kindergarteners, and record reflecting learning and loving.
- Background including courses in Childhood Development, Early Childhood Education, and Educational Psychology.
- CPR/First Aid certified and valid driver's license, with perfect driving record.

DAY CARE, TEACHING, AND CHILD CARE EXPERIENCE

2004–Present   PRIVATE RESIDENCE, Livermore, CO
Nanny: Care for twin boys from the age of two months through two years. Provide environmental enrichment, personal care, and play supervision.
- Accompanied family on numerous trips and cared for children during illnesses.

2002–2004   BABY BEAR PRESCHOOL, Keystone, CO
Teacher: Taught infant, preschool, and after-school programs. Planned curriculum, organized activities, communicated with parents and staff regarding children's growth and development.
- Responded to annual increase in students and move to new facility.
- Worked with owner on goals and assisted with annual licensing documentation and visitation.

2000–2002   THIS LITTLE PIGGY DAYCARE CENTER, Dove Creek, CO
Teacher: Planned and implemented infant program, blending developmental with custodial needs. Communicated with parents and colleagues regarding daily progress of children.
- Enhanced skills development through interactive play and song.

1998–2000   THE KID CORRAL, Wild Horse, CO
Teacher: Planned and implemented curriculum for toddler program. Enriched children's experiences through play, music, and art.

SPECIAL CARE EXPERIENCE

2000–Present   COALITION FOR RETARDED CITIZENS, Ivywild, CO
Volunteer

EDUCATION

1995–1998   METROPOLITAN STATE COLLEGE, Denver, CO
- Completed 30 credits in Education, with an emphasis on the day care setting.

REFERENCES

Furnished upon request.

Dental Hygienist

Francis Williams

123 Main Street • Hometown, NJ 00000 • (555) 555-1234

DENTAL HYGIENIST QUALIFICATIONS

- Progressively responsible experience as a Hygienist, Assistant, and Office Administrator.
- Sound knowledge of medical terminology and clinical procedures.
- Certified in first aid, cardiopulmonary resuscitation, and electrocardiography.
- Additional experience as receptionist/secretary with an executive search/management consulting firm, financial management company, and realty firms.

LICENSURE

- New Jersey Dental Hygiene License National Board Dental Hygiene Exam (Written: 90)
- N.E.R.B. Dental Hygiene Exam (Clinical: 93; Written: 90)

DENTAL HYGIENE AND OFFICE MANAGEMENT EXPERIENCE

HERBERT DICKEY, D.D.S.   Brooklyn, NY
Dental Hygienist, Surgical Dental Assistant, and Assistant Office Manager   2004–Present
- Provide state-of-the-art individualized prophylaxis treatment to adult and adolescent patients.
- Administer teeth cleaning, gum massage, oral hygiene education, and periodontal scaling procedures, and supervise interns undertaking similar procedures.
- Schedule patients for appointments for surgical procedures and provide presurgical preparation.
- Record temperature and blood pressure, insert intravenous units, and administer sedatives.
- Provide postoperative care in person and via telephone follow-up.
- Record vital signs every 10 minutes until patient is conscious; establish patient comfort; provide necessary information to patients regarding new medications and possible side effects.
- Handle accounts payable and receivable and health insurance transactions.

DR. RETTMAN, D.M.D.   Upper Montclair, NJ
Dental Hygienist   2003–2004
- Provided prophylaxis treatment, teeth cleaning, oral-hygiene education, and periodontal scaling.
- Administer Novocain prior to painful procedures.

Dental Assistant   2001–2003
- Assisted dentist in prophylactic procedures: provided necessary tools, sterilized equipment, comforted patients.
- Provided secretarial assistance, same as above.

Dental Trainee/Extern   1999–2001
- Initially, served in rudimentary observation and support roles, then advanced to Dental Assistant.
- Sterilized instruments, processed X-rays, scheduled appointments, maintained patient relations.

PROFESSIONAL TRAINING

KELLY SCHOOL OF DENTAL HYGIENE, New York, NY
A.S. in Dental Hygiene   June, 2001
Coursework included Radiology, Periodontology, Pathology, Dental Equipment, Oral Biology, and Pharmacology.

Dentist

Chris Smith, D.D.S.

123 Main Street • Hometown, WA 00000 • (555) 555-1234 • csmith@company.com

PROFESSIONAL DENTISTRY EXPERIENCE

1995–Present   PAYNE DENTAL ASSOCIATES, Bellingham, WA
Owner—General Practice
- Purchased large dental practice through a leveraged buyout.
- Determined and successfully implemented long-term growth strategies.
- Supervised a staff consisting of two other dentists and six support personnel.
- Provided comprehensive care for 2,000+ patients.
- Lead the office in steadily increasing production and revenues.
- Updated practice and computerized equipment.
- Presently facilitating transition of practice to new owner.

1993–2001   SEATTLE UNIVERSITY DENTAL SCHOOL, Seattle, WA
Clinical Instructor and Assistant Dental Clinic Director
- Supervised clinic with rotating groups of dental students and support personnel.
- Evaluated student performance via videotape voice-overs and written reports.
- Annually analyzed financial viability of clinic, instituted regularly revised plans to increase profitability, and managed business-related activities.

1991–1993   UNIFIED DENTAL CENTERS, Moses Lake, WA
Dentist
- Provided comprehensive dental care and trained staff members.
- Developed marketing plan, established and allocated marketing budget, and oversaw business operations of practice composed of one dentist, one hygienist, and one support professional.

1986–1991   UNIVERSITY OF WASHINGTON, Seattle, WA
Instructor of Clinical Periodontics
- Supervised small groups of students during their first contact with patients.
- Developed lessons, demonstrated periodontal procedures, and evaluated students.

PROFESSIONAL AND UNDERGRADUATE EDUCATION

UNIVERSITY OF WASHINGTON SCHOOL OF DENTISTRY, Seattle, WA
Doctor of Dental Surgery, 1986
- Completed comprehensive studies, including 2000 hours of clinical experience.
- Graduated 10th in a class of 400.
- Served as mentor for 1st- and 2nd-year students.

SEATTLE INSTITUTE OF TECHNOLOGY, Seattle, WA
Bachelor of Science Degree, Biology, 1982

Corey Davis

123 Main Street • Hometown, CA 00000 • (555) 555-5340 • cdavis@company.com

Editing, Writing, and Reporting Qualifications

- Research, writing, and editorial talents for interviewing, fact checking, script writing, and proofreading.
- Book, magazine, newspaper, and broadcast writing and editing experience.
- Confidence drafting, editing, and finalizing news, features, and sports stories.
- Production experience within varied print and broadcast media.
- Abilities gained through graduate studies and positions within magazine, newspaper, and television.
- Bilingual Spanish-English skills as well as Mac and Windows platforms and Internet.

Editorial, Writing, and Reporting Experience

BOOKS R COOL, INC., Long Beach, CA
Senior Editor, 2007–Present
- Evaluate general trade reference titles and assess profit potential, acquire titles, and negotiate contracts.
- Oversee publication, from development and editing to production, publicity, and marketing.
- Serve as in-house editor for internal and external newsletters and Web documentation.

BOP and *BB* MAGAZINES, Studio City, CA
Staff Writer, 2005–2007
- Wrote and researched music- and celebrity-related stories.
- Interviewed various celebrities and wrote and maintained a monthly column.

TEEN MAGAZINE, Los Angeles, CA
Editorial Assistant, 2004–2005

THE BEACON HILL TIMES, Boston, MA
Reporting Intern, 2003

WHDH CHANNEL 7 NEWS, Boston, MA
Reporting and Production Intern, 2002

Professional Development

- New York University Graduate Publishing Program, 2002–Present.
- American Society of Magazine Editors Junior Editorial Seminar Series, Summer 2004.
- American Society of Newspaper Editors Training Seminars, 2002–Present.

Graduate and Undergraduate English and Communication Degrees

SIMMONS COLLEGE, Boston, MA
Master of Arts, English, January 2003

UNIVERSITY OF THE PACIFIC, Stockton, CA
Bachelor of Arts, Communication, with English minor, May 2001

Jamie Brown

123 Main Street • Hometown, Texas 00000 • (555) 555-9873 • jbrown@company.com

ELECTRICAL ENGINEERING QUALIFICATIONS

- Success leading product development efforts for commercial, OEM, and government markets.
- Experience administering research and development activities, managing vendor and partner technology relationships, and satisfying customer expectations.
- A decade of project management, design, testing, and troubleshooting experience.
- Specialized knowledge of microprocessor development, marketing, and implementation.

ELECTRICAL ENGINEERING ACCOMPLISHMENTS

AEROSPACE SYSTEMS, Dallas, Texas
Systems Engineering OEM Section Manager, 1999–Present

- Managed development of customized versions of personal computer products, meeting requirements of OEM customers, Japanese, and United States government agencies.
- Supplied personal computer products with customized security and networking functionality.
- Provided OEM customers with problem-solving support and systems integration engineering.
- Managed development of laptop PC in support of U.S. Navy Lightweight Computer Unit.

Design Evaluation Manager, 1995–1999

- Managed development support engineering group established to complete personal computer competitive analysis and design verification testing.
- Developed competitive analysis process resulting in more compact computer designs.
- Initiated test processes including electrostatic discharge; conducted susceptibility, emissions, and related problem solving to meet regulatory requirements.
- Developed test plans and processes to verify functionality of computer products.

BELL SYSTEMS, Arlington, Texas
Senior Principal Design Engineer, 1991–1995

- Developed bus architecture enhancements to a Goldstone 10000-based in-store processor to meet customer performance requirements.
- Developed Goldstone 15000-based cluster terminal controller, emulating an IBM 3050.
- Developed a PCL 2/6 Channel interface in partnership with Expectations, Inc.

MITASHA CORPORATION, Galveston, Texas
Microcontroller Operations Product Engineer, 1989–1991

- Designed wafer-sort production test hardware for the 6235 microcontrollers, incorporated as a plug-in card to a test system.
- Developed test process improvements, resulting in 85% gross margin and less returns.

AIR DESIGN CORPORATION, Houston, Texas
Electrical Engineer Coop Student, Summer 1988

ENGINEERING EDUCATION

MASSACHUSETTS INSTITUTE OF TECHNOLOGY, Cambridge, MA
Bachelor of Science, Electrical Engineering, *cum laude,* June 1989

Chris Smith

123 Main Street • Hometown, MA 00000 • (555) 555-9873

Teaching Qualifications and Achievements

- Certification in Elementary Education, Music, and Secondary English.
- Experience teaching Elementary, Junior High, and High School Students.
- Competencies teaching choral and instrumental classes and directed choirs and bands.
- Success developing youth music programs by creating musicals tailored to student abilities.
- Musicals involved students composing, acting, choreographing, playing instruments, and singing.
- As classroom and private teacher, used audiovisual and electric piano computer systems.
- Formed **Music & More,** a civic musical theater company composed of multicultural youth.
- Accomplished pianist, singer, accompanist, conductor, composer, and writer.

Music Teaching Experience

1982–Present   E.M. VOICE AND PIANO, Boston, MA
Voice and Piano Teacher

- Instruct approximately 70 voice, piano, and composition students.
- Present 6 recitals annually, working with students to select and prepare performance pieces.
- Regularly use video and electronic piano computer system to provide audio and visual feedback.
- Students applied for admissions, auditioned for, and attended selective music programs; then progressed to professional performance and composition.

1990–99   MASSACHUSETTS METHODIST CHURCH, Boston, MA
Director of Youth Choirs

- Prepared and conducted weekly rehearsals and performances for students grades K–12.
- Composed and directed 8 Christmas pageants televised on local station.

1992–94   "MUSIC AND MORE," Boston, MA
Musical Director

- Founded after-school musical theater company for students grades 2–12.
- Composed, directed, and accompanied original scores and scripts for various productions.

1977–82   CHESTNUT HILL SCHOOLS, Chestnut Hill, MA
Primary Schools Choral Director/Show Choir Director

- Directed choral groups associated with 6 elementary schools.
- Introduced students kindergarten through 2nd grades to music appreciation and vocal performance.
- Nurtured vocal performance skills within students 3rd grades through 6th grades.
- Oversaw extracurricular Show Choir composed of approximately 175 students grades 9–12.
- Coached students in composing, choreographing, and performing original musicals.

Education and Credentials

Berklee College of Music, Boston, MA
Master of Music, 1983, and Bachelor of Music, 1975
Massachusetts Elementary and Secondary Teaching Credentials with certification in Music and English

Dana Johnson

123 Main Street • Hometown, CA 00000 • (555) 555-5543 • djohnson@company.com

EMERGENCY MEDICAL QUALIFICATIONS

- Knowledge of and experience implementing state-of-the-art Emergency Medical procedures.
- Proven capabilities assisting in emergency childbirth and heart attacks.
- Familiar with procedures for critical burns, shock, gunshot wounds, physical manifestations of child abuse, and spousal battering.
- Provided emergency treatment for rape victims while staying within the guidelines of the law.
- Certified to teach and administer CPR.

EMERGENCY MEDICAL EXPERIENCE

DOLAN AMBULANCE SERVICES, Visalia, CA
Head Emergency Medical Technician, 2003–Present

RUSSELL AMBULANCE SERVICES, Modesto, CA
Emergency Medical Technician, 2001–2003

MEDICAL LICENSES, CERTIFICATIONS, AND EDUCATION

- Certified, EMT License Visalia Hospital, 2001
- License # 4490223 State of California, 2001

MODESTO JUNIOR COLLEGE, Modesto, CA
Emergency Medical Technician Certification Program, 2000–2001

ATHLETIC TRAINING EXPERIENCE

UNIVERSITY OF THE PACIFIC ATHLETIC TRAINING INTERNSHIP, Stockton, CA
Sports Medicine Clinic, 1997–2000
Men's and Women's Tennis, Spring 1999 and 2000
Men's Basketball, Fall 1999 and 2000
- California Interscholastic Federation Wrestling Tournament, Spring 1998, 1999, and 2000
- Northern California Sectional High School Basketball Tournament, Spring 1998, 1999, and 2000
- Nike Volleyball Festival, Spring 1998, 1999, and 2000

ATHLETIC TRAINING EDUCATION

UNIVERSITY OF THE PACIFIC, Stockton, CA
Bachelor of Arts, Sport Sciences, with Biology minor, June 2000

Chris Smith

123 Main Street • Hometown, PA 00000 • (555) 555-1234 • csmith@company.com

OBJECTIVE

Executive Assistant Position

QUALIFICATIONS AND CAPABILITIES

- Extensive knowledge of bank administrative policies and procedures through six years of experience.
- Able to supervise employees and work with all levels of management in a professional, diplomatic, and tactful manner. Rapidly analyze/recognize department problems and solutions.
- Work on multiple projects under pressure and meet strict deadlines and budget requirements.
- Literate in MS Office Suite: Word, Excel, PowerPoint, Outlook, Access.
- Confidence drafting and proofreading correspondence.
- Proficient using shorthand, dictation machines, and multifunction calculators.

ADMINISTRATIVE SUPPORT EXPERIENCE

ERIE SAVINGS BANK, Erie, PA

Administrative Assistant to the Chief Executive Officer, 2003–Present

Coordinated and prioritized daily activities of Board Chairman. Performed administrative functions in support of CEO. Required an in-depth knowledge of the bank, financial community, investors, and customers. Assisted with preparation for Board of Directors and Shareholder meetings. Recorded and distributed minutes of Board, Shareholder, and Executive Committee meetings. Maintained CEO's travel and appointment schedule, using computerized scheduling system.

Executive Secretary to the Senior Vice President Commercial Division, 1999–2003

Set up Commercial Loans on System. Prepared monthly reports for Board of Directors. Updated financial statements. Maintained appraisal files. Coordinated loan renewals.

SPARTAN TRUST COMPANY, Erie, PA

Administrative Assistant to the President and Chief Executive Officer, 1995–1999

Prioritized daily activities of CEO. Set up and maintained "tickler system." Composed, and edited correspondence for President. Assisted CEO with sensitive customer and employee relationships. Recorded and distributed Management Committee minutes. Maintained and distributed monthly department reports.

Executive Secretary to Executive Vice President and Senior Loan Officer, 1991–1995

Managed secretarial staff supporting Commercial Loan Officers. Coordinated staff meetings and presentations to Board of Directors. Prepared monthly departmental and divisional reports for distribution. Updated and maintained Policy and Procedure Manual on a timely basis.

Commercial Finance Assistant, 1988–1991

Prepared daily client loan advances and payment activity. Maintained client loan/collateral statements. Assisted with preparation of departmental reports and loan agreements.

EDUCATION

PENNSYLVANIA STATE UNIVERSITY PITTSBURGH CAMPUS, Pittsburgh, PA
Continuing Education Program Participant, 1986–1991

ERIE INSTITUTE OF BUSINESS STUDIES, Pittsburgh, PA
Associate of Arts, Administrative Studies, 1986

Chris Smith

123 Main Street • Suite 234 • Hometown, NE • (555) 555-1234 • csmith@company.com

OBJECTIVE

Financial Analyst Position

FINANCE, ACCOUNTING, AND RELATED QUALIFICATIONS

- Experience working as liaison with accounting, treasury, and finance professionals.
- Confidence collecting and analyzing data to identify trends, make projections, and assist with managerial decision making.
- Specialized knowledge of banking industry, regulations, and auditing techniques.
- Proficient in Excel, Lotus Notes, Word, PowerPoint

FINANCE AND BANKING EXPERIENCE

September 2005 to Present

BRIDELL BANK AND TRUST CO., Omaha, NE
Comptrollers Division Corporate Accounting Analyst
- Prepared and analyzed income statements, balance sheets, and earnings schedules for $9 billion corporation.
- Compiled 10k federal reserve, management, and analyst reports.
- Utilized trend reports to analyze balance sheet and income statement key ratios.

September 2002 to August 2005

CARTEL BANK, Wayne, NE
Intern Audit Trainee
- Conducted audits to complete Federal and State regulatory documentation associated with the FDIC.
- Assessed efficacy of policies and procedures related to fiscal, regulatory, and customer service standards.
- Gained knowledge of operating procedures associated with departments including Personal Banking, Small Business Banking, and Home Equity Loans.

Summers 2000 and 2002

Account Group Intern
- Supported efforts of Relationship Managers, servicing depositors with accounts in excess of $500,000.
- Supported transactions and addressed inquiries, developed reports, and assisted colleagues and customers.

FINANCE AND BUSINESS EDUCATION

UNIVERSITY OF NEBRASKA AT OMAHA, Omaha, NE
Bachelor of Science, Finance, May 2002
Selected Courses: Tax Accounting, Advanced and Intermediate Accounting, Auditing, Strategic Management, Cost Accounting, Financial Management, International Business, and Operations Management.

UNIVERSITY OF ROCHESTER'S EUROPEAN INTERNSHIP PROGRAM, Rome, Italy
Completed banking internship while studying Italian language, economics, and history.

Francis Williams

123 Main Street • Hometown, New Jersey 00000
(555) 555-0987 • fwilliams@company.com

Financial Planning Qualifications and Credentials

- Over a decade of progressively significant roles and achievements within planning, portfolio management, and client services.
- Personal responsibilities for more than $210 million in client assets.
- Recognized for outstanding asset-based performance and customer service.
- After completion of ABC Financial Consultant Sales Training and Advanced Training, served as trainer and curriculum developer.
- Licensed Series 6, 7, 63, and health and life insurance.

Financial Planning Accomplishments

1995–Present

ABC FINANCIAL CONSULTANTS, Princeton, NJ
Financial Consultant/Financial Planner
Serve in comprehensive financial planning and roles. Oversee individual and group portfolios. Serve as manager, supervisor, and trainer within corporate headquarters of firm responsible for over $800 million in client assets.

- Developed $210 million client asset base through aggressive prospecting and targeting campaign.
- Successfully built portfolio that includes stock, bonds, options, and insurance products for more than 450 clients.
- Gained expertise associated with estate planning, asset allocation, and wealth succession.

1993–1995

Sales Associate

- Worked directly with firm's top producer, profiling high net worth individuals for future business.
- Generated $90,000 for top producer through new account openings.
- Analyzed existing portfolios, assisting in development of accounts.

1992–1993

Account Executive Trainee/Intern

- Completed more than 35,000 account transactions annually.
- Completed comprehensive training related to trade settlement, NASD regulations, and customer service.
- Acted as liaison between sales force and New York operations.

Summers 1991 and 1992

MAPLEWOOD INVESTMENTS, Maplewood, NJ
Prospecting Intern

Education

IONA COLLEGE, Iona, New York
Bachelor of Arts in Economics, with Concentration in Management, 1993

CHRIS SMITH

123 Main Street • Hometown, TN 00000 • (555) 555-1234 • csmith@company.com

HUMAN RESOURCES EXPERIENCE

TENNESSEE MUTUAL INSURANCE   MEMPHIS, TN
Director of Human Resources and Staff Development   **2002–Present**

Develop and implement overall human resource policies. Provide leadership in the areas of personnel, payroll, labor relations, training, and affirmative action for operations with over 2,000 employees. Administer personnel and payroll procedures, policies, and systems to meet management and employee needs. Consult with Chairman, Executive Board, managerial staff, and supervisors to ensure policy compliance with applicable statutes, rules, and regulations. Advance agency Affirmative Action Plan. Determine appropriate grievance procedures required to resolve labor disputes. Act as liaison for regulatory agencies: EOHS, OER, DPA, State Office of A.A., and PERA. Maintain staff training program. Interface with Legal Staff when addressing discipline and grievances.

WILMONT INSURANCE CO.   NASHVILLE, TN
Director of Human Resources   **1992–2002**

Oversaw hiring, training, and all personnel responsibilities for insurance broker with 400 employees. Determined technology and procedures related to maintaining and updating personnel files, ensuring compliance with federal and state regulations pertaining to benefits and wages. Supervised grievance adjudication. Performed claim payment internal audits. Coordinated activity with reinsurance carriers.

Central Personnel Administrator   **1990–1992**

Coordinated statewide reclassification study. Organized questionnaires and individual interviews. Evaluated, analyzed, and rewrote job descriptions; prepared study package for senior management approval. Established related managerial files. Dealt with diverse personnel-related projects.

DEPARTMENT OF EMPLOYMENT AND TRAINING   NASHVILLE, TN
Supervisor   **1987–1990**
Claims Adjudicator   **1985–1987**

HUMAN RESOURCE AND BUSINESS EDUCATION

MILLIGAN COLLEGE   MILLIGAN, TN
Course work in Personnel Management and Human Resources   **1995–Present**

TENNESSEE WESLEYAN COLLEGE   NASHVILLE, TN
B.A. Management, with Personnel Track   **1985**

PROFESSIONAL PROFILE

- Over 15 years of human resource experience; 5 as a Director of comprehensive programs.
- Expertise recruiting, training, performance reviews, compensation, and affirmative action.
- Capacities to work with senior management to develop, implement, and monitor HR strategies including recruitment outsourcing, vendor management, and Web technology for contingent workforce management.
- Specialized knowledge of issues, policies, and procedures associated with the insurance industry.
- Commitment to ongoing professional development through continued courses and seminars.

Human Services Counselor

Jamie Brown

123 Main Street • Hometown, IL 00000 • (555) 555-1234 • jbrown@company.com

OBJECTIVE

Human Services Counselor/Administrator Position

QUALIFICATIONS

- Comprehensive case management experience for juveniles and families.
- Expertise assessing cases, developing treatment plans, facilitating crisis intervention procedures, and family therapy.
- Diverse counseling skills applicable to developmental and physical disabilities, and substance abuse.
- Experience with child abuse and neglect cases, as well as the needs of developmentally disabled youth.

EXPERIENCE

1993 to Present — SOCIETY FOR PREVENTION OF CRUELTY TO CHILDREN, Chicago, IL
Investigator/Case Manager
- Conduct assessments and develop treatment plans for family caseload.
- Maintain documentation of contracts and provide crisis intervention and family therapy.
- Serve as advocate for clients in court and with community agencies.

1991 to 1992 — FARMINGTON JUVENILE COURT, Farmington, IL
Intern
- Tracked abuse/neglect cases to ensure that status reports and petitions were filed accurately and on time.
- Observed court hearings and trials and established court expectations.

1990 to 1991 — PEORIA JUVENILE COURT, Peoria, IL
Intern
- Provided individual and group counseling for juvenile offenders in detention.
- Reviewed, updated, and cited findings of case files and incident reports.

2002 to Present — TEMPORARY RESOURCES, Peoria, IL
Human Service Worker
- As a temporary associate, served clients in hospitals, day programs, and private residences.
- Counseled and supervised adolescents in group homes and serve as substitute teacher at institutions such as the Stafford School for the Deaf.

2000 to 2003 — ALLIED GROUP HOMES, Columbus, IN
Residential Manager
- Worked in several residential programs for all levels of developmentally delayed clients.
- Counseled and taught daily living, hygiene, and community awareness skills.

Summers 1998 to 2000 — DEPARTMENT OF MENTAL HEALTH, Gardena, IL
Intern
- Assisted developmentally delayed adults, encouraging development of self-sufficiency.

EDUCATION — BRADLEY UNIVERSITY, Peoria, IL
Bachelor of Science, Human Services, 2000

Corey Davis

123 Main Street • Hometown, AZ 00000 • (555) 555-8767 • cdavis@company.com

Underwriting Qualifications

- Underwriting and analytical skills, sales and marketing knowledge, and technical skills exhibited throughout past 20 years.
- Record of productivity and profitability in progressively responsible positions.
- Efficient supervisor, planner, organizer, and manager of time, projects, and professional peers.

Underwriting and Marketing Experience and Achievements

SCRIMSHAW INSURANCE CO., Tempe, AZ

2003–Present **Personal Lines Insurance Underwriter**
- Analyzed all personal lines of business to determine acceptability and to control, restrict, or decline, according to company guidelines.
- Supervised all personal lines of business for Arizona and New Mexico.
- Kept current with changing policies, rates, and procedures, explaining coverage, rules, forms, and decisions to agents, staff, and insured.

2001–03 **Manual Rating and Policy Writing Supervisor**
- Delegated responsibilities, set objectives, and monitored work.
- Evaluated performance, established supervisory controls, and conducted audits.
- Implemented staff briefings, ongoing training, and updating materials.

CALIFORNIA INDEMNITY INSURANCE COMPANY, Sacramento, CA

1996–01 **Senior Marketing Representative**
- Managed assigned territory including prospecting new distribution sources, rehabilitating nonperforming agencies, and terminating relationships.
- Served in lead role for all insured sales presentations by conducting strategy negotiations, making presentations, and facilitating actual presentation.

1994–96 **Underwriting Manager—Commercial and Special Accounts**
1992–94 **Senior Underwriter**
- Developed book of $25,000 to $1,000,000 SIR deductible contracts.
- Served as Property/Inland Marine Specialist for Division by handling all referrals, audits, and facultative reinsurance negotiations.

FIREMAN'S FUND INSURANCE COMPANY, Sacramento, CA

1989–92 **Commercial Underwriter/Inland Marine Specialist**
1985–89 **Personal Lines Underwriter/Client Customer Service Representative**

Professional Development, Seminars, and Education

- Insurance 21, 22, and 23 Courses, Underwriting School (6-week program), Senior Underwriting Seminar, Listening Seminar, Supervisory Seminar.
- Bachelor of Arts, University of Phoenix, 1993

Chris Smith

123 Main Street • Hometown, Ohio 00000 • (555) 555-6654 • csmith@company.com

Laboratory and Technical Expertise

- Proven ability in analysis, scientific theories, and procedures.
- Experience collecting and studying data from various biological sources.
- Proficient at producing and processing blood components.
- Skilled at performing tissue experiments using electron microscopy.
- Quickly and accurately learn and perform complicated tasks.
- Understanding of the differences between research within biotechnology and academic research.
- Experience organizing, writing, and editing detailed reports and research papers.
- Trainer for biochemists in routine blood-banking procedures.
- Experience within Web design, graphic arts, layout, and related roles.
- Proficient in: Excel, Word, PowerPoint, PhotoShop, InDesign, Flash, DreamWeaver, and Internet research.

Laboratory and Technical Experience

American Red Cross, Cleveland, OH
Laboratory technician: produce and process blood components. Label and release for transfusion and manufacture. Perform viral immunology testing and irradiation of blood products. 2006–Present

Biogen Inc., Cambridge, MA
Analytical Development Department Intern: qualified an SEC-HPLC method with subtraction of a twin peak in an Avonex formulation for use in the Quality Control Department. Edited images using PhotoShop to illustrate a PowerPoint presentation delivered to corporate colleagues and internship peers. Summer 2006

Case Western Reserve University Hospital, Cleveland, OH
Department of Biochemistry and Molecular Biology Intern: Expressed proteins in E. Coli for use in protein translocation projects. Performed SDS-Page gels and Western blots to test protein expression. Summer 2005

Teaching and Computer Experience

Case Western Reserve University, Cleveland, OH
Biochemistry Laboratory Teaching Assistant: Assisted students in biochemistry laboratory. Worked with professors to prepare materials for use in the laboratory and graded quizzes and laboratory reports. Created Web page allowing students access to test results. 2006–2007
Educational Technology Consultant: Assisted faculty and students with computer-related problems with scanning and photographic manipulations. 2005–2007

Biological Sciences Education

Case Western Reserve University, Cleveland, OH
Bachelor of Science, Biology/Chemistry, with a major GPA of 3.3, May 2006
Courses include: Organic Chemistry I and II, Molecular Cell Biology, Biochemistry, Molecular Biology, Anatomy, Physiology, Biochemistry Laboratory, Immunology, and Topics of Biological Macromolecules.

DANA JOHNSON

123 Main Street • Hometown, NM 00000 • (555) 555-1234 • djohnson@company.com

LOCAL AREA NETWORK AND TECHNICAL COMPETENCIES

- Expertise in configuring, installing, and administering network infrastructure and telecommunications systems that support staff of up to 300 personnel.
- Skilled in planning and implementing network security, including building firewalls.
- Knowledge of Windows 2000, 2003, and NT4 network operating systems; Active Directory, NT4 domain administration, and primary network services.

TECHNICAL EXPERIENCE AND ACHIEVEMENTS

JEFFERSON MANUFACTURING CORP., Albuquerque, NM
LAN Coordinator, 2003–Present
- Analyze, develop, and maintain application software for multi-site engineering LAN.
- Provide training and user support for all applications to LAN users.
- Maintain departmental PC workstations including software installation and upgrades.
- Reduced data entry errors and process time by developing an online program allowing program manager to submit model number information.
- Replaced time-consuming daily review board meetings by developing a program which allowed engineers to review and approve model and component changes online.
- Developed an online program which reduced process time, standardized part usage, and which allowed engineers to build part lists for new products and components.

Computer Systems Analyst, 1999–2003
- Completed database management, systems analysis and design, workstation maintenance and repair, and LAN management tasks.
- Reduced process time and purchasing errors by developing an online program which allowed the purchasing department to track the status of all purchasing invoices.
- Developed purchase order program that improved data entry speed and reduced data entry errors.

LAFAYETTE, INC., Albuquerque, NM
Engineering Technician, 1994–1999
- Prototyped and tested new PC products, drawing schematics and expediting parts for these new PC products. Designed and coded multi-user database management software for engineering use.
- Expedited the parts for 25 or more telecommunications terminal prototypes. Built, troubleshot, and transferred those prototypes to various departments for testing.

ELECTRONICS AND TECHNICAL EDUCATION

UNIVERSITY OF NEW MEXICO, Albuquerque, NM
Bachelor of Science, Electronics, 1999

SAN THOMAS COMMUNITY COLLEGE, Albuquerque, NM
Associate of Arts, Information Technology, 1995

Francis Williams

123 Main Street • Hometown, VT 00000 • (555) 555-1234 • fwilliams@company.com

PROFESSIONAL PROFILE

- Library professional with community, secondary school, and university experience.
- Capacities to translate services, policies, and procedures into patron focused and educational outcomes.
- Specialized focus on community outreach, patron education, program planning, and public speaking roles.
- Experience using and instructing peers and patrons to use NLM Classification System, ALA filing rules, as well as various indexes and Internet resources.

LIBRARY EXPERIENCE AND ACHIEVEMENTS

KATHRYN F. BELL LIBRARY, Burlington, VT

Librarian, 2001 to Present

- Provide excellent patron services when covering circulation and reference desks.
- Give instructional guidance to patrons, including use of computerized and manual index tools and catalogs.
- Focus interactions on empowering and instructing patrons while creating positive relationships.
- Address reference questions by demonstrating proper Internet and printed resources.
- Plan and present regular community education programs.
- Record incoming periodicals and journals on computerized system and strip resources for security.
- Compile statistics on door count, circulation, photocopies, and reference activities.
- Serve on Acquisition Committee and provide quarterly and annual recommendations to Budget Committee.

Evening Librarian, 1999 to 2001

- Performed overall patron services and library operations, and supervised the evening clerk.
- Compiled and circulated specialized reference packet for series of community health seminars.

EAST CATHOLIC HIGH SCHOOL, Rutland, VT

Librarian/Audiovisual Coordinator, 1995 to 1999

- Supervised comprehensive secondary school library, overseeing volunteer, professional, and student staffs.
- Established annual educational plans and regularly supported instructional efforts of teachers.
- Completed daily patron services and operations efforts and supervised student study periods.
- Interacted with Budget Committee to establish and monitor annual budgets.
- Ordered publications as well as software, and maintained audiovisual equipment.

SIMMONS COLLEGE, Boston, MA

Library Graduate Intern, 1994 to 1995

- Via supervised rotations, learned about reference, periodical, acquisition, and special collection areas.
- Researched, wrote, and presented four special reports to library professionals and graduate student peers.

EDUCATION

SIMMONS COLLEGE, Boston, MA

Masters of Library Science, 1995

UNIVERSITY OF VERMONT, Burlington, VT

Bachelor of Arts in English, 1993

Management Consultant

Jamie Brown
123 Main Street NW • Apartment 12 • Hometown, VA 00000 • (555) 555-6777 • jbrown@company.com

Consulting *Experience*	**American Management Systems** *Senior Consultant Government Practice*	**Washington, D.C.** *2005–Present*

- Ensured operational readiness of a division of the Internal Revenue System by preparing a staffing gap analysis and developing a database to record staffing demand of new organization; prepared package to submit new organizational design charts and functional statements to Commissioner.
- Developed operational policies, procedures, and responsibilities handbook for IRS management.
- Developed survey tool to baseline office characteristics.

Consultant   *2003–2005*

- Evaluated underutilization of grant funds for Housing and Urban Development program. Analyzed grant expenditure data, developed hypotheses, led interviews, and wrote sections of final report.
- Provided analytical and technical support to Department of Energy, Office of Environmental Management. Tracked appropriations legislation, managed the research, maintenance, and production of a portion of EM's FY 2005 Budget Request that was submitted to Congress.

Research Analyst   *2002–2003*

- Developed organizational redesign and change management initiatives for the District of Columbia Metropolitan Police Department. Facilitated client team working groups, conducted best practices research, developed data collection and analysis tools, and developed new process diagrams.

Computer *Experience*	**University of Rochester Press** *Web Developer*	**Rochester, NY** *Fall 2001*

- Developed Web page; provided general public access to UR Press publication profiles and order forms, and enabled authors and editors to submit work.

Government *Experience*	**Labour Party Headquarters** *Intern*	**London, England** *Spring 2001*
	Democratic Congressional Campaign Committee *Intern*	**Washington, D.C.** *Spring 2000*
Education	**University of Rochester** *Bachelor of Arts in Political Science, with Concentration in Journalism, cum laude*	**Rochester, NY** 2002
	European Programs Abroad *Overseas Studies Program Participant*	**London, England** 2001

Qualifications

- Ability to manage cases from evaluation and data collection to analysis, presentation, and implementation.
- Significant knowledge of government systems, structures, funding, and organizational oversights.
- Ability to use Excel and Access to create financial models and related databases and Word, PowerPoint, LexisNexis for research, presentation development, and report writing.

Dana Johnson

123 Main Street • Hometown, NC 00000 • (555) 555-3456 • djohnson@company.com

Management Information Systems Profile

- Extensive and diverse computer hardware and software knowledge related to personal computer usage within business and educational settings.
- Expertise assessing hardware and software needs, estimating costs, purchasing, and installing.
- Capacities to hire, train, and monitor performance of Information Systems professionals.
- Experience working with outside consultants, service and product vendors, and third-party temporary and permanent placement agencies.
- Ability to use, teach, and support programming languages, operating systems, network configurations, as well as word-processing, Internet, database, and spreadsheet applications.

Technical Qualifications

- Programming Languages: Borland C, C++, XML, JavaScript, HTML, Visual Basic.
- Operating Systems: Windows, Windows NT Server, UNIX, Linux, and Novell Netware.
- Network Technologies: LAN, WAN, VPM, Wireless Networks, Satellite Networks.
- Database: Access.
- Spreadsheet: Lotus 123 and Excel.
- Word Processing: Word for Windows and Word for Mac.
- Presentation and Publishing: Quark Xpress, PowerPoint, FrontPage.
- Web Page Development: PageMill and Fireworks.

Summary of Achievements

- Researched, wrote, and edited proposal used to identify needs and fund networks and desktop configurations composed of 8 personal computers and two printers.
- Supervise 3 Technology and Systems Consultants for office with 30 full-time employees.
- Planned and oversaw completion of special project teams related to existing and future technology needs and potential purchases.
- Regularly conduct software- and hardware-related troubleshooting and audit activities.
- Interact with product vendors and customer service and technology support professionals.
- Designed 24/7 backup and retrieval system for accounting databases and word-processing data.

Management Information Systems Experience

Maximum Data Systems, Charlotte, NC
Information Systems Manager, 2001–Present

Touchestone Systems, Inc., Charlotte, NC
Computer Consultant, 1999–2001

Gilford College, Greensboro, NC
Introduction to Computer Science Instructor, Part-time and Summers 1998–2000
Information Technology Consultant, Part-time 1997–1999

Education

Duke University, Durham, NC
Bachelor of Science, Computer Science, June 1999

COREY DAVIS

123 Main Street • Hometown, OR 00000 • (555) 555-1234

Brand Management Accomplishments

- Accountabilities include P&L for $500 million covering 100+ film products and 80+ cameras.
- Developed and implemented comprehensive annual marketing and strategic plans covering 150 products.
- Delivered and executed 5 national marketing plans and 25 new product launches.
- Created 4 new imaging categories and negotiated $40 million in first-year sales with a projected 20% increase in high-tech market sales in newly established distribution.
- Fully profiled and conducted outreach to 30 multi-location customers and won them back to Cressidine, securing $20 million in sales.
- As Product Manager of the International Division, traveled for 5 years between 5 South American countries and 10 European subsidiaries building product launch plans and developing relationships and knowledge of foreign customs and business protocols.
- Provide leadership for national sales force of 500+.
- Mentored and promoted numerous managers into key positions.

Brand Management and Marketing Experience

CRESSIDINE CORPORATION   Corvallis, OR
Brand Manager and Director of Marketing Operations for Technical Imaging   *1997–Present*
- Spearhead implementation of corporate objectives within the Technical Imaging Division.
- Conceive and energize all marketing strategies and provide feedback on program performance and recommendations to corporate senior managers.
- Direct and supervise staff of 10 with responsibilities for generating $250 million in sales with a $150 million margin for core products.
- Prepare and effectively control a $7 million marketing expense and a $4 million advertising budget.
- Created first end-user direct mail strategy, generating a 30% response rate and selling 400,000 units in first year.
- Mounted trade show exhibitions including designing booths, collateral materials, and advertisements. Secured $200,000 in prebooked sales within a month of tradeshow presentations for 4 new products.

Group Marketing Manager for Technical Imaging   *1993–1997*
- Responsible for developing relationships with major imaging companies and securing long term contracts for core products within a vertical market framework.
- Directed and monitored new product launch programs; developed pricing and selling strategies.
- Fostered and maintained key account relations.

Business, Marketing, and Management Studies

UNIVERSITY OF OREGON   Eugene, OR
Masters of Business Administration   *1995*
Bachelor of Science in Business Administration   *1993*

CHRIS SMITH

123 Main Street • Hometown, NH 00000 • (555) 555-1234 • csmith@company.com

PROFESSIONAL PROFILE

- Expertise conducting research required to develop strategically sound business plans and used to generate capital.
- Confidence addressing consumer product, health care, government agencies, and nonprofit issues.
- Capacities to develop state-of-the-art statistically viable projects and cite findings in comprehensive reports.

MARKET RESEARCH ACHIEVEMENTS

SEARCHER ASSOCIATES, Ossipee, NH

2006–Present **Market Research Consultant:** Established firm, conducted client outreach, recruited 3 associates, and oversee all operations activities. Build consumer behavior models using multivariate techniques, including regression and discriminate analysis, and cluster analysis. Analyze data from national survey to identify purchase intents and patterns for business-to-consumer direct marketers. Present information to senior management of client organizations. Specialized in entrepreneurial start-up activities, business plan development, and venture capital solicitation.

STEVEN ICE, INC., Derry, NH

2003–2006 **Vice President of Marketing:** Identified target markets, constructed complex questionnaires, conducted telephone interviews, compiled and analyzed data for research activities associated with entrepreneurial start-up. Conducted focus groups to identify market segments and penetration. Wrote and presented report to management including strategic recommendations. Addressed all marketing research needs. Gathered data to develop comprehensive business plan and marketing reports.

HAWTHORNE MANAGEMENT, Washington, D.C.

1995–2003 **Market and Strategic Management Research Consultant:** Conducted large-scale quantitative research projects based in customer satisfaction measurement and total quality implementation, including design, coordination, statistical analysis, and report generation. Specialized in business-to-business services, e-commerce, and health care.

1991–1995 **Research Associate:** Managed behaviorally based research projects including proposal writing; methodology, instrument and sample development; field coordination; data coding, analysis; and report writing. Included customer and employee studies, communication audits, market analysis, name/logo testing, constituency relations, positioning, and consumer studies.

INTERNATIONAL RESEARCH GROUP, Miami, FL

1988–1991 **Management Consultant:** Provided Marketing, Behavior, and Research counsel for advertising, public relations, and marketing consulting firm. Participated in internal and external strategic planning for *Fortune* 500 firms, government agencies, nonprofits, and health-care providers.

WEBBER AND SONS, INC., Washington, D.C.

1983–1988 **Research Assistant:** Completed projects for insurance providers, hospitals, and private practices.

EDUCATION

GEORGETOWN UNIVERSITY, Washington, D.C.
Master of Arts, Applied Psychology, with concentration in Health Care Research, 1985
Arts Baccalaureate, Psychology, *cum laude,* 1983

Military to Business Transition

Jamie Brown

123 Main Street • Hometown, CA 00000 • (555) 555-1234 • jbrown@company.com

BUSINESS QUALIFICATIONS

- Knowledge gained from comprehensive business courses, including accounting and economics.
- Capacities to conduct topic-specific or problem-focused research and analysis.
- Confidence presenting research results verbally and via detailed reports and illustrated presentations.
- Experience prioritizing tasks and completing assignments accurately and on time.
- Comfortable within reporting hierarchies and motivating peers.
- Strong task management and personnel motivation capabilities gained through military training.
- Cross cultural skills enhanced through travel in Iraq, Africa, and Asia.
- Technical and mechanical aptitude applicable to manufacturing, troubleshooting, and technical settings and projects.
- Basic Russian language abilities.

EDUCATION

SACRAMENTO STATE UNIVERSITY, Sacramento, CA
Bachelor of Arts, Liberal Studies, anticipated June 2009.

AMERICAN RIVER COLLEGE, Sacramento, CA
Completed general education courses, 2000.

BUSINESS-RELATED COURSES

Macro- and Microeconomics	Financial Accounting
Managerial Accounting	Contemporary World Issues
Public Speaking	Social Research Methods

MILITARY EXPERIENCE AND TRAINING

2003–Present   EXPLOSIVES DISPOSAL UNIT, Mare Island, CA
US Navy EOD Diver
- As Bomb Disposal Unit team member, give and receive briefings to task-related personnel, maintain and update classified publications, procure operations-related equipment, and process after-action documentation such as Dive logs and equipment usage reports.

2000–2003   USS *BERGALL* (SSN-667) SUBMARINE SQUADRON
Submariner, Machinist Mate 2nd Class and Operations-Diver
- Operated and maintained submarine's atmosphere control equipment, such as breathing air/gas mixture levels, and potable water.
- Ordered and kept accounting of repair parts and supplies for both Auxiliary Division and Dive locker.
- Nuclear Weapons Armed Security Guard. Security Swimmer.

Dana Johnson

123 Main Street • Hometown, CA 00000
(555) 555-1234 • djohnson@company.com

Education

2005–2007	**University of California Los Angeles (UCLA),** Los Angeles, CA Masters of Music, with a major in Conducting, June 2007
2003–2005	**University of the Pacific (UOP),** Stockton, CA Bachelor of Music, with a major in Music Education, May 2005
2001–2003	**California State University, Northridge (CSUN),** Northridge, CA Completed Music and General Education Courses

Music Performance Experience

University of California Los Angeles, Los Angeles, CA
2005–2007   Conductor, Pianist, Composer, Studio Vocalist
2006–2007   Gospel Choir Accompanist and Vocalist

University of South Carolina, Columbia, SC
Summer 2005   Conductors Institute Participant

University of the Pacific, Stockton, CA
2003–2005   Trumpeter, Pianist, and Vocalist

California State University, Northridge, Northridge, CA
2001–2003   Trumpeter, Pianist, and Vocalist

Morris Chapel and St. Mary's Church, Stockton, CA
2003–2005   Conductor, Pianist, Organist, and Vocalist

Conducting and Music Teaching Experience

Marymount High School, Los Angeles, CA
2005–Present   Conductor and Teacher of Music Theory

UCLA Music Department, Los Angeles, CA
2005–2007   Choral Ensembles Student Conductor

Presentation Elementary School, Stockton, CA
2003–2005   Instrumental Music Teacher

Central Valley Youth Orchestra, Stockton, CA
2003–2005   Assistant Conductor

UOP Morris Chapel, Stockton, CA
2003–2005   Choir Director for Catholic Mass

Dana Johnson   Page Two

Employment History

Marymount High School, Los Angeles, CA
2005–Present   Director of Music

Audiences Unlimited, Inc., Los Angeles, CA
2005–Present   Studio Audience Coordinator

Honors and Affiliations

2005–Present   Conductor's Guild

2001–Present   California Music Educators Association, Southern California School Band
                    and Orchestra Association, International Association of Jazz Educators,
                    California Music Educators Conference, and International Trumpet Guild

Works Conducted

Beethoven's Symphony No. 8, First Movement
Mayer's Andante for Strings
Hindemith's Five Pieces for String Orchestra
Haydn's Symphony No. 49, "La Passione"
Elgar's Serenade for Strings
Grieg's Holberg Suite
Mozart's Symphony No. 29
Sibelius's Andante Festivo for Strings
Bizet's Carmen Suite

Conducting Instructors

Steven Smithers, Stockton, CA
Dr. Mitchell Pearson, Los Angeles, CA

Trumpet Instructors

Peter Smith, Northridge, CA
Robert Horn, Los Angeles, CA

Jazz and Classical Piano Instructors

Stephanie Best, Los Angeles, CA
Patricia Peterson, Pasadena, CA

References/Performance CD

Available upon request

Nanny

Jamie Brown

123 Main Street • Hometown, CA 00000 • USA
Phone (409) 555-1234 • Cell (409) 555-5678 • jbrown@company.com

Objective   Live-In Nanny/Au Pair Position.

Qualifications

- Ability to develop trusting relationships with children and parents.
- Certified Teacher with strong classroom and private tutoring experience.
- Skills to plan educational and recreational activities.
- Command of teaching conversational English.
- Cross cultural and European travel experiences, with passport, international driver's license, and working papers, and conversational abilities in Italian.
- Experience supporting children with special needs.

Childcare Experience

ROBERT AND THERESA SANTANA, Santa Clara, CA

2005 to Present *Nanny:* Provide live-in childcare for two boys, currently ages 2 and 4. Supervise play, transport children to preschool and other activities, and assist with meals. Reinforce parental rules and values. Accompany family on short and long trips and vacations.

Teaching Credential and Training

NATIONAL UNIVERSITY, San Jose, CA
California Multiple Subject Credential, June 2004
Curriculum included: whole language instruction, curriculum, and instruction, and literature based integrated language arts.
Courses included: Foundations of Education, Curriculum and Instruction, Literature Based Integrated Language Arts, and Exceptional Children in the Classroom.

Teaching and Tutoring Experience

CATHOLIC DIOCESE OF SANTA CLARA, Santa Clara, CA

Summer 2004 *Summer School English Teacher:* Planned and implemented lessons focusing on literature, grammar, writing, and research. Addressed remedial needs of students.

PRESENTATION SCHOOL, Cupertino, CA

Spring 2004 *3rd Grade Student Teacher:* Independently established and presented lesson and unit plans. Created specific interdisciplinary Reading and Work unit, focusing on reading skills for varied jobs, and including visiting career field representatives.

2001 to 2003 1st, 2nd, and Kindergarten Teacher's Aide

Education   UNIVERSITY OF SANTA CLARA, Santa Clara, CA
Bachelor of Arts, English, May 1994

References and Letters of Recommendation Upon Request

FRANCIS WILLIAMS, R.N., N.P.

123 Main Street • Hometown, Michigan 00000 • (555) 555-2322 • fwilliams@company.com

OBJECTIVE

Nurse Practitioner in a clinical, educational, research, or administrative setting

QUALIFICATION SUMMARY

- Eighteen years as an Adult Nurse Practitioner in Primary Care and Women's Health Care
- Skilled in medical histories, physical exams, microscopy, laboratory testing, and medical prescription
- Expertise evaluating and managing wide scope of acute, chronic, and complex problems, and preventive and routine medical care
- Strong interpersonal/communication skills with patients and colleagues
- Skilled with elderly, adults, teens, mentally retarded, and the hearing impaired (using medical Sign Language)
- Provide counseling for mood problems and other health issues
- Abilities to develop health education materials; teach in-service lessons; and act as preceptor
- Experienced in committee leadership and participation

CLINICAL NURSING EXPERIENCE AND ACHIEVEMENTS

Ann Arbor Gynecologic & Obstetric Associates, P. C., Ann Arbor, MI
Nurse Practitioner, 1996–Present
- Provide gynecologic, obstetric, and primary care in collaboration with physicians in private practice
- Evaluate and manage acute and chronic gynecologic and obstetric problems, including: abdomino-pelvic pain, genitourinary problems, infections, breast concerns, endocrine-related problems, osteoporosis, and postoperative and pregnancy complications
- Evaluate and manage wide array of primary-care problems including EENT, allergic conditions, dermatological problems, infectious diseases, chest pain, and respiratory, gastrointestinal, and musculoskeletal problems
- Perform annual and employment exams and prenatal and postpartum care
- Counsel and prescribe for cholesterol and weight management, contraception, menopause, osteoporosis, and mood disorders
- Developed health education handouts and presented staff in-service training
- Performed periodic Quality Assurance review for on-site laboratory
- Acted as preceptor for nurse practitioner and physician assistant students

University of Michigan University Health Service, Ann Arbor, MI
Senior Nurse Practitioner, 1992–1995
- Evaluated and managed health problems including: infectious diseases; allergic conditions; dermatological problems; respiratory, gastrointestinal, genitourinary, endocrine, and musculoskeletal problems; traumatic injuries; and occupational health issues
- Provided routine and preventive care and employment and sports physical exams
- Initiated gynecologic services for Eastman School of Music
- Made health education presentations, acted as preceptor, and served on Training and HIV Task Force
- Coordinated University Health Services Library used by nurses, nursing students, and patients

FRANCIS WILLIAMS
Page Two

University of Michigan University Health Service, Ann Arbor, MI
Nurse Practitioner, 1989–1992
- Evaluated and managed wide variety of health problems for students
- Performed routine and preventive care and sports physical exams
- Became proficient in Sign Language used in medical context
- Made health education presentations to staff and students, acted as preceptor for students, and served on various committees

NURSING EDUCATION AND LIBERAL ARTS STUDIES

University of Michigan School of Nursing, Ann Arbor, MI
MS, Family Health Nurse Clinician, 1995, and BS, *magna cum laude*, Nursing, 1988

Ann Arbor County Community College, Ann Arbor, MI
Completed prerequisite science and pre-nursing courses, 1985–1986

Albion College, Albion, MI
BA, Religion, 1985

CREDENTIALS AND AFFILIATIONS

- American Nurses' Association Certification, Adult Nurse Practitioner
- Michigan State Certification, Family Health Nurse Practitioner with Prescription Privilege
- Michigan State License, Registered Professional Nurse
- Certified in CPR, most recent update 2006

COREY DAVIS

123 Main Street • Hometown, NM 00000 • (555) 555-5555 • cdavis@company.com
345 Mission Boulevard • Hometown, CA 00000 • (555) 555-0987

PARALEGAL QUALIFICATIONS AND ACHIEVEMENTS

- Outstanding case research, client relations, document management, and writing skills gained in progressively responsible positions over a 13-year period.
- Expertise gained as law office manager, compiling a training manual and supervising administrative support personnel, revamping accounting, debit, and credit systems.
- Trained and accomplished interviewer, negotiator, and mediator.
- LexisNexis, WestLaw, Word, FileMaker Pro, Excel, QuickBooks, and Internet skills.

PARALEGAL AND MANAGEMENT EXPERIENCE

LAW OFFICES OF BRENDAN ELLIS   Santa Fe, NM
Civil Litigation Specialist/Office Manager   1995–Present
- Manage office and staff of 3 secretaries, ensuring smooth operation of firm with 3 attorneys and billings in excess of $1.5 million and awards of over $10 million annually.
- Interview clients; prepare files and discovery; handle multiple cases.
- Request and review medical documentation; ascertaining evidence from appropriate parties.
- Negotiate and settle cases with defense attorney and insurance companies.
- Attend mediations and conciliations.
- Prepare clients for depositions and trials.
- Control and maintain law office accounts, utilizing accounting and billing software.
- Regularly attended seminars on personal injury law.

SANTA FE DISTRICT ATTORNEY'S OFFICE DOMESTIC VIOLENCE UNIT   Santa Fe, NM
Witness Advocate   Spring–Summer 1995
- Interviewed victims and witnesses, prepared documents, and organized information for court appearances.
- Assisted attorneys during trials, taking notes and facilitating access to evidentiary documents.

NEW MEXICO PUBLIC DEFENDER'S OFFICE   Santa Fe, NM
Legal Intern   Summers 1993 and 1994
- Researched and drafted motions on criminal law and procedural issues. Interviewed clients at New Mexico correctional institutions.
- Argued bail motions in several state district courts.
- Negotiated plea and bail agreements for defendants accused of misdemeanors. Attended criminal trials and depositions.

ATTORNEY DANIEL GALL   Santa Fe, NM
Legal Secretary/Legal Assistant   1991–1995
- Greeted clients, maintained files, and completed administrative tasks.
- Prepared documents for legal proceedings involving real estate transactions.
- Entered client information into Excel- and Access-driven computer system.

EDUCATION

SAINT JOHN'S COLLEGE   Santa Fe, NM
B.S., Human Resource Management, with Honors   1995
- Completed degree while employed and served as peer advisor to nontraditional students.

Dana Johnson

123 Main Street • Hometown, CA 00000 • (555) 555-1234 • djohnson@company.com

OBJECTIVE Pharmacist Position

EDUCATION UNIVERSITY OF THE PACIFIC SCHOOL OF PHARMACY, Stockton, CA
Pharm. D., May 2000
Pre-Pharmacy Studies, 1994–1996

PHARMACY ACCOMPLISHMENTS

2000–Present DAVID GRANT MEDICAL CENTER, Travis Air Force Base, Fairfield, CA
Pharmacist: Provide comprehensive pharmaceutical services for patients, assist physicians with identification of appropriate drug regimens, and support educational efforts targeting health care professionals and patients.

Spring 2000 *Internal Medicine Rotation:* Attended rounds with physicians; assisted physicians selecting proper drug regimens; monitored drug-to-drug interactions and patient lab results.

Fall 1999 *Clinical Psychiatric Rotation:* Monitored patient charts for drug-to-drug interactions; enhanced patient medication compliance; instructed patients regarding medication; and consulted with patients regarding discharge medications.

Winter 2000 VETERANS ADMINISTRATION OUTPATIENT CLINIC, Martinez, CA
Ambulatory Care Rotation: Monitored PT/INR in anticoagulation clinic; monitored patient status in cardiovascular and hypertension clinic; evaluated proper medication renewal in pharmacy refill clinic.

Winter 1999 LONGS DRUGS CORPORATE OFFICE, Walnut Creek, CA
Community Pharmacy Management Rotation: Undertook inventory control efforts and RXD orders; updated prices; completed key tagging for billing purposes; and developed positive customer service approaches and attitudes.

Summer 1999 WALGREENS PHARMACY, Cupertino, CA
Community Pharmacy Rotation: Processed new prescriptions and refills; took new prescriptions from physicians; processed third-party claims to Aetna, Blue Shield, and Foundation; labeled and organized inventory; assisted customers with OTC purchases and prescriptions.

June 1998-
June 1999 SMART FOOD PHARMACY, Stockton, CA
Pharmacy Intern

PROFESSIONAL AFFILIATIONS

California Pharmacists' Association
American Pharmacists' Association
Kappa Psi Pharmaceutical Fraternity

Chris Smith

123 Main Street • Hometown, IN 00000 • (555) 555-5094 • csmith@company.com

Physical Therapy, Sports Medicine, and Massage Therapy Qualifications

- Background in physical therapy and sports medicine, and clinical experience with adults, student athletes, and pediatric patients.
- Over 2,000 hours as Physical Therapist; 1,000 hours as Athletic Trainer; 4,000 hours as Physical Therapy Aid; 200 hours as Nurse; and 350 hours as certified Massage Therapist.

Physical Therapy, Massage Therapy Experience

MIDWEST MEMORIAL HOSPITAL, Indianapolis, IN
Orthopedic In- and Outpatient Clinic Therapist, 2004–Present
- Develop treatment plans for chronic-pain and cardiac patients.
- Present regular in-service on hip and knee prostheses.

DEARBORN COUNTY HOSPITAL, Richmond, IN
Cardiac Rehabilitation Therapist, 2003–2004
- Acted as program coordinator for exercise regimen and provided treatments using ultrasound, electric stimulation, massage therapy, and stretching/strengthening exercises.
- Coordinated aquadynamics program for chronic-pain patients.

CINNAMON MOUNTAIN, Mishawaka, WI
Pediatric Rehabilitation, Summers 2001–2003
- Coordinated treatment of amputee children and children with congenital birth defects.
- Created "Alive with Pride" program now functional at 30 national hospitals.
- Developed child-oriented play program and trained teachers via elementary school seminars.

XCEL ORTHOPAEDIC PHYSICAL THERAPY, Bloomington, IN
Physical Therapy Aid, Spring 2002–Spring 2003
- Assisted with ultrasound, muscle stimulation, massage, and interferential treatments.
- Served as translator, using Spanish-language skills with selected patients.

INDIANA UNIVERSITY, Bloomington, IN
Student Trainer, Spring 1999
Massage Therapy Intern, Fall 1999

Physical Therapy, Sports Medicine, and Nursing Training

INDIANA UNIVERSITY, Bloomington, IN
Bachelor of Science in Physical Therapy, May 2003
Performed independent research evaluating back and shoulder strength of musicians suffering from tendonitis. Presented findings to department and published in *Indiana Journal of Medicine*.

BLOOMINGTON COMMUNITY COLLEGE, Bloomington, IN
General Education Nursing, and Science Courses, 1999–2001
Massage Therapy Certificate, Summer 2001

FRANCIS WILLIAMS

123 Main Street • Hometown, MD 00000 • (555) 555-1234 • fwilliams@company.com

PROFESSIONAL PROFILE

- Over a decade of progressively responsible roles in private and municipal law enforcement.
- Specialized skills associated with community relations and maintenance of positive and professional attitudes among colleagues.
- Proven abilities to hire, train, evaluate, and motivate officers and support staff.
- Trained and certified law enforcement professional in front line and management roles.
- License to carry firearms. Emergency Medical Technician. Certification in Radar Usage, Breathalyzer, and Identi-Kit Systems.

LAW ENFORCEMENT AND SECURITY EXPERIENCE

JOHNS HOPKINS UNIVERSITY POLICE DEPARTMENT   Baltimore, MD
Assistant Chief of Campus Police   2003–Present
- Assist with personnel, budget, and procedural oversights associated with a department of 20 full-time and 20 part-time security professionals.
- Recruit, train, and review performance of professional and administrative personnel.
- Protect life and property on and about the campus of Johns Hopkins University.
- Patrol on foot and via automobile, using strong observational and interaction skills.
- Uphold laws and codes of the State of Maryland and Johns Hopkins University.
- Cooperate with law enforcement agencies, regularly interacting with Deputy Sheriff.
- Conduct community outreach and educational efforts, focusing on alcohol use and abuse, safe dating, and property protection.
- Serve on Student Life Committees and assist with judicial investigations.

BUCKMAN ASSOCIATES   Bethesda, MD
Head of Security   2000–2003
- Managed all aspects of security for hotels and adjoining properties.
- Hired, scheduled, supervised, and evaluated personnel.
- Provided all policing functions, with emphasis on defusing potentially violent situations.
- Cooperated extensively with Baltimore and Bethesda Police Departments.

TOWN OF ROCKVILLE POLICE DEPARTMENT   Rockville, MD
Patrolman   1995–2000
- Performed all standard policing functions, earning excellent ratings annually.
- Interacted and communicated with town officials regarding proactive and reactive efforts.

LAW ENFORCEMENT TRAINING

BALTIMORE POLICE ACADEMY   Baltimore, MD
Graduate   2000

ROCKVILLE POLICE ACADEMY   Rockville, MD
Graduate   1995

COREY DAVIS

123 Main Street • Hometown, WA 00000 • (555) 555-1234 • cdavis@company.com

PROFESSIONAL PROFILE

- Experience as publicist, media consultant, publicity professional, and television booker.
- Extensive contacts within broadcast and print media, yielding successful placements of stories as well as interviews.
- Talents to establish and implement strategic media and promotional campaigns to generate multimedia coverage.
- Capacities to work with clients to attain marketing, attendance, and general publicity goals.

PRESS RELATIONS AND PROMOTIONS ACHIEVEMENTS

COVERAGE CONCEPTS CONSULTING, Pullman, WA
Personal Publicist and Consultant: Personally support media relations, campaign development, and implementation efforts associated with professional athletes, education, and not-for-profit clients. Interact with clients regularly to address needs and fine-tune annually updated strategic media plans. Draft, edit, and finalize news releases, speeches, and press packets. Develop and maintain relationships with regional and national print and broadcast media, supporting efforts to maximize desired coverage. Serve as client spokesperson and as press conference coordinator. 2003–Present

CNBS TELEVISION, Pullman, WA
Production Assistant for "Confrontations": Booked main guests and panelists for weekly topical talk show. Generated and researched story ideas. Conducted video research. Edited teasers for show. Organized production details for studio tapings. Coordinated publicity ads in local newspapers. 2000–2003

BARSTOW PUBLISHING COMPANY, Seattle, WA
Publicity Assistant: Publicized new books and authors. Assisted with television, radio, and print media tours and individual appearances. Created and implemented author questionnaire to maximize publicity generated through professional contacts. Wrote press releases and designed press packets. Responded to review copy requests. 2001–2003

WNBN-TV, Tacoma, WA
Production Intern for "Sports Talk": Assisted producers of live daily sports interview and call-in show. Researched and generated story ideas. Preinterviewed guests. Covered shoots and wrote promos. Produced 5 segments. 2000–2001

UNIVERSITY OF WASHINGTON, Seattle, WA
Sports Information Promotional Assistant: Implemented promotional campaigns, wrote copy, and designed advertisements. Enhanced attendance via creative competitions and corporate sponsored giveaways. 1999–2000

THE CHERRY HAIKU, INC., Seattle, WA
Art Assistant: Produced paste-ups and mechanicals for full service advertising agency. Operated Photostat camera and coordinated logistics for photo shoots. Brainstormed with creative team. Summers and Part-time 1997–1999

EDUCATION

UNIVERSITY OF WASHINGTON, Seattle, WA
B.A. in Communications, cum laude, with a Minor in English, 2000

Public Relations Account Executive

JAMIE BROWN

123 Main Street • Hometown, NY 00000 • (555) 555-5555 • jbrown@company.com

PUBLIC RELATIONS EXPERIENCE

SYRACUSE HEART ASSOCIATION, Syracuse, NY
Public Relations Manager, 2005–Present
- Serve as consultant to 7 state chapters regarding campaign problems and activities.
- Organize regional campaign meetings; speak at several campaign conferences.
- Review legislation and bring specific bills to the attention of the proper committee or individual.
- Staff the Legislative Advisory Committee and follow through on specific bills.
- Develop fundraising programs.
- Conducted the previous two annual campaigns for the newly merged Central Chapter.

Campaign Assistant for Greater Syracuse Chapter, 2000–2002
- Supervised chapter campaign duties and assisted the Executive Director with administrative responsibilities, such as personnel and budget.

BIG APPLE NATURAL FOODS, Syracuse, NY
Special Events Coordinator, 2003–2005
- Created and coordinated special events and promotions, within $425,000 marketing budget.
- Selected and wrote event advertising, promotional materials, and publicity copy.
- Handled charity fundraising, corporate image positioning, and community outreach efforts.

Assistant to the Director of Public Relations, 2002–2003
- Assisted in promotion and publicity of special events.
- Developed press kits and releases to initiate, maintain, and maximize media relations.
- Compiled easy to access and update computerized publicity files using FileMaker Pro.
- Researched prospective consumer markets using Internet and direct contact techniques.
- Created direct-mail lists, updated media lists, and maintained task priority lists.

SYRACUSE UNIVERSITY, Syracuse, NY
Teacher's Assistant, Fall and Spring 2003

COMMUNICATION AND PUBLIC RELATIONS EDUCATION

SYRACUSE UNIVERSITY, Syracuse, NY
Bachelor of Arts in Public Relations, *magna cum laude*, June 2003

QUALIFICATIONS

- Ability to plan and direct successful fundraising, public relations, and promotions programs.
- Campaign development and implementation experience with major health agency.
- Extensive volunteer recruitment experience and success motivating diverse teams.
- Supervisory experience with both professional and nonprofessional staffs.
- Capacity to use Word, Excel, PowerPoint, and FileMaker Pro for drafting and editing features and promotional materials, for budgeting tasks, and for graphics projects.

Dana Johnson

123 Main Street • Hometown, CA 00000 • (555) 555-2311 • djohnson@company.com

REAL ESTATE LENDING EXPERIENCE AND ACHIEVEMENTS

SAN JOSE AND SANTA CLARA HOME LOANS, San Jose, CA
Real Estate Loan Officer, 2006–Present
- Originate real estate loans, develop plan to expand business in Santa Clara County.
- Conduct cold calls, create individualized mortgage broker packets, complete individual and group presentations designed to generate Conventional, FHA/VA, PERS, JUMBO, and CHAFA loan business.

BAY AREA BANK, Santa Clara, CA
Real Estate Loan Officer, 2003–2006
- Originated real estate loans, developed marketing plan to expand business in Santa Clara County.
- Conducted cold calls, created individualized mortgage broker packets, completed individual and group presentations designed to generate loan business, and implemented first-ever real estate expo promotional event.

HOUSING LENDING, Fresno, CA
Wholesale Account Executive, 2001–2003
- Marketed loan and financing programs to financial institutions and mortgage brokers in San Joaquin, Merced, Fresno, and Stanislaus counties.

CALIFORNIA MORTGAGE SPECIALISTS, INC., San Mateo, CA
Professional Real Estate Loan Auditor, 1997–2001

SANTA CLARA SAVINGS, Santa Clara, CA
Loan Officer in Residential Lending Department, 1991–1997
Loan Underwriter/Processor in Residential and Government Loan Departments, 1987–1991
Loan Underwriter in Secondary Market Department, 1985–1987
Loan Packager in Loan Processing Department, 1983–1985

BUSINESS AND FINANCE DEGREE

SANTA CLARA UNIVERSITY, Santa Clara, CA
Bachelor of Science in Business Administration, 1985

PROFESSIONAL PROFILE

- Over 20 years of experience in mortgage banking and finance, with emphasis on customer service loan qualifications and accurate risk analysis.
- Experience as loan consultant enhancing qualification potential and prospective customers.
- Expertise with Conventional, FHA/VA, PERS, JUMBO, Community Home Buyer, and CHAFA loan programs for homes in Santa Clara, San Joaquin, Merced, and Stanislaus counties.

Chris Smith

123 Main Street ■ Hometown, CA 00000 ■ (555) 555-1234 ■ csmith@company.com

Real Estate Sales Qualifications

- Record of productivity and profitability as real estate sales professional.
- Proven accountability, dependability, and decisiveness, servicing needs of buyers and sellers.
- Sales and marketing talent gained via experience, achievements, and customer relationships.
- Efficient planner, organizer, and effective manager of time and territory.
- Self-starter, tenacious with ability to service existing business while prospecting new accounts.
- Competencies from Century 21 Sales Curriculum, Dale Carnegie's Face-to-Face Selling Skills, Xerox Selling Skills, Creating Customer Focus, and other varied seminars and training courses.

Real Estate Sales Achievements

2003–Present   CENTURY 21, Walnut Creek, CA
Residential and Commercial Associate
- Serve in comprehensive sales as well as mortgage and lease advisory capacities for residential and commercial clients for one of the Bay Area's largest branch offices.
- Prospect new buyers and sellers via monthly seminars, direct mail, and e-mail campaigns, appearances on radio programs, and printed and television ads.
- Regularly exceeded sales goals, twice receiving national Gold Jacket recognition for top 10% production, three times receiving $100 million Club recognition for annual sales and leases, and annually receiving Top Producer recognition for regional and state sales figures.
- One of three "interdisciplinary producers," licensed in residential and commercial sales, property management, and financing and leasing.

General Sales Achievements

1997–2003   AMERICAN COMMERCIAL COMPANY, Walnut Creek, CA
Commercial Insurance Product Services for Northern California
- Developed internal structures for prospecting new production sources.
- Generated territory volume of $10 million from $3 million.

1995–1997   CENTURION INSURANCE COMPANY, San Francisco, CA
Territory Manager for Northern California
- Recruited to open and develop Bay Area for multiline commercial accounts.
- Generated territory volume of $4 million from $250,000.

1992–1995   INDUSTRIAL INDEMNITY, Sacramento, CA
Marketing Representative

1982–1992   FIREMAN'S FUND INSURANCE COMPANY, Sacramento, CA
Commercial Lines Underwriter

Education   UNIVERSITY OF THE PACIFIC, Stockton, CA
Bachelor of Arts, Communication, May 1982

JAMIE BROWN

123 Main Street • Hometown, CT 00000 • (555) 555-1234 • jbrown@company.com

Recruiting Qualifications

- Experience developing and implementing comprehensive college recruiting program.
- Capacities to source, screen, and select candidates based upon strategic qualification criteria.
- Abilities to conduct interviews, train interviewers, and facilitate decision making regarding offers.
- Developed recruiting, selection, and training associated with internship program.
- Broad-based human resources knowledge to effectively interact with senior management.
- Extensive knowledge of recruitment Web sites for candidate mining, job postings, and resume review.

Recruiting, Human Resources, and Management Achievements

NORMAN'S DEPARTMENT STORES   NEW LONDON, CT

Manager of Executive Recruitment   *2005–Present*

Oversee all logistical and financial aspects of program recruiting 20 Management Development Program participants annually for regional chain of 15 stores. Involves on-campus interviews, career fairs, and information sessions held at 7 target schools and participation in three multi-school consortium events.

- With VPs of Human Resources, Merchandising, and Operations, review and revise annual college recruiting strategies and yield targets.
- Develop, propose, and monitor annual college recruiting budgets of approximately $75,000.
- Regularly review and establish target school listings, contacts, and recruiting dates.
- Train college team liaisons and leaders to make effective campus recruitment presentations.
- Organized senior executive involvement in Career Days second interview processes.
- Facilitate College Recruiting Team discussions regarding Management Development Program offers.
- Recruit for, hire, and oversee 15 Summer Interns and 10 Academic Year Interns annually.
- Assist training staff with planning educational and social activities associated with initial portions of a 10-week program that blends classroom instruction with career networking and skills training.

Assistant Store Personnel Manager   *2001–2005*

- Hired, reviewed, and supported the needs of full-time and part-time sales professionals.
- Tracked daily, weekly, and monthly coverage data, to minimize costs and maximize coverage and service.
- Conducted various training sessions including: customer service, register operations, and security.
- Received award for overall achievement and outstanding performance in human resources.

Children's Department Manager   *1999–2001*

- Merchandised children's clothing and accessories, analyzing and marketing a $2 million inventory.
- Trained and developed staff of 15 sales associates in customer-service skills and selling techniques.
- Achieved 20% sales increase over one-year period and chosen manager of the year in 2000.

Education

CONNECTICUT COLLEGE   NEW LONDON, CT

B.A., Spanish Modified with Government Studies   *June 2000*

Francis Williams

123 Main Street • Hometown, CA 00000 • (555) 555-8876 • fwilliams@company.com

Restaurant Management and Service Experience

NORDSTROM, San Francisco, CA
Champaign Exchange Café Manager, 2004–Present
- Oversee operations of 250-seat facility averaging over $10,000 daily sales, offering American cuisine luncheon and dinner service to store patrons.
- Schedule, motivate, and supervise staff of 25 full-time and part-time servers per shift.
- Monitor daily and monthly receipts and expenditures.
- Communicate with store and corporate management regarding sales targets and profit strategies.

SHAKESPEARE'S TAVERN, London, ENGLAND
Assistant Manager, 2002–2004
- Oversaw operations of 175-seat facility averaging over £2,000 daily food sales and £2,000 wine and alcohol sales, offering luncheon, dinner, and after-dinner service.
- Supervised staff of 30 employees per shift.
- Monitored food costs, effectively communicated with chef and prep staff regarding costs.
- Prepared and submitted weekly, monthly, and quarterly reports to owners.
- With chef, planned weekly menus.

CLUB METROPOLIS, Montreal, CANADA
Assistant Manager, 2000–2002
- Scheduled and supervised staff, controlled inventory, deposited cash, maintained physical plant, and completed daily and weekly reports for after-hours club catering to elite patrons.
- Supervised up to 20 employees per shift.
- Completed management training program.
Bartender and Bar Manager, 1999–2000
- Served patrons, purchased wine, alcohol, beer, and mixes.

Food Services Training and Experience

CALIFORNIA SCHOOL OF CULINARY ARTS, San Francisco, CA
Restaurant Management Certificate, 2004

PROFESSIONAL BARTENDING SCHOOL OF MONTREAL, Montreal, CANADA
Certificate, 1999

ROYAL CANADIAN AIR FORCE, Toronto and Montreal, CANADA
Completed Class A & C Cooking School, 1996–1999

Languages

Bilingual French-English

Retail Buyer

DANA JOHNSON

123 Main Street • Hometown, MD 00000 • (555) 555-1234 • djohnson@company.com

BUYING EXPERIENCE AND ACCOMPLISHMENTS

CALVIN CLOTHES COMPANY, Baltimore and Bethesda, MD and Washington, D.C.

2002–Present *Baltimore Junior Apparel Department Buyer*
- Developed sales volume from $5.5 million to $7.5 million.
- Consistently achieved net operating profit of 50%, highest in company.
- Implemented promotional strategies and developed key classifications directly responsible for volume increase.
- Developed electronic and direct communication networks supplying product knowledge to sales staff and impacting strategic planning of vendor programs.
- Instituted e-mail communication strategies and status-tracking efforts.
- Chosen as Merchant of the Year 2003, 2005, and 2006.

2000–2002 *Bethesda Divisional Sales Manager*
- Handled furniture, electronics, and basement store, with 2000 volume of $5.6 million.
- During mall expansion, held store sales volume within plan by achieving 12% increase.
- Priorities included constant evaluation of stock levels and content, goal setting, development of key personnel, and achieving a high motivational level.

1998–2000 *Washington Assistant Buyer*
- Acted as liaison with vendors and warehouse to assure timely merchandise delivery of men's coordinates, coats, swimwear, and activewear.
- Interpreted, analyzed, and responded to OTB, selling reports, and seasonal plans.

1996–1998 *Washington Assistant Store Manager*
- Promoted from trainee to Assistant Manager within 12 months.
- Conceptualized and implemented employee training and effectiveness program.

1995–1996 *Executive Trainee*

PROFESSIONAL DEVELOPMENT AND EDUCATION

CALVIN CLOTHES COMPANY EXECUTIVE TRAINING SEMINARS, Baltimore, MD
Computerized Buying Techniques, Loss Prevention, Sales Motivation, Buyer-Store Communication Skills, Retail Mathematics and Quantitative Techniques, Buying Segmentation and Consumer Behavior, Merchandising, Personnel Management, and Profits

UNIVERSITY OF DELAWARE, Newark, DE
Bachelor of Science in Marketing, 1995

QUALIFICATION SUMMARY

- Capacities to translate strategic plans into profitable purchases and merchandising plans.
- Experience using communication programs and talents to maximize sales at store level.
- Quantitative skills required to establish market segmentations, maximize profits, and analyze sales figures.
- Commitment to understanding consumer attitudes, developing relationships with suppliers, and reinforcing positive achievements of sales professionals and operations personnel.

Corey Davis

123 Main Street • Hometown, CA 00000 • (555) 555-1234 • cdavis@company.com

Retail sales position using:

- Experiences within retail sales in diverse department and specialty store settings.
- Curiosity regarding consumer attitudes and behaviors and desire to sell based upon product qualities.
- Marketing and consumer behavior skills gained via business and psychology courses and projects.
- Outgoing personality, persuasive skills, and excitement about meeting sales goals.
- Time and task management and leadership skills nurtured as campus office holder.
- Knowledge of computerized registers and inventory control, and abilities to use Word, Power-Point, and Excel to create sales materials and reports.

Sales, Marketing, and Customer Service Experience

NORDSTROM, San Mateo, CA
Salesperson, Seasonally 2002–Present and Summers 2005 and 2006

NATIONAL SHOPPING SERVICE, Los Angeles, CA
Mystery Shopper, Part-time 2003–Present

THE LIMITED, San Mateo, CA
Salesperson, Part-time and Summers 2001–2003

CRYSTAL MOON JEWELRY, San Mateo, CA
Stockperson and Administrative Support Person, Part-time 2000–2003

WEINSTOCKS, Sacramento, CA
Sales Associate, Part-time 1998–2001

Education

SAINT MARY'S COLLEGE, Miraga, CA
Bachelor of Arts, anticipated May 2009
Major in Psychology and minors in Business and Studio Art
Delta Gamma Sorority Treasurer, 2007–2008 and Activities Committee, 2006–2007

CALIFORNIA STATE UNIVERSITY HAYWARD, Hayward, CA
Completed psychology and business courses, Summer 1999

Marketing and General Business Courses and Projects

Marketing Management, Management and Organizational Behavior, Financial Accounting, Consumer Behavior, and Designing Effective Organizations
- Create hypothetical business to assess and create overall marketing plan.
- Developed, administered, and interpreted survey distributed at St. Mary's athletic events to determine target market profiling.
- Examined organizational structure of QVC Shopping Network.

Francis Williams

123 Main Street • Apartment 13 • Hometown, CA 00000 (555) 555-1234 • fwilliams@company.com

RETAIL MANAGEMENT AND SALES ACHIEVEMENTS

SPINNER RECORDS CORPORATION   LOS ANGELES, CA
Manager   **2004–Present**
- Manage Spinner's largest-volume store, with sales of approximately $30,000 per week.
- Handle all merchandising, inventory control, ordering, cash control, and maintenance.
- Oversee store opening and closing procedures.
- Direct sales floor activities, assist customers, and address customer concerns.
- Input data to prepare daily sales reports and regularly use weekly and monthly data to develop sales and promotional strategies.
- Hire, train, and coordinate a staff of 26.
- Work with Spinner corporate colleagues as well as record company professionals to develop local marketing and advertising strategies, supplementing national campaigns.
- Inspire sales staff to develop and implement special promotions and events.
- Won two merchandising display contests.
- Received the "Super Spinner" Sales Award for exceeding sales goals.

Assistant Manager   **2002–2004**
- Fulfilled all management responsibilities in absence of manager.
- Opened and closed store, handled customer service issues, and oversaw cash control.
- Supervised and motivated employees.
- Assisted with merchandising and promotions efforts.

SANTA ANA MEN'S SHOPPE   SANTA ANA, CA
Assistant Manager   **1997–2002**
- Hired, trained, and supervised staff of six serving customers of specialty men's clothing store.
- Provided exceptional customer service to high-end consumers, regularly including direct e-mail and phone contact, and relationship building.
- Tallied daily receipts and made bank deposits.
- Maintained inventory levels, monitored merchandise, provided feedback to owner/buyer regarding trends and need for reorders.

LENNY'S TOYS   SANTA ANA, CA
Assistant Manager   **Summers and Part-time 1993–1997**
- Hired, trained, and supervised three shifts of four sales associates daily.
- Tallied daily receipts and made bank deposits.
- Maintained inventory levels, ordered merchandise, and independently tracked all special orders.

BUSINESS AND RETAIL EDUCATION

COMMUNITY COLLEGE OF LOS ANGELES   LOS ANGELES, CA
Associate of Arts, Business Administration, with Retail Management Certificate   **2002**
SANTA ANA COMMUNITY COLLEGE   SANTA ANA, CA
Completed General Education and Business Courses Part-time   **1995–1999**

Chris Smith

123 Main Street • Hometown, New York 00000 • 555-555-1234 • csmith@company.com

Graduate and Undergraduate Counseling and Psychology Education

LOYOLA MARYMOUNT UNIVERSITY, Los Angeles, California
Ph.D., Counseling and Human Development, Dissertation to be defended July 2008
- Dissertation: "Ethnic Identity Development of Multi-ethnic College Students"
- As Rotary Scholarship Recipient received Full Tuition Award and Counseling Assistantship Stipend

M.A., School Counseling, May 2003
TOWSON UNIVERSITY, Towson, Maryland
B.S., Psychology, August 1999

College Counseling and Teaching Experience

LOYOLA MARYMOUNT UNIVERSITY, Los Angeles, California
Counseling and Mental Health Services Intern, September 2005–July 2006, January 2007–May 2007
- Counseled undergraduate and graduate students with personal, academic, and career issues.
- Addressed psychological and developmental needs of multicultural and diverse 3,600 undergraduate and 1,000 graduate students.
- Assessed and diagnosed clients on the basis of presenting problem, history, and rating on Personality Assessment Inventory (PAI).
- Participated in two hours of individual supervision and one hour of group supervision per week.
- Served as a liaison between Counseling Center and University Health Services through involvement in the development of "Feel Fit in February" speakers series and outreach program designed to meet the health needs of student populations.

Graduate Assistant, September 2004–May 2007
- Facilitated the CACREP accreditation process by designing program curriculum to meet standards by researching programs, developing and presenting graphs and charts, and attending faculty meetings.
- Designed the Counseling Student's Handbook for the Master's and Doctoral programs.
- Researched trends in Client-Centered Therapy, examining the influence of Carl Rogers on the field of professional counseling.
- Contribute to the enhancement of the Counseling and Human Development program by attending faculty meetings related to the development of the program, and by investigating new ideas to strengthen the curriculum and overall structure of the program.

Instructor/Supervised Intern in School and Community Counseling Course, September 2006–May 2007
- Planned and presented lectures, hosted guest speakers, and facilitated weekly discussions based on topics relevant to students' internship experiences in either a school setting or a community agency setting. Topics included diversity, confidentiality and ethics, eating disorders, and crisis intervention.
- Supervised students individually and in group via taped sessions and experiences at internship sites.

Counselor Supervisor for Practicum Course, January 2006–May 2006 and January 2007–May 2007
- Supervised four Masters students individually who were counseling students within a K–12 school setting.

Counselor Supervisor for Professional Orientation and Practice, January 2006–May 2006
- Supervised Masters students learning counseling techniques through the use of role playing.

Chris Smith
Page Two

School Counseling and Teaching Experience

TORRANCE UNIFIED SCHOOL DISTRICT, Torrance, California
School Counselor, September 2003–June 2004
- Counseled students individually and in groups; designed specific counseling programs to meet needs.
- Responded effectively to various on-campus crises via crisis intervention strategies.
- Coordinated and oversaw IEP meetings and specific meetings designed to help high-risk students become more successful in school.
- Consulted daily with teachers and parents regarding student performance.
- Teamed with psychologist presenting information for special education students to parents and teachers.
- Facilitator of workshops, presentations, and programs for students, teachers, and staff.

WISEBURN SCHOOL DISTRICT, Hawthorne, California
School Counselor Intern, December 2002–June 2003
- Developed and implemented guidance services in a multicultural setting; included social skills groups, divorce groups, and disability awareness program.
- Conducted individual and group counseling for students in grades K–5.

CULVER CITY HIGH SCHOOL, Culver City, California
School Counselor Intern, January 2003–June 2003
- Counseled students on personal, educational, and career issues.
- Worked with the "Latinos Unidos" club to improve cultural awareness.
- Developed and implemented preschool curriculum to enhance language skills of developmentally delayed students.
- Coordinated with parents on designing an educational plan to facilitate the development of their children.

REDONDO BEACH UNIFIED SCHOOL DISTRICT, Redondo Beach, California
Substitute Teacher, September 2001–January 2003
- Instructed academic lessons to K–12 population; lesson development and classroom management.
- Worked with developmentally challenged students.

Professional Affiliations

Member, American Counseling Association
Member, Association for Counselor Education and Supervision
Member, Association for Multicultural Counseling and Development
Member, American College Counseling Association

Language Development

Spanish Grammar Course, University of Rochester, January 2007–Present
Spanish Language Course, University of Navarra, Spain, August 2006–September 2006
Spanish Language Course, Eurocenters Salamanca, Spain, July 2005–August 2005

COREY DAVIS

123 Main Street • Hometown, WA 00000 • (555) 555-1234 • cdavis@company.com

TEACHING ACCOMPLISHMENTS

Tacoma High School, Tacoma, WA

Chairperson, Mathematics Department, 2003–Present
- Serve as math instructor and Director of the Math Evaluation Committee.
- Develop report for submission to the National Association of Schools and Colleges.
- Develop and monitor budgets, assess goals, programs, plans, and professional performance.
- Select and approve departmental texts, and write and upgrade course descriptions as necessary.
- Evaluate instructional staff, advise on contract renewal, and evaluate candidates for new hires.

Mathematics Instructor, 1999–Present
- Instruct grades 9–12 in Trigonometry, Algebra I & II, Geometry, Pre-Calculus, and Business Math.
- Develop curricula and lesson plans, select texts, and design tests.
- Initiated remedial math program and after-school tutorial sessions for problem math students.
- Conduct summer-school sessions in remedial math and SAT preparation.

Stagg High School, Stockton, CA

9th–12th Grade Mathematics Student Teacher, Fall 1999
- Implemented lessons for and assessed students in Honors Algebra, and Honors Trigonometry.

9th–10th Grade Algebra and Geometry Mathematics Field Work Teacher's Assistant, Spring 1998

TUTORIAL EXPERIENCE

Private Tutoring, Stockton, CA and Tacoma, WA

Tutor for Middle and High School Mathematics Students, 1997–Present
- Helped students with homework assignments and enhanced general understanding of concepts and approaches associated with Algebra, Trigonometry, Calculus, and General Math.

University of the Pacific, Stockton, CA

Mathematics Department Grader for Inferential Statistics, 1998–1999

Mathematics Resources Center Proctor for Algebra and Trigonometry, 1998–1999

Mathematics Department Grader for Finite Mathematics, Statistics, and Calculus, 1997–1998

Parklane Elementary School, Stockton, CA

Teacher's Aide for Summer Youth Employment Training Program, Summers 1994 and 1995

EDUCATION AND MATH DEGREES

University of Washington, Seattle, WA

M.S. in Secondary Education and Curriculum and Instruction, with Mathematics Specialization, 2001

University of the Pacific, Stockton, CA

B.S. in Mathematics, with Mathematics Education major, Single Subject Credential, Fall 1999

San Joaquin Delta Community College, Stockton, CA

Associate of Arts in Mathematics, June 1997

Jamie Brown

123 Main St. • Apt. 13 • Hometown, MD 00000 • (555) 555-9821 • jb@company.com

Social Work Experience

Baltimore Central School District, Baltimore, MD
District Social Worker, 2005–Present
- Provide direct social work services to elementary, middle, and high school students and families.
- As member of interdisciplinary team, establish, implement, and monitor effectiveness of Independent Educational Programs.
- Regularly communicate with parents, teachers, and special-education professionals regarding individual students.
- Conduct group discussions with students and parents pertaining to developmental, behavioral, and medical issues.

Johns Hopkins University Children and Teen Clinic, Baltimore, MD
Clinical Social Worker, 2003–2005
- Diagnosed, evaluated, and treated children, adolescents, adults, and families living within the guidelines of Care and Protection Petitions.
- Interacted with legal, medical, and psychological professionals.
- Provided individualized social-work services for children and adolescents, including pregnant teens, foster-home residents, and those meeting court-mandated criteria.
- Maintained accurate and thorough documentation via case records.

Baltimore County Juvenile Court Clinic, Baltimore, MD
Field Placement Intern, 2002–2003
- Diagnosed, evaluated, and treated children, adolescents, adults, and families.
- Conducted evaluations and supported Family Services team by handling research, field assessments, and administrative follow up.

Johns Hopkins University Hospital, Baltimore, MD
Pediatric Social Work Intern, 2001–2002
- Provided clinical services, family counseling, and referrals for patients and families.
- Conducted home visits and completed follow-up evaluations.
- Participated in classroom-based education program for potential kidney transplant patients.

Education

Social Work and Psychology Studies
Johns Hopkins University, Baltimore, MD
Master of Social Work, May 2003

Colby College, Waterville, ME
Bachelor of Arts, Psychology and Bachelor of Arts, Sociology, cum laude, June 2001

Qualification and Capabilities

- Capabilities to serve within comprehensive social work capacities in school or health care settings.
- Experience creating and implementing treatment plans for clients with psychosocial, behavioral, and health-related disorders.
- Capacity to manage cases, maintain accurate case records, and create detailed reports.

CHRIS SMITH

123 Main Street, Apartment 13 • Hometown, UT 00000 • (555) 555-1234 • csmith@company.com

OBJECTIVE   Speech and Language Pathology Position with Clinical Fellowship Year.

QUALIFICATIONS

- Experience diagnosing and treating children displaying apraxia, language delay, hearing impairment, and articulation disorders and adult-exhibiting motor speech disorders and aphasia.
- Ability to accurately administer hearing screenings and tympanometry readings.
- Perspectives and skills required to effectively work on diagnostic evaluation team.
- Skills to document cases, communicate with colleagues, and correspond with clients and families.
- Fluency using Visual Phonics and American Sign Language.

GRADUATE AND UNDERGRADUATE PROFESSIONAL DEGREES

Brigham Young University, Salt Lake City, UT
Master of Arts in Communicative Disorders, December 2007
Bachelor of Arts in Communicative Disorders, *magna cum laude*, May 2005
- Graduate Overall GPA 3.98 and Undergraduate Major GPA 3.91 (out of 4.0)
- Outstanding Senior Award in Communicative Disorders Department, May 2005
- Phi Kappa Phi Honor Society Member and Utah Speech and Hearing Association Member

CLINICAL AND RESEARCH EXPERIENCE

Elmwood Elementary School, Salt Lake City, UT
Language, Speech, and Hearing Intern, February–May 2007
- Administered group therapy to Preschool–6th grade students with articulation and language disorders.
- Worked with students in classroom and independently outside of the classroom.
- Involved in Individualized Education Plan (IEP) assessments and meetings.

Brigham Young University Speech and Hearing Center, Salt Lake City, UT
Student Clinician, September 2005–Present
- Diagnosed, then planned and administered therapy to children with apraxia, language delay, hearing impairment, and articulation disorders.
- Used Visual Phonics and American Sign Language with hearing-impaired child client.
- Diagnosed, then administered therapy to adult displaying motor speech disorders and aphasia.
- Established home programs to effectively train and motivate parents, spouses, and others.
- Wrote case summaries documenting clinical goals, approaches, and achievements.
Clinical Diagnostic Team Member, 2003–2005
- Interviewed, assessed, and wrote reports on stuttering, articulation, and language delay disorder cases.

Brigham Young University Language Disorders Department, Salt Lake City, UT
Visual Phonics and Down Syndrome Researcher, 2005–2007

Bret Harte High School, Salt Lake City, UT
Special Education Classroom Volunteer and ASL Tutor, Summers 2004 and 2005

Jamie Brown

123 Main Street • Hometown, NC 00000 • (555) 555-1234 • jbrown@company.com

Systems Engineering Profile

- Extensive and diversified hardware and software knowledge.
- Expertise in prototype computer testing.
- Comprehensive investigative and research skills.
- Knowledge of programming languages, operating systems, as well as word processing, database, and spreadsheet software applications including: Windows, Macintosh, UNIX, Assembler Natural, Cs, Java, Pascal, COBOL, Visual Basic, Word, Excel, Access, and Oracle.

Systems Engineering and Programming Experience

Maximilian Data and Computer Systems   **Charlotte, NC**

Systems Engineer   *2002–Present*

Coauthored software test plan for computer prototypes. Researched, wrote, and edited test procedures. Developed computer engineering test tools. Wrote database application to track and generate reports on problems found during development. Organized preproduction testing of prototypes. Analyzed requirements for new processes to improve product testing. Created software that automated work-related processes, such as generating status- and engineering-change request reports.

Systems Programmer   *1999–2002*

Maintained over 300 assembler modules and developed 75. Formulated screen manager program to trace input and output to the VTAM buffer. Developed program to monitor complete security control blocks.

University of Georgia School of Law   **Atlanta, GA**

Systems Programmer   *Summers 1995–1997 and Full-time 1997–1999*

Initiated start-up and implemented operations. Designed and managed implementation of a network providing the legal community with a direct line to Supreme Court cases. Developed a system that catalogued entire library's inventory. Used Cs to create a registration system for a university registrar.

Engineering and Technical Education

Georgia Tech University   **Atlanta, GA**

B.S. in Computer Science   *May 1997*

Georgia Tech University   **Atlanta, GA**

Post-baccalaureate coursework   *1997–Present*

Courses included: JavaScript, Visual Basic, Web Services, ASP/NET, CH/NET, VB/NET, Web Forms, Advanced IBM 370 Assembler, SNA Fundamentals, MVS/ESA Architecture, Natural 2 Programming Language, MVS/XA Concepts and Facilities, MVS/XA Job Control Language, MVS/XA Using and Creating Procedures.

Technical Writer

Dana Johnson

123 Main Street • Hometown, FL 00000 • (555) 555-1234 • djohnson@company.com

TECHNICAL WRITING EXPERIENCE

2004–Present   RIZZO ASSOCIATES, Melrose, FL
Technical Writer and Senior Project Administrator
- Research data and accurately describe the installation, removal, erection, and maintenance of all military hardware.
- Outline wiring diagrams, draw part breakdowns for illustrators, draft and finalize all descriptions associated with use of and training to use military hardware.
- Serve as overall program lead for specific projects in A-3, EA-3, and EP-3E programs.
- Work on IPB, MIM, and IFMM for all maintenance levels.
- Transform various source materials, including engineering drawings and wiring diagrams into user-targeted written and disc-driven documentation and illustrations.

1999–2004   CAPABIANCO PUBLISHING, Winter Park, FL
Technical Writer
- Supported efforts to develop and finalize illustrations and documentation associated with military hardware.
- Served as project lead, including editing, layout, and corrections.

1995–1999   DARK WILLOW ENGINEERING CORPORATION, Killarney, FL
Editor/Writer
- Edited and wrote large proposals for government contracts.
- Designed format and coordinated production.
- Organized and maintained up-to-date dummy book through several revision cycles.
- Interpreted client requirements and determined applicability of proposal responses.

EDUCATION

UNIVERSITY OF FLORIDA, Gainesville, FL
B.S. in Civil Engineering, 1995
Additional coursework in Computer Science, Mathematics, English Literature, and Journalism.

TECHNICAL WRITING AND PROJECT MANAGEMENT QUALIFICATIONS

- Proven abilities to structure technical writing projects and motivate others to complete components accurately and on time.
- Capacities to transform technical information into detailed illustrations and documentation.
- Sensitivities related to creation of classified training and support materials for military hardware.
- Security Clearance Level IA.
- Project and team management skills nurtured via observation and experience.
- Capacities to identify specific task components, set realistic deadlines, then monitor and motivate others.
- Expertise associated with the use of Word, PowerPoint, Excel, and CAD.

Telemarketer

Francis Williams

123 Main Street • Hometown, FL 00000 • (555) 555-1234 • Cell (555) 555-5678 • fwilliams@company.com

TELEMARKETING QUALIFICATIONS

- Outstanding selling and closing capabilities illustrated by a proven track record of exceeding goals.
- Well versed in active listening techniques, nurturing conversations through appropriate questioning.
- Drive and focus required to meet contact and sales quotas, meeting established deadlines.
- Confidence in cold calling and direct sales roles, marketing services and products to businesses and clients.
- Pride associated with using earnings as telemarketer to pay for college tuition and expenses.
- Business Administration, Public Speaking, Persuasive Writing, and Marketing courses.

ACHIEVEMENT SUMMARY

- Induction into national club of Top Ten Percent 2005, 2006, and 2007.
- Awarded Golden Ring Award for meeting sales goals throughout Fiscal Years 2005 and 2006.
- Personally responsible for over $500,000 FY 2006–2007 annual sales as a result of accounts gained.
- Record of consistently reaching or exceeding established goals for over 4 years.

TELEMARKETING EXPERIENCE

2005–Present   ESP TELECOMMUNICATIONS, Saint Petersburg, FL
                Telemarketing Professional
                - Cold-called residential and commercial consumers, assessing domestic and international calling needs, and then recommending and marketing long-distance programs.
                - Consistently achieved at least 125% of sales goals.
                - Landed largest commercial accounts during 2006–2007 and 2005–2006 Fiscal Years.

2003–2005   TEST REVIEW EDUCATION GROUP, Miami, FL
                Marketing Assistant
                - Cold-called high school and college students and parents, marketing college and graduate school entrance exam preparation courses.
                - Yielded 35% attendance at seminars and simulations used to market services.

RETAIL SALES EXPERIENCE

2000–2003   KAYBEE TOYS, Miami, FL
                Sales Associate
                - Addressed inquiries of customers, maintained inventory levels, and trained salespersons.

EDUCATION

ROLLINS COLLEGE, Winter Park, FL
Bachelor of Arts, English, May 2009
MIAMI DADE JUNIOR COLLEGE, Miami, FL
Associate of Arts, Liberal Studies, August 2007

COREY DAVIS

123 Main Street • Hometown, MA 00000 • (555) 555-1234 • cdavis@company.com

SPORTS MEDICINE STUDIES

ITHACA COLLEGE, Ithaca, NY
BA Sports Medicine, May 2002

ATHLETIC TRAINING EXPERIENCE

ITHACA COLLEGE, Ithaca, NY
Senior Trainer, 2002–Present
Conduct hydrostatic weighing and skin-fold body fat tests. Set up individual rehab and strengthening programs, and serve as nutrition and fitness consultant to all teams. Oversee all student trainers.
Rehabilitation Trainer, 2000–2002
Student Trainer, 1999–2002

WORLD WRESTLING FEDERATION, Syracuse, NY
Athletic Trainer for Syracuse and Rochester Appearances, 2001–Present

FITNESS EXPERIENCE

MIDTOWN RACQUETBALL CLUB, Milford, MA
Aerobic Instructor, Summers 1998–2001

TOTAL HEALTH AND FITNESS STOP, Hopedale, MA
Aerobic Instructor, Summer and Part-time 1997

FOCUS ON FITNESS, Ashland, MA
Aerobic Instructor, Summers and Part-time 1995–1997

WORLD GYM, Framingham, MA
Aerobic Instructor, Part-time 1995–1999

CERTIFICATIONS AND AFFILIATIONS

A.C.E. (American Council on Exercise) Personal Trainer Certification and Fitness Instructor Certification Basic Life Saving and Cardiac Care Certified, American Heart Association. Standard First Aid Certified, American Red Cross. Member N.A.T.A. (National Athletic Trainers Association).

QUALIFICATIONS

- Experience implementing programs designed to prevent and treat injuries of athletes in variety of sports including football, wrestling, volleyball, basketball, swimming, water polo, and tennis.
- Taught a variety of weekly classes including hi-lo, low impact, body sculpting, and step. Introduced funk aerobics to participants ages 15–65.
- Taught "FITKIDS" classes for ages 3–6 and ages 7–11.

Chris Smith

123 Main Street • Hometown, IL 00000 • (555) 555-1234 • csmith@company.com

Travel Industry Qualifications

- Four years of experience acquired via travel industry employment and training.
- Thorough knowledge of various reservation transactions, including booking, bursting, ticketing, sales, customer service, and dealing with contracted vendors to ensure customer reservation specifications.
- Expertise assisting individuals, groups, and corporate accounts with specialized knowledge of cruise industry and Disney packages.

Professional Experience and Achievements

SURGE AND SIEGE TRAVEL, INC. Joliet, IL
Air and Sea Coordinator 2004–Present

- Coordinate air ticketing requests and tour departures using APOLLO and SABRE systems.
- Serve as agent specialized for cruise industry.
- Regularly attend sessions hosted by cruise and air carriers, educating regarding options and plans.
- Track international and domestic fares, sharing data with colleagues daily.
- Issue tickets and final itineraries for air and cruise customers.
- Maintain and file pertinent materials and assist with updating of Web site (www.surgetravel.com).
- Assist with projects associated with marketing of Disney World, Disneyland, and Disney Cruises.
- Serve as group leader for numerous cruise and resort familiarization trips.
- Prepare detailed financial reports and assist senior management with development of strategic goals.

QUICK TRIP TRAVEL Evanston, IL
Travel Consultant 2002–2004

- Arranged individual and group travel, regularly yielding monthly billings in excess of $10,000.
- Promoted agency via weekly visits to senior residences as well as college campuses.
- Regularly attended training sessions related to airline offerings and reservation systems updates.

GOTTA FLY TOURS Wheaton, IL
Computer Operator/Intern 2000–2002

- Trained to use SABRE and other airline, cruise, and resort reservation systems.
- Administered ARC ticket stock and accountable documents.
- Rotated through specialty areas and assisted with accounting activities.

Professional Training and Education

MIDWEST TRAVEL SCHOOL, Chicago, IL
Certificate, 2002

DEPAUL UNIVERSITY, Chicago, IL
Bachelor of Arts, History, 2000

WINDY CITY COMMUNITY COLLEGE, Chicago, IL
Associate of Arts, Geography, 1998

Jamie Brown

123 Main Street • Hometown, MD 00000 • (555) 555-1234 • jbrown@company.com

Tutorial and Teaching Qualifications

- Capacities to teach and tutor various high school subjects, including English, Literature, Creative Writing, U.S. and World History, and self-paced SAT Preparation and GED curriculum.
- Tutored and taught English as a Second Language to university students in the U.S. and abroad.
- Experience as tutor, instructor, and teaching assistant addressing needs of college and high school students with varied backgrounds, abilities, and motivations.
- Multicultural sensitivities gained through overseas studies and successes within ESL roles.

Undergraduate and Overseas Studies

Loyola College, Baltimore, MD
Bachelor of Arts in English, emphasis in Professional Writing, May 2007
- Overall GPA, 3.6; English GPA, 3.8; and Dean's List 6 of 6 Eligible Semesters

Josef Eotvos Kollegium, Budapest, HUNGARY
Hungarian Language, Literature, and Politics courses, Fall 2006

University of Koln, Koln, GERMANY
German Language, History, Government, and Literature courses, Spring–Summer 2006

University of Edinburgh, Edinburgh, SCOTLAND
Took Scottish History course, Summer 2005

Tutorial and Teaching Experience

Loyola College, Baltimore, MD

Summer 2007 — Summer Enrichment Program Advisor and Tutor: Advised, tutored, and taught specialized courses to selected group of High School students. Planned and implemented 10-week Study Skills, SAT Preparation, and Writing Skills seminars, focusing on at-risk students with the potential to succeed in college. Created assignments-based "Reality Academy," an ideal high school.

2003–2007 — International Students Association Tutor: Taught and tutored English as a Second Language to Japanese, German, and Russian students.

2005–2007 — Writing Center Tutor and Persuasive Paper Writing Seminar Instructor

2003–2007 — Study Skills Center English and History Tutor

St. Luke's School, Baltimore, MD

2006–Present — Substitute Teacher and Tutor Grades 8–12

Baltimore County Women's Facility, Baltimore, MD

2006–Present — GED Student Teacher

Private English Tutoring, Budapest, HUNGARY and Koln, GERMANY

2006 — English as a Second Language Tutor

DANA JOHNSON

123 Main Street • Hometown, OR 00000 • (555) 555-1234 • djohnson@company.com

CERTIFICATIONS AND QUALIFICATIONS

- State of Oregon Licensed Animal Health Technician.
- 7 years of progressively responsible clinical, research, and supervisory experience.
- Generalist experience with all species and varied procedures in private practices and state-affiliated research and treatment facility.
- Specialist skills and competencies associated with surgery.

ANIMAL CARE EDUCATION

UNIVERSITY OF OREGON, Eugene, OR
B.A. in Animal Health Technology, 2004

UNIVERSITY OF PORTLAND, Portland, OR
A.S. in Animal Health Technology, 2000

VETERINARY AND ANIMAL CARE EXPERIENCE

UPPER VALLEY ANIMAL CARE CLINIC, Marylhurst, OR
Senior Surgical Assistant, 2004–Present
- Perform pre- and postoperative care and emergency care.
- Monitor ventilation and vital statistics of premature and critically ill animals.
- Collect and ship blood samples, perform intravenous and arterial catheterization, intubation of endotracheal and nasogastric tubes.
- Organize labs for and oversee veterinary students and clinical instruction sessions.

Surgical Assistant, 2002–04
- Assisted clinicians and students treating patients, and provided room pre- and post-operative care.

NEWMAN ANIMAL CARE CLINIC, Medford, OR
Surgery Intern, Part-time 2002–04

CHRIS SMITH, D.V.M., Portland, OR
Veterinary Assistant, Part-time 1998–2000
- Assisted with daily diagnosis and treatment, and served as ICU specialist, completing oral, IV, IM, SQ, fluid therapy, radiology, hematology, immunology, chemotherapy-related tasks.
- Administered, assisted, and maintained anesthesia during surgery.

UNIVERSITY OF OREGON RESEARCH CENTER, Eugene, OR
Animal Technician/Research Assistant, Part-time 1998–2000
- Directed hygienic procedures on 300 animals, including surgery and necropsies.
- Conducted research on pet food products and analyzed studies on nutrition, zinc, urine, feces, fluid therapy, medication, breeding, and artificial insemination.
- Collaborated in testing new vaccine for feline leukemia, submitting reports for FDA approval.
- Supervised and scheduled 20 center and union employees in conducting research.

VOLUNTEER EXPERIENCE

HURRICANE KATRINA RELIEF
Served two weeks on rescue team with members of Oregon Humane Society to find missing pets, rescue animals, and assist with relief efforts in aftermath of Katrina.

Francis Williams

123 Main Street • Apartment 13 • Hometown, HI 00000
(555) 555-0988 • fwilliams@company.com

FOOD SERVICES EXPERIENCE

THE PALMS   Kaneohe, HI
Head Waiter   2005–Present

- Manage, open, and close high-volume four-star restaurant.
- Hire, train, schedule, and supervise wait staff.
- Lead weekly quality assurance and menu discussion sessions.
- Oversee special catering events held on-site and at residences of patrons.
- Address concerns and special requests.
- Reconcile gratuity intake in accordance with tax regulations.

PALUA SAILS RESTAURANT   Kaneohe, HI
Head Waiter   2003–2005

- Provided efficient service to full bar, serving area, and catered affairs.
- Trained new wait staff.

CANDLE IN THE WIND   Honolulu, HI
Barback   Part-time 2001–2003

- Handled customer service and cash intake.
- Assisted with liquor inventory.
- Performed security services.

BLUE HAWAII RESTAURANT   Honolulu, HI
Busboy   Part-time 1999–2001

- Set and cleared about 20 tables of large dining room per evening.
- Trained new bus people.

SPECIALIZED TRAINING AND RECOGNITION

- Completed Palms Patron Services Training offered to Head Waiters and tenured servers.
- Regularly rated "superior" in all weekly, monthly, and annual performance reviews.
- Certified in the SIPS program for responsibly serving alcohol.
- Attended Restaurant Association training sessions: "Customer Satisfaction Is in Your Hands" and "Teaching Others to Service."

EDUCATION

HAWAII LOA COLLEGE   Kaneohe, HI
B.A. in Liberal Arts   expected 2008

Before-and-After Resumes

The following resume samples are under very tight space requirements. On a normal sheet of paper, you could fit more lines and have wider margins, thus allowing for more content. A good rule of thumb is to allow half-inch margins on the top, bottom, left, and right.

- Times New Roman font is professional and space-efficient.

- Identifying information for two addresses uses four lines that may not e-mail well.

- Soon-to-be college graduate's multipurpose resume.

- Education presented first under general header.

- Experience under basic and general header in reverse chronological order.

- Experience and courses presented in paragraph form to conserve space.

CHRIS SMITH

123 Main Street   csmith@company.com   987 Centre Avenue
Hometown, NY 00000   Hometown, NY 10001
(555) 555-1234   (555) 555-5678

EDUCATION

2004–2007   UNIVERSITY OF ROCHESTER, Rochester, NY
Bachelor of Arts, French, with a major GPA of 3.5, May 2007.
Bachelor of Arts, Psychology, with a major GPA of 3.3, May 2006.
Minor: **Economics,** with a minor GPA of 3.4.
- Management Studies Certificate, for completion of courses taught by faculty of College and the William E. Simon School of Business Administration.
- Economics Council, Activity Board, and *Campus Times* Staff Writer.

2003–2004   HOBART AND WILLIAM SMITH COLLEGES, Geneva, NY

EXPERIENCE

Spring 2006   THE FINANCIAL GROUP DISCOUNT BROKERAGE, Pittsford, NY
Intern/Assistant to Operations Manager: Used computerized financial transactions and market tracking systems. Updated customer databases using Excel. Interacted with and completed administrative projects for licensed representatives and addressed client inquiries from throughout the United States.

Summer 2006   DAYS ADVERTISING, INC., Pittsford, NY
Intern/Assistant to an Account Manager: Assisted with design of television and radio ads and proposals for varied products and clients, including Wegmans and Bausch & Lomb. Developed customer database.

2005–2006   ADEFFECTS, Rochester, NY
Intern/Assistant to an Account Manager: Researched and developed promotional materials for local retail, manufacturing, and restaurant clients. Gained knowledge of small business marketing. Recommended changes in client advertising materials, consumer outreach strategies, and marketing literature.

Summer 2006   PEARLE VISION CENTER, Pittsford, NY
Sales Representative: Implement strategy targeting upscale markets.

Summer 2004   IT HAPPENS, Antwerp, Belgium
Marketing Intern: Determined target markets and developed ad budget for concert, event planning, and entertainment agency. Conducted market penetration surveys. Assisted graphic artists producing ads, posters, brochures, and reports.

Advertising Account Executive (After)

CHRIS SMITH

123 Main Street • Hometown, NY 00000 • (555) 555-1234 • csmith@company.com
987 Centre Avenue, Apartment 13 • Rochester, NY 00000 • (555) 555-5678

ADVERTISING ACCOUNT MANAGEMENT QUALIFICATIONS

- Marketing research, strategic planning, promotions, customer service, and sales talents nurtured by diverse advertising, promotions, and retail internships and employment.
- Skills gained via courses including: Marketing, Marketing Projects and Cases, Motivation, Public Relations Writing, Advertising, and Consumer Behavior.
- German, French, Dutch, and Farsi fluency, and conversational Spanish capabilities.
- UNIX, HTML, Word, Excel, PowerPoint, InDesign, PhotoShop, and Internet skills.

ADVERTISING AND MARKETING EXPERIENCE

DAYS ADVERTISING, INC., Pittsford, NY
Account Management Intern: Assisted with design of TV and radio ads and proposals for clients, including Wegmans and Bausch & Lomb. Developed client database. Summer 2006

ADEFFECTS, Rochester, NY
Account Management Intern: Researched and developed promotional materials for retail, manufacturing, and restaurant clients, using knowledge of small business marketing. Suggested client changes in outreach strategies, and marketing literature. 2005–2006

PEARLE VISION CENTER, Pittsford, NY
Sales Representative: Implemented strategy targeting upscale markets. Summer 2006

IT HAPPENS, Antwerp, Belgium
Marketing Intern: Determined target markets and developed advertisement budget for concert, event planning, and entertainment agency. Conducted surveys to determine market penetration. Assisted graphic artists with ads, posters, brochures, and reports. Summer 2003

BUSINESS, ECONOMICS, AND LANGUAGE STUDIES

UNIVERSITY OF ROCHESTER, Rochester, NY
Bachelor of Arts, French, with a major GPA of 3.5, May 2007.
Bachelor of Arts, Psychology, with a major GPA of 3.3, May 2007.
Minor: **Economics,** with a minor GPA of 3.4.

WILLIAM E. SIMON SCHOOL OF BUSINESS ADMINISTRATION, Rochester, NY
Management Studies Certificate, Marketing and Finance/Accounting Tracks, May 2007

FINANCE EXPERIENCE

THE FINANCIAL GROUP, INC. DISCOUNT BROKERAGE FIRM, Pittsford, NY
Intern/Assistant to Operations Manager, Spring 2006

- Identifying information uses only two lines.
- Left-justified block text format is e-friendly; can be uploaded to Web sites and copied and pasted into e-mail.
- Experience presented under targeted headline.
- Education presented under targeted headline to highlight specialized studies.
- Courses presented in qualification summary to highlight significance.
- Chris is a focused yet typical soon-to-be graduate. His before resume is multipurpose. Chris's strategy of having a multipurpose and a targeted resume is sound.
- Both possess qualities worthy of modeling.
- Think about the headlines used in the after version and about changes in the order of presentation.
- How did the qualification summary change your reaction to this resume?

Day Care Worker (Before)

- Watch choice of font. Use a font that is easy to read and universal so that poor font substitutions or errors won't occur for your audience; i.e. Times, Bookman, Garamond, or Arial.

- Education presented first, without dates, under general header is confusing format.

- Experience under basic and generic header is presented in a confusing format.

- Difficult to see chronological or functional progress year to year or job to job.

Jamie Brown

123 Main Street
Home (555) 555-5555

Hometown, CO 00000
Cell (555) 555-9999

EDUCATION

30 Education credits, with day care emphasis, and English minor.
Metropolitan State College, Denver, CO

EXPERIENCE

2004-Present
NANNY
Care for twin boys from the age of two months through two years. Assist in selecting toys and equipment, provide environmental stimulation, personal care, and play.
Private residence, Livermore, CO

2002-04
TEACHER
Taught infant, preschool, and after-school programs. Planned curriculum, organized activities, communicated with parents and staff regarding growth and development. Suggested equipment to enrich children's experiences and helped create a stimulating environment.
Baby Bear Preschool, Keystone, CO

2000-03
TEACHER
Planned and implemented curriculum for infants. Communicated with parents and other staff regarding daily progress of children.
This Little Piggy Daycare Center, Dove Creek, CO

1998-00
TEACHER
Planned and implemented curriculum for toddler program. Enriched children's experiences through play, music, and art.
The Kid Corral, Wild Horse, CO

1996-98
CAREGIVER
Provided care in clients' homes, administering physical therapy when necessary. Planned activities to stimulate and improve children's skills and environment.
Residences, Dove Creek, and Keystone, CO

2000-Present
VOLUNTEER
Ivywild Coalition for Retarded Citizens, Ivywild, COSKILLS AND INTERESTS
Valid driver's license; perfect driving record. CPR/first aid certified. Skiing, reading, music, arts and crafts.

Day Care Worker (After)

Jamie Brown

123 Main Street • Hometown, CO 00000 • (555) 555-1234 • Cell (555) 555-9999

DAY CARE QUALIFICATIONS AND COMPETENCIES

- More than 9 years of diverse experience within home and school settings, teaching and caring for children ranging in ages from 2 months to 7 years.
- Commitment to the needs of infants, preschoolers, and kindergarteners.
- Academic background including courses in: Childhood Development, Early Childhood Education, Educational Psychology, and Assessments.

DAY CARE, TEACHING, AND CHILD CARE EXPERIENCE

2004–Present   PRIVATE RESIDENCE, Livermore, CO
Nanny: Care for twin boys from the age of two months through two years. Provide environmental enrichment, personal care, and play supervision.
- Accompanied family on trips and cared for children during illnesses.

2002–2004   BABY BEAR PRESCHOOL, Keystone, CO
Teacher: Taught infant, preschool, and after-school programs. Planned curriculum, organized activities, communicated with parents and staff regarding children's growth and development.
- Responded to annual increase in students and move to new facility.
- Worked collegially with owner on goal development.
- Assisted with annual licensing documentation and visitation.

2000–2002   THIS LITTLE PIGGY DAYCARE CENTER, Dove Creek, CO
Teacher: Planned and implemented infant program, blending developmental and custodial needs. Communicated with parents regarding student progress.
- Enhanced skills development through interactive play and song.

1998–2000   THE KID CORRAL, Wild Horse, CO
Teacher: Planned and implemented curriculum for toddler program. Enriched children's experiences through play, music, and art.

1998–2004   PRIVATE CAREGIVER, Wild Horse, Dove Creek, and Keystone, CO

2000–Present   COALITION FOR RETARDED CITIZENS VOLUNTEER, Ivywild, CO

EDUCATION

1995–1998   METROPOLITAN STATE COLLEGE, Denver, CO
- 30 credits in Education, with an emphasis on day care.

REFERENCES

Provided upon request.

- Professional and e-friendly Garamond font.

- Qualifications and competencies appearing first serve as objective and preview of assets.

- Experience under targeted headline in easy-to-review format.

- Date timeline shows chronological and functional progress.

- Okay to use "References provided upon request" for this type of position. Be sure to have separate sheet of professional references with full contact information available.

- Jamie is an experienced nanny and day care professional. Her current employer has informed her that she will no longer be needed full time. For the increasingly professional worlds of day care, private child care, and preschools, she has created a very appealing and marketable resume.

- Jamie has kept her audience in mind and her resume targets upscale day care facilities and parents.

- Watch choice of font! Remember, typeface must be easily read by all and convenient to e-mail.

- Identifying information spread out over three lines.

- Resume lacks any kind of targeted objective, which is a disadvantage to an experienced candidate.

- Experience is presented first under general header, with dates appearing first, then entries presented in reverse chronological order. Confusing to reader.

Dana Johnson
123 Main Street
Hometown, New Jersey 00000

(555) 555-1234
djohnson@company.com

Experience

ABC FINANCIAL CONSULTANTS, Princeton, NJ
July 1995–Present
Financial Consultant/Financial Planner
- Developed $210 million client base via prospecting.
- Build portfolio that includes stock, bonds, options, and insurance products for more than 450 clients.
- Implemented financial plans and operations through account development and growth.

October 1993–July 1995
Sales Associate
- Worked directly with firm's top producer, profiling high net worth individuals for future business.
- Generated $90,000 for top producer via new accounts.
- Analyzed portfolios to expand account performance.

September 1992–October 1993
Account Executive Trainee/Intern
- Supervised about 35,000 accounts in the area of trade settlement, NASD regulations, and customer inquiries.
- Reported recommendations to upper management.
- Acted as liaison with New York operations.

MAPLEWOOD INVESTMENTS, Maplewood, NJ
Summers 1991 and 1992
Prospecting Intern
- Planned, created documents for, and oversaw invitations and confirmations for 3 annual Summer Financial Seminars.
- Researched stock and updated transactions.

Related Training

Successfully completed ABC Financial Consultant Sales Training and Advanced Training program in Princeton, NJ, headquarters. Licensed in Series 6, 7, 63, and health and life insurance.

Education

IONA COLLEGE, Iona, New York
Bachelor of Arts degree in Economics, 1993

Financial Planner (After)

Dana Johnson

123 Main Street • Hometown, NJ 00000 • (555) 555-1234 • djohnson@company.com

Financial Planning Qualifications and Credentials

- Over a decade of progressively significant roles and achievements in planning, portfolio management, and client services.
- Personal responsibilities for more than $210 million client assets.
- Recognized for asset-based performance and customer service.
- Served as trainer and curriculum developer.

Financial Planning Accomplishments

1995–Present

ABC FINANCIAL CONSULTANTS, Princeton, NJ
Financial Consultant/Financial Planner
Serve in comprehensive financial planning roles. Oversee individual and group portfolios. Serve as senior manager, supervisor, and trainer within corporate headquarters of firm responsible for over $800 million in client assets.

- Developed $210 million client asset base through aggressive prospecting and targeting campaign.
- Successfully built portfolio that includes stock, bonds, options and insurance products for more than 450 clients.
- Implemented financial plans and operations through account development and growth.
- Gained expertise associated with estate planning, asset allocation, and wealth succession.
- Completed ABC Financial Consultant Sales Training and Advanced Training Program. Licensed in Series 6, 7, 63, and health and life insurance.

1993–1995

Sales Associate

- Worked directly with firm's top producer, profiling high net worth individuals for future business.
- Generated $90,000 through new account openings.
- Analyzed portfolios to expand account performance.

1992–1993

Account Executive Trainee/Intern

- Completed about 35,000 account transactions annually.
- Completed comprehensive training related to trade settlement, NASD regulations, and customer service.

Summers 1991 and 1992

MAPLEWOOD INVESTMENTS, Maplewood, NJ
Prospecting Intern

Education

IONA COLLEGE, Iona, New York
Bachelor of Arts degree in Economics, 1993

- Bookman Old Style is good font choice.

- Dana is an experienced financial services professional. She is not in active job search mode, but because she is frequently called upon to serve as a spokesperson and seminar leader, she regularly updates her resume.

- The before version appears professional, but lacks focus. It doesn't highlight achievements. The after version, introduced via a qualifications and credentials section, is achievement-oriented, and it highlights career growth.

Francis Williams

123 Main Street
Hometown, NY 00000
(555) 555-1234

fwilliams@company.com

987 Centre Ave.
Homeville, NY 10001
(555) 555-5678

EDUCATION

UNIVERSITY OF ROCHESTER, Rochester, NY
Bachelor of Arts, Health and Society, Anticipated May 2008
Management Certificate in Public Sector Analysis, May 2007
Completed Language and Cultural Studies in Rome, Italy Spring 2006

ACTIVITIES AND LEADERSHIP

SIGMA DELTA FRATERNITY
President, 2007–2008, Secretary, 2005–2006, and Member, 2004–Present
STUDENT HEALTH ADVISORY COMMITTEE
Member, 2007–2008

EXPERIENCE

CHECK YOUR PULSE AMERICA RESEARCH STUDY, Rochester, NY
Research Assistant: Helped design aspects of nationwide research study dealing with stroke prevention. Responsibilities included distribution of questionnaire, data entry, and report writing and editing. Fall 2006

NYS VETERANS NURSING HOME, Wood Cliff, NY
Human Resource Assistant: Supported various recruiting, payroll, and benefits activities. Collected, reviewed, and rated resumes. Communicated with candidates by phone and e-mail. Summer 2007

THE CARDIOLOGY GROUP, Wood Cliff, NY
Administrative Assistant: Greeted and scheduled patients, maintained files, assisted with billing, communicated with insurance carriers and pharmacies, and completed special tasks as assigned. 2003–Present

YOUR INSURANCE GROUP, White Plains, NY
Office Assistant, Summer 2006

COMPUTER AND OFFICE SKILLS

Word, Excel, PowerPoint, Access, and Internet capabilities.
Abilities to serve in receptionist, billing, and human resource roles.

Francis Williams

123 Main St. • Hometown, NY 00000 • (555) 555-1234 • fwill@company.com
987 Centre Ave. • Homeville, NY 10001 • (555) 555-5678

MEDICAL PRODUCT SALES QUALIFICATIONS

- Knowledge of health care, business, and economics-related topics gained from courses including: Accounting, Microeconomics, Business Administration, Changing Concepts of Disease, Medical Sociology, Domestic Social Policy, Organizational Psychology, and Statistics.
- Confidence and experience communicating with physicians, health care practitioners, patients, and others associated with medical devices.
- Research, project management, time management, writing, and oral communication skills gained from employment, education, and activities.
- Capacities to conduct topic-specific research, identify trends or key issues, and document findings in reports as well as presentations.
- Persuasive communication style, required to educate regarding protocols and studies specific to medical products and treatment techniques.
- Word, Excel, PowerPoint, Access, and Internet capabilities.

HEALTH AND SOCIETY AND BUSINESS EDUCATION

UNIVERSITY OF ROCHESTER, Rochester, NY
Bachelor of Arts, Health and Society, anticipated May 2008
- Health and Society Major focused on study of Community and Preventive Medicine, as well as history and economics of health care delivery.
- Sigma Delta Fraternity President, Secretary, and Member.
- Student Health Advisory Committee, Member and Class of 2007 Senator.

WILLIAM E. SIMON SCHOOL OF BUSINESS ADMINISTRATION, Rochester, NY
Management Certificate in Public Sector Analysis, anticipated May 2008
- Certificate for completion of business, economics, and policy-focused courses taught by faculty of the College and of the Simon School.

TEMPLE UNIVERSITY ROME, Rome, Italy
Completed Language and Cultural Studies, Spring Semester 2006

HEALTH CARE, BUSINESS, AND RESEARCH EXPERIENCE

CHECK YOUR PULSE AMERICA RESEARCH STUDY, Rochester, NY
Research Assistant: Helped design aspects of nationwide research study dealing with stroke prevention. Fall 2006

NYS VETERANS NURSING HOME, Wood Cliff, NY
Human Resource Assistant: Supported recruiting, payroll, and benefits activities. Summer 2007

THE CARDIOLOGY GROUP, Wood Cliff, NY
Administrative Assistant, Summers and Part-time 2002–Present

YOUR INSURANCE GROUP, White Plains, NY
Office Assistant, Summer 2006

- Left-justified block text header format is visually appealing.

- Objective is presented via a qualification summary.

- Marketing, business, and health care courses are presented first in qualifications section, highlighting significance.

- A goal targeted summary of qualifications is first, immediately followed by detailed education. This gives primary emphasis to the most important information.

- Summary of qualifications supplemented by a cover letter shows commitment and the capabilities to succeed.

- Times New Roman typeface is q professional-looking font.

- Identifying information omits e-mail address. Many job seekers choose to also include a cell phone number.

- This is an experienced candidate with ten years of post-college experience in one field.

- Experience under one generic headline includes law, retail, and administrative.

- Bullets used as effective highlighting technique.

COREY DAVIS

123 Main Street • Santa Fe, NM 00000 • (555) 555-5555

EXPERIENCE

BRENDAN ELLIS CIVIL LITIGATION SPECIALIST/OFFICE MANAGER
Santa Fe, NM 2003–Present

- Manage office and staff of 3 secretaries, ensuring smooth operation of firm.
- Interview clients; prepare files and discovery.
- Request and review medical documentation; ascertain evidence information, and process all with the appropriate parties.
- Negotiate and settle cases with defense attorney and insurance companies.
- Attend mediations and conciliations.
- Prepare clients for depositions and trials.
- Control and maintain law office accounts.

BROWNINGTON, INC. ADMINISTRATIVE ASSISTANT
Albuquerque, NM 1998–2003

- Confirmed all manpower hours and prepared logs to bill various sites.
- Provided clerical support to 24 software engineers.
- Recognized for "Excellence in Customer Satisfaction Southwest Region."

WILD RAIN EXOTIC GIFTS MANAGER/SALESPERSON
Silver City, NM 1995–98

- Sold art and memorabilia on consignment.
- Hired, trained, and supervised 8 sales personnel.
- Handled accounts, managed orders, and created promotions.

SANTA FE DISTRICT ATTORNEY'S DOMESTIC VIOLENCE WITNESS ADVOCATE
Santa Fe, NM Spring–Summer 1995

- Interviewed victims and witnesses, prepared documents, and organized information for court appearances.
- Assisted attorneys during trials.

NEW MEXICO PUBLIC DEFENDER'S LEGAL INTERN
Santa Fe, NM Summers 1993 and 1994

- Researched and drafted motions on criminal law and procedural issues.
- Interviewed clients at Illinois correctional institutions.
- Negotiated plea and bail agreements for defendants.

ATTORNEY DANIEL GALL LEGAL SECRETARY/LEGAL ASSISTANT
Santa Fe, NM 1991–95

EDUCATION

SAINT JOHN'S COLLEGE B.S., HUMAN RESOURCE MANAGEMENT
Santa Fe, NM 1995

Paralegal (After)

COREY DAVIS

123 Main Street • Hometown, NM 00000 • (555) 555-5555 • cdavis@company.com
After May 2008: 987 Centre Avenue • Hometown, CA 00000 • (555) 555-1234

PARALEGAL QUALIFICATIONS AND ACHIEVEMENTS

- Case research, client relations, document management, and writing skills gained in progressively responsible positions over a 12-year period.
- Expertise as law office manager, compiling training manual, supervising support personnel, revamping accounting, debit, and credit systems.
- Trained and accomplished interviewer, negotiator, and mediator.
- LexisNexis, WestLaw, Word, FileMaker, Excel, QuickBooks, and Internet skills.

PARALEGAL AND MANAGEMENT EXPERIENCE

LAW OFFICES OF BRENDAN ELLIS Santa Fe, NM
Civil Litigation Specialist/Office Manager 1995–Present
- Manage office and staff of 3 secretaries, ensuring operation of firm with 3 attorneys and billings of $1.5 million and awards over $10 million annually.
- Interview clients; prepare files and discovery; handle multiple cases.
- Request and review medical documentation; ascertain evidence information and process all with the appropriate parties.
- Negotiate and settle cases with defense attorney and insurance companies.
- Attend mediations and conciliations.
- Prepare clients for depositions and trials.
- Control and maintain office accounts, using accounting and billing software.

SANTE FE DISTRICT ATTORNEY'S DOMESTIC VIOLENCE UNIT Santa Fe, NM
Witness Advocate Spring–Summer 1995
- Interviewed victims and witnesses, prepared documents, and organized information for court appearances.
- Assisted attorneys during trials, taking notes, and facilitating access to evidentiary documents.

NEW MEXICO PUBLIC DEFENDER'S OFFICE Santa Fe, NM
Legal Intern Summers 1993 and 1994
- Researched and drafted motions on criminal law and procedural issues. Interviewed clients at Illinois correctional institutions.
- Negotiated plea and bail agreements for defendants accused of misdemeanors. Attended criminal trials and depositions.

ATTORNEY DANIEL GALL Santa Fe, NM
Legal Secretary/Legal Assistant 1991–1995

EDUCATION

SAINT JOHN'S COLLEGE Santa Fe, NM
B.S., Human Resource Management, with Honors 1995
- Completed degree part-time while employed.

- Qualifications and achievements summary supports objective and showcases experience.

- Experience under specialized headline focuses on legal background.

- Capitalization, italics, and bullets are used effectively.

- Education makes mention of receiving degree while working full time as a legal secretary. This fact should also be highlighted in a cover letter.

- Candidate calls attention to geographic move with new relocation address and date.

- Bullets showcase career progression and growth within field. Achievements are cited, as are job titles.

- Poor choice of font; resume is visually unappealing.

- Lengthy objective contains unnecessary wording—fluff.

- Experience and Education appear under basic and generic header.

- Titles use old-fashioned underlining technique (looks dated and is often unreadable to resume scanning technology).

- Paragraph experience descriptions are difficult to read quickly.

- Internship information is poorly presented.

Chris Smith

123 Main St., Hometown, CA 00000 (555) 555-1234, cs@company.com

CAREER OBJECTIVE

Challenging pharmaceutical sales position with a progressive organization seeking dynamic and driven sales professional.

EXPERIENCE

Pearls and Gemstones Corporation, San Francisco, California
6/06–Present
Sales Associate: Sell and market polished gemstones for the San Francisco office of international gemstone and pearl distributor and jewelry manufacturer.

Bank of Hong Kong, Hong Kong   6/05–8/05
Trader: International Securities Dealing Room: Responded to customers' executing orders in the areas of American and foreign equities, bonds, and options. Received training in and gained working knowledge of Bloomberg and Reuters information systems.

Bank of Hong Kong, San Francisco, California   11/02–10/04
Credit Analyst: International Lending Department: Prepared proposals on prospective customers and renewals and reaffirmations of existing facilities for credit committee. Performed financial statement, cash flow, and projection analysis. Conducted research using Bloomberg, Moody's, and S&P analysts and publications.

Computer Associates International, San Jose, California   1/02–9/02
Quality Assurance Analyst: Implemented quality assurance for inter/intranet-enabled, multiplatform, enterprise management solution used worldwide.

EDUCATION

University of California, Berkeley, California
Bachelor of Arts   Class of 2002
Major: Political Science. Minor: Economics.
Dean's List Fall 2001 and Spring 2000 and Overall GPA: 3.34/4.0

University of New South Wales, Sydney, Australia   Spring 2001

HONORS

International Internships, London, England
Gordon McMaster, MP: British Parliament   9/00–12/00
Performed research, assisted in speech writing, aided constituents.
IPA Political Internships, Washington, DC
Senator Barbara Boxer: U.S. Senate   6/00–8/00
Wrote research briefs on pending legislation.

Pharmaceutical Sales (After)

Chris Smith

123 Main Street • Hometown, California 00000 • (555) 555-1234 • csmith@company.com

OBJECTIVE

Pharmaceutical Sales Position using and expanding upon ...

- Record of success within direct marketing and information-driven sales roles.
- Confidence nurturing relationships via direct calls using information dissemination strategies.
- Capacity to understand and share knowledge of pharmaceutical products and protocols.
- Abilities to set goals, document efforts and outcomes, and maximize achievements.
- Bilingual English-Mandarin abilities and cross-cultural sensitivities.

SALES AND SALES SUPPORT ACHIEVEMENTS

PEARLS AND GEMSTONES CORPORATION, San Francisco, California   2006–Present
Sales Associate for Loose Diamond Division: Sell gemstones for international distributor and manufacturer. Sales methods include appointments onsite, telemarketing, trade show exhibiting, and Internet. Customers include manufacturers, retail and department stores, and catalogues.

- *Directly involved in sales to house accounts totaling $2.5 million in 2006.*
- *Indirectly involved in sales to salespersons accounts totaling $3 million in 2006.*

COMPUTER ASSOCIATES INTERNATIONAL, San Jose, California   2002
Quality Assurance Analyst: Analyzed business applications for functionality and marketability. Reviewed RFPs (Request For Proposal) and identified key marketing leverage points. Implemented quality assurance for worldwide projects and software products.

- *Supported customer service and sales representatives in refining product to match customer needs.*

BUSINESS AND FINANCE EXPERIENCE

BANK OF HONG KONG, Hong Kong   Spring 2005
Securities Trader: Executed American and foreign equities, bonds, and option orders.

BANK OF HONG KONG, San Francisco, California   2002–2005
Department Credit Analyst: Prepared proposals on prospective customers and renewals for credit committee. Researched using Bloomberg, Moody's, and S&P analysts and publications.

BUSINESS, ECONOMICS, AND LIBERAL ARTS EDUCATION

UNIVERSITY OF CALIFORNIA, BERKELEY, Berkeley, California   1998–2002
Bachelor of Arts Political Science, with minor in Economics,

- Intern for Member of British Parliament, Fall 2000, and Senator Boxer, Summer 2000.

HAAS SCHOOL OF BUSINESS ADMINISTRATION, Berkeley, California   1998–2002

- Management Certificate for completion of Marketing and Business courses.

- Garamond font is good choice for attractive layout.

- Objective and candidate's assets are effectively blended together.

- Experience is set off by specific achievements as noted in the header.

- Bilingual skills are cited.

- Sales experience gets greater emphasis with specific numeric achievements noted in italics.

Public Relations Account Executive (Before)

JAMIE BROWN

123 Main Street, Hometown, NY 00000 (555) 555-1234

EXPERIENCE

SYRACUSE HEART ASSOCIATION, Syracuse, NY
Public Relations Manager, 2005–Present
Organizing: Serve as consultant to the 7 state chapters. Organize statewide and regional campaign meetings; speak at campaign conferences. Lobbying: Review legislation regarding the Society and bring specific bills to attention of proper committee or individual. Staff the Legislative Advisory Committee and follow through on specific bills. Fundraising: Develop fundraising programs. Conducted two annual campaigns for newly merged Central Chapter. Serve as chair for New York Independent Health Agency Committee and secretary for Combined Federal Campaign. Training: Developed orientation courses held for new employees; acted as training coordinator.
Directorial Assistant for Greater Syracuse Chapter, 2000–2002
Assisted the Executive Director with administrative responsibilities, such as personnel and budget.

BIG APPLE NATURAL FOODS, Syracuse, NY
Special Events Coordinator, 2003–2005
Created and coordinated special events and promotions. Selected and wrote event advertising and promotional materials. Managed $425,000 marketing budget. Handled charity fundraising, corporate image positioning, and community outreach activities.
Assistant to the Director of Public Relations, 2002–2003
Assisted in promotion and publicity of special events. Drafted press releases. Developed press kits; maintained media relations. Compiled publicity files. Researched prospective consumer markets.

SYRACUSE UNIVERSITY, Syracuse, NY
Teacher's Assistant, Fall and Spring 2003
Assisted professor in editing book. Developed lesson plans. Graded midterm exams for class of 18.

ABC KID KAMP, Syracuse, NY
Coordinator, Summers 2002 and 2003
Organized daily activities program for 45 children. Developed promotional strategies for potential markets.

COMPUTER SKILLS

Word, InDesign, PowerPoint

EDUCATION

SYRACUSE UNIVERSITY, Syracuse, NY
Bachelor of Arts in Public Relations, magna cum laude, June 2003

Public Relations Account Executive (After)

JAMIE BROWN   123 Main Street • Hometown, NY 00000 • (555) 555-1234 • jbrown@company.com

PUBLIC RELATIONS ACHIEVEMENTS

SYRACUSE HEART ASSOCIATION, Syracuse, NY
Public Relations Manager, 2005–Present
- Serve as consultant to 7 state chapters regarding campaign problems and activities.
- Organize statewide and regional campaign meetings; and speak at several campaign conferences.
- Review related state legislation activities and bring specific bills to the attention of proper committee or individual.
- Staff the Legislative Advisory Committee and follow through on specific bills.
- Develop fundraising programs and conducted two annual campaigns for newly merged Central Chapter.
- Serve as chair for New York Independent Health Agency Committee and secretary for Federal Campaign.
- Assisted with developing and teaching new employee orientation courses.

Campaign Assistant for Greater Syracuse Chapter, 2000–2002
- Supervised chapter campaigns and assisted Executive Director with campaign personnel and budget.

BIG APPLE NATURAL FOODS, Syracuse, NY
Special Events Coordinator, 2003–2005
- Managed $425,000 budget to coordinate special events and create advertising and promotional materials.
- Handled charity fundraising, corporate image positioning, and community outreach efforts.

Assistant to the Director of Public Relations, 2002–2003
- Assisted in promotion and publicity of special events.
- Drafted, edited, finalized, and distributed press releases and kits to initiate and maximize media relations efforts.
- Researched prospective consumer markets using Internet and direct contact techniques.
- Created direct-mail lists, updated media lists, and maintained task priority lists.

SYRACUSE UNIVERSITY, Syracuse, NY
Teacher's Assistant and Proofreader for "Working with the Media" Class and Text, Fall and Spring 2003

PUBLIC RELATIONS AND COMMUNICATION EDUCATION

SYRACUSE UNIVERSITY, Syracuse, NY
Bachelor of Arts in Public Relations, magna cum laude, June 2003

QUALIFICATIONS AND CAPABILITIES

- Campaign development and implementation experience with major health agency.
- Supervisory experience with both professional and nonprofessional staffs.
- Ability to plan and direct successful programs for fundraising, public relations, and promotions-oriented clients.
- Extensive volunteer recruitment experience and success motivating diverse teams.
- Experience representing agency interests to legislators and lobbyists.
- Capacity to use Word, InDesign, and PowerPoint for drafting and editing features and promotional materials, budgeting and financial tasks, and graphics projects.

- Identifying information is presented on one line.

- Resume format has more visual appeal for a creative field.

- Headlines use descriptive phrases, and italics and bold are used for emphasis.

- Use of lines to set off content continues to give this resume a more creative edge.

- Bullets set off responsibilities and content and allow reader to peruse resume quickly.

- Qualifications offer good conclusion and "close" the reader.

- Bold use of job titles showcases upwardly mobile career progression.

- Summer college position omitted—dated and no longer necessary.

Real Estate Professional (Before)

Dana Johnson

123 Main Street
(555) 555-1234

Hometown, CA 00000
djohnson@company.com

EDUCATION

SANTA CLARA UNIVERSITY, Santa Clara, CA
Bachelor of Science in Business Administration, 1985

EXPERIENCE

SAN JOSE AND SANTA CLARA HOME LOANS, San Jose, CA
Real Estate Loan Officer, 2006–Present
- Originated real estate loans, developed marketing plan to expand business.
- Conducted cold calls, created individualized mortgage broker packets, completed individual and group presentations designed to generate Conventional, FHA/VA, PERS, JUMBO, Community Home Buyer, and CHAFA loan business.

BAY AREA BANK, Santa Clara, CA
Real Estate Loan Officer, 2003–2006
- Originated real estate loans, developed marketing plan to expand business.
- Conducted cold calls, created individualized mortgage broker packets, completed individual and group presentations designed to generate loan business.
- Planned and implemented first-ever real estate expo promotional event.

HOUSING LENDING, Fresno, CA
Wholesale Account Executive, 2001–2003
- Marketed loan and financing programs to financial institutions and mortgage brokers in San Joaquin, Merced, Fresno, and Stanislaus counties.
- Conducted cold calls, created customer specific material packets, completed individual and group presentations designed to generate loan business.
- Train mortgage brokers, loan officers, and real estate agents in Conventional, Jumbo, FHA/VA, PERS, Community Home Buyer, and other niche programs.

CALIFORNIA MORTGAGE SPECIALISTS, INC., San Mateo, CA
Professional Real Estate Loan Auditor, 1997–2001
- Audited loans determining FHLMC/FNMA, FSLIC, or private investor marketability.
- Reviewed notes and deeds of trust to determine accuracy and legality.
- Interacted with Savings and Loan and Mortgage professionals in Western U.S.

SANTA CLARA SAVINGS, Santa Clara, CA
Loan Officer in Residential Lending Department, 1991–1997
- Responsible for residential and commercial loans in California and throughout U.S.
- Managed loan processing and underwriting staff of 10.
- Evaluated residential loans for approval or denial and FHLMC/FNMA conformance.
- Coordinated loan closing with production, closing, and with legal staffs.
- Traveled to project sites to establish positive relations with builders and sales representatives and outline financing and efficient loan procedures.

Loan Underwriter/Processor of Residential and Government Loans, 1987–1991
Loan Underwriter in Secondary Market Department, 1985–1987
Loan Packager in Loan Processing Department, 1983–1985

Real Estate Professional (After)

Dana Johnson

123 Main Street • Hometown, CA 00000 • (555) 555-1234 • djohnson@company.com

REAL ESTATE LENDING ACHIEVEMENTS

SAN JOSE AND SANTA CLARA HOME LOANS, San Jose, CA

Real Estate Loan Officer, 2006–Present

- Originated real estate loans, developed marketing plan to expand business in Santa Clara County.
- Conducted cold calls, created broker packets, completed presentations to generate Conventional, FHA/VA, PERS, JUMBO, and CHAFA loans.

BAY AREA BANK, Santa Clara, CA

Real Estate Loan Officer, 2003–2006

- Conducted cold calls, created individualized mortgage broker packets, completed individual and group presentations designed to generate loan business.
- Planned and implemented first-ever real estate expo promotional event.

HOUSING LENDING, Fresno, CA

Wholesale Account Executive, 2001–2003

- Marketed loan and financing programs in San Joaquin, Merced, Fresno, and Stanislaus counties.
- Conducted cold calls, created customer-specific material packets, completed individual and group presentations designed to generate loan business.

CALIFORNIA MORTGAGE SPECIALISTS, INC., San Mateo, CA

Professional Real Estate Loan Auditor, 1997–2001

- Audited loans to determine marketability to FHLMC/FNMA, FSLIC, or private investors.
- Interacted with Savings and Loan and Mortgage professionals in Western U.S.

SANTA CLARA SAVINGS, Santa Clara, CA

Loan Officer in Residential Lending Department, 1991–1997

- Evaluated residential loans for approval or denial and FHLMC/FNMA conformance.
- Traveled to project sites to establish positive relations with builders and sales representatives.

Loan Underwriter/Processor in Residential and Government Loan Departments, 1987–1991

Loan Underwriter in Secondary Market Department, 1985–1987

Loan Packager in Loan Processing Department, 1983–1985

PROFESSIONAL PROFILE

- More than 15 years in mortgage banking, customer service, finance, loan qualifications, and risk analysis.
- Expertise with Conventional, FHA/VA, PERS, JUMBO, and CHAFA loans.
- B.S. in Business, from Santa Clara University, in 1985 and continuing professional studies.

- Good mix of fonts between Arial for headlines and Century Schoolbook for content.

- Identifying information condensed to two lines.

- Headlines are clearly defined.

- Achievements presented first to showcase promotions and accomplishments.

- Profile offered last as a closing statement to the reader.

- The before and after resumes of this candidate are both good, with largely style and format preference up to individual taste.

Student Seeking Internship (Before)

- Times New Roman font is good choice, very traditional.

- This is a good multipurpose resume, but candidate may want to develop alternative with stronger career focus.

- Education and Work Experience use generic, non-descriptive headers.

- Good use of italics for highlighting.

- Bullets might help reader to peruse quickly and extract information.

- Zip code and street address not necessary for Employment information.

Francis Williams

123 Main Street
Hometown, Ohio 00000-0000
555. 555.1234

PO Box 987
Homeville, Ohio 00001-0000
fwilliams@college.edu

EDUCATION

The Ohio State University
Columbus, Ohio 43210
GPA: 3.30/4.0

Degree: BSBA
Major: Business, Marketing
Expected Graduation Date: 2008

WORK EXPERIENCE

February 2007–April 2007
46 East Sixteenth Avenue

Intern, Birthright Israel
Columbus, Ohio 43201

Recruited and interviewed candidates for national Birthright Israel program. Recruitment included campus-wide telephone and marketing campaign.

July 2006–August 2006
2880 San Thomas Expressway

Intern, NetAds, Inc.
Santa Clara, California 95051

Designed database tracking sales leads and developments. Initiated and developed early stages of contact with potential clientele. Marketed product to more than 400 potential clients, including Visa, DreamWorks Inc. and Knight-Ridder Press.

October 2005–January 2007
106 West Vine Street

Server, World Cuisine Café
Columbus, Ohio 43215

Used thorough knowledge of varied food menu and over 75 different fine wines and spirits to guide guests through fine-dining experience. Demonstrated prompt, accurate service.

October 2003–December 2003
4 Limited Parkway

Intern, Abercrombie and Fitch Co.
Columbus, Ohio 43068

Analyzed sales and presented findings to supervisors. Photographed students at local college campuses for research and development. Designed men's garment for Spring line.

October 2001–September 2005
882 High Street

Receptionist, Worthington Realtors
Worthington, Ohio 43085

INTERESTS, ACTIVITIES, AND HONORS

Alpha Phi Women's Fraternity Alumni Relations Director: January 2007–Present
American Business Women's Association Fundraising Chair: April 2007–Present
Ohio State University Community Commitment Volunteer: September 2004–Present
Project Open Hand Columbus, Volunteer: April 2005–Present
Susan G. Komen Breast Cancer Foundation, Fundraiser: 2002–Present
America Israel Public Affairs Committee Member: February 2007–Present
The Ohio State University Trustees Scholar: 2006

Student Seeking Internship (After)

FRANCIS WILLIAMS

PO Box 987 • Homeville, OH 00000 • Cell: 000.000.0000 • fwilliams@college.edu
123 Main Street • Hometown, OH 00000 • 555.555.1234

LOBBYING AND FUNDRAISING INTERNSHIP QUALIFICATIONS

- Experienced as fundraiser and program recruiter for campus organizations.
- Confidence in event planning, marketing strategy development, and outreach.
- Capacity to draft and finalize correspondence, promotional materials, and brochures.
- Research, analytical, and presentation skills associated with lobbying and topical reports.
- Business knowledge gained from courses including: Accounting, Finance, and Marketing.

BUSINESS AND MARKETING EDUCATION

THE HOME STATE UNIVERSITY, Columbus, Ohio
Bachelor of Science, Business Administration, anticipated May 2008
- Major: *Business, Marketing* and Secondary Major: Business, Transportation Logistics
- Overall GPA: 3.30, Trustees Scholar, and National Dean's List Scholar
- University of Dreams Internship and Professional Development Program, 2007

FUNDRAISING, OUTREACH, AND LEADERSHIP ACHIEVEMENTS

- Susan G. Komen Breast Cancer Foundation, Fundraiser, 2002–Present
- America Israel Public Affairs Committee, Member, February 2007–Present
- Alpha Phi International Fraternity, Director, Alumni Relations, January 2007–Present
- American Business Women's Association, Chairperson, Fundraising, April 2007–Present
- The Ohio State University Community Commitment, Volunteer, September 2004–Present
- Project Open Hand Columbus, Volunteer, April 2005–Present

OUTREACH, MARKETING, AND ADMINISTRATIVE ACHIEVEMENTS

BIRTHRIGHT ISRAEL, Columbus, Ohio
Recruiting and Marketing Intern, Spring 2007
- Recruited and interviewed candidates for national program providing free travel to Israel.
- Recruitment included campus-wide telephone and marketing campaign.

NETADS, INC., Santa Clara, California
Marketing Intern, Summer 2006
- Designed database tracking sales leads and initiated contact with potential clientele.
- Marketed to 400 potential clients, including Visa, DreamWorks Inc., and Knight-Ridder Press.

ABERCROMBIE AND FITCH CO., Columbus, Ohio 43068
Marketing Intern, Fall 2003
- Analyzed sales and presented findings to supervisors.

WORTHINGTON REALTORS, Worthington, Ohio
Receptionist, Summers and Part-time 2001–2005

- Book Antiqua font is good alternative type choice. Candidate may want to experiment with resume in different fonts to see if one generates more employer interest than another.

- Qualification summary gives focus to Internship sought by candidate.

- Headlines highlight significant entries and make good use of key words.

- Bullets give reader opportunity to peruse quickly for facts.

- Most important information appears first.

- This candidate chose to have one multipurpose resume and one targeted resume. Good strategy for an effective job (or internship) search.

Corey Davis

123 Main Street • Hometown, NJ 00000 • (555) 555-1234 • cd@company.com

Experience

EDISON TECHNICAL AND VOCATIONAL HIGH SCHOOL, Edison, NJ
9th Grade General Science Teacher, September 2006–Present

EDISON TECHNICAL AND VOCATIONAL HIGH SCHOOL, Edison, NJ
Biology Teacher (Contract Substitute), January–June 2006

MAPLEWOOD-SOUTH ORANGE SCHOOL DISTRICT, Rochester, NY
Substitute Teacher K-12, October–December 2006

NEWARK ACADEMY, Rochester, NY
Substitute Teacher K-5, October–December 2006

Education

FAIRLEIGH DICKINSON UNIVERSITY, Madison, NJ
M.S., Math/Science/Technology Education, expected August 2008
- Received Eisenhower Grant to study critical thinking in classrooms
- Researched and wrote thesis: Problem Based Learning to Increase Engagement in an Urban Science Classroom
- Created Interdisciplinary Biology, English, and Social Studies unit
- Developed and used problem-based learning projects as well as inquiry-based learning units within classroom settings

DREW UNIVERSITY, Madison, NJ
B.S., Ecology and Evolutionary Biology, May 2005

Selected Courses

Human Genetics & Evolution, Biochemistry, Ecology, Evolution, Cell Biology, Mammalian Anatomy, Evolution of the Earth (geology), Calculus I and II, Statistics for Biologists, Probability, History and Philosophy of Education, Foundations of Math/Science/Technology, Teaching Math/Science, Inquiry in the Classroom, Classroom Dynamics, Differentiating Instruction, Developing Literacy Skills, Literacy through Math/Science/Technology, Assessment, Problem-Based Learning

Teaching Certifications and Qualifications

NJ STATE CERTIFICATION IN BIOLOGY, 7TH THROUGH 12TH GRADES, June 2007
NJ STATE CERTIFICATION IN GENERAL SCIENCE, June 2007

Teacher (After)

Corey Davis

123 Main Street · Hometown, NJ 00000 · (555) 555-1234 · cdavis@company.com

Teaching Certifications and Qualifications

- NJ State Certification in Biology, 7th through 12th grades, received June 2007
- NJ State Certification in General Science, received June 2007
- Creativity and knowledge to create lessons for students at various readiness levels
- Interest in teaching science, mathematics, as well as Spanish
- Experience co-teaching in an inclusion classroom

Science, Mathematics, and Education Studies

FAIRLEIGH DICKINSON UNIVERSITY, Madison, NJ
Master of Science, Math/Science/Technology Education, anticipated August 2008

- Received Eisenhower Grant to study how to bring critical thinking into classrooms
- Thesis: Problem Based Learning to Increase Engagement in an Urban Science Classroom
- Created a unit incorporating literacy building strategies into science
- Developed and used problem-based and inquiry-based learning units within classroom settings
- Developed unit differentiated for three different readiness levels

DREW UNIVERSITY, Madison, NJ
Bachelor of Science, Ecology and Evolutionary Biology, Psychology minor, May 2005

Science, Mathematics, and Education Coursework

- Human Genetics & Evolution, Genetics, Biochemistry, Ecology, Evolution, Cell Biology, Principles of Experimental Biology Lab, Animal Behavior, Mammalian Anatomy, Evolution of the Earth
- Calculus I and II, Statistics for the Sciences, Statistics for Biologists, Probability
- Foundations of Math/Science/Technology, Teaching Math/Science, Inquiry in the Classroom, Classroom Dynamics, Differentiating Instruction, Literacy through Math/Science/Technology, Assessment, Problem Based Learning

Teaching Experience

EDISON TECHNICAL AND VOCATIONAL HIGH SCHOOL, Edison, NJ
9th Grade General Science Teacher, September 2006–Present
Biology Teacher (Contract Substitute), January–June 2006

MAPLEWOOD-SOUTH ORANGE SCHOOL DISTRICT, Rochester, NY
Substitute Teacher K–12, October–December 2006

NEWARK ACADEMY, Rochester, NY
Substitute Teacher K–5, October–December 2006

- Century Schoolbook is a professional and appropriate font.
- Certifications and Qualifications presented as lead to reader. Sets tone for resume.
- Summary entries replace individual job descriptions.
- Headlines highlight significant education and courses, the strengths of this candidate.
- Corey is about to complete a Master's degree which is prompting this job search for improved career opportunity.
- After several interviews, Corey determined employers were very focused on most recent coursework, so candidate emphasized this content.
- Headlines stress candidate's strengths in specific subject matter.

Appendix B

Helpful Web Sites

This section identifies some additional obvious and not-so-obvious research and job-search support tools. In this Web 2.0 world, you really should maximize whatever Internet resources are available to advance your career. This may mean taking advantage of job boards (where openings are posted), employer Web sites (where internal opportunities are listed or you can apply online), and other sites such as business networking sites, career guidance sites, and blogs (where people make comments about an industry, company, type of job, or other work-related matters). Use a mix of technology resources along with traditional print publications, industry associations, and of course, your local library, to get as much information as you can about a prospective employer or job openings that might be a good fit for your skills, experience, and career goals.

Web-Based Resources

Web-based resources are critical because job seekers and resume writers have a lot of homework to do. They must conduct preresearch, set goals, enhance field-focused vocabulary, and develop a hit list of prospective employers.

The following list of Web sites is offered to facilitate your efforts for job-search success. Identify those that address your needs, and use those that are appropriate to your strategies and goals. This is just a small representation of what is available on the Web.

The Big Three Job Boards

✍ *www.careerbuilder.com*

One of the most popular multiple industry and national sites for posting, resume collection, and job-search information. It includes help wanted ads from more than 200 newspaper markets and metropolitan areas in electronic format. Beyond resume posting, participants are able to browse jobs and apply online, distribute resumes, take career tests, use the site's free salary calculator, look for local and regional career fairs, get career advice from experts, and have a resume critiqued. You can search jobs by a wide variety of variables including company, industry, category, and location.

✍ *www.monster.com*

Literally and figuratively, one of the monsters of all posting, resume collection, and career advice sites. This creatively advertised and widely recognized job board offers employer research, search-agent capabilities, and job search advice. Like all the big boards, it is very user-friendly. This site promotes with great pride the fact that it contains millions of resumes and millions of postings for job seekers of all stages and ages, including internship candidates, soon-to-be and recent college grads, and experienced professionals. Additional site amenities include: scholarship research, information about online degrees, and Monster en Español.

✑ *www.hotjobs.com*

This site, a subsidiary of Yahoo!, is the force behind Yahoo!'s career channel. It offers industry information, job search advice, and a relocation center. Postings may be accessed by categories including company, staffing firm, U.S. location, international location, and industry. You can distinguish your search between search firms and direct employers or by the number of years required by an employer for an opening. You can also see the number of opportunities by region or category. Additional features offer information on work-life balance and retirement. Specific newsletters by job interest are also available through subscriptions.

Additional Excellent Job Board Sites

✑ *www.indeed.com*

Indeed calls itself "a search engine for jobs." It collects job listings from many job boards, newspapers, company career pages, and other sites. At the time of this writing, it listed more than 1 million jobs posted in the last seven days.

✑ *www.simplyhired.com*

Another job board search engine. You can browse by state, job title, company name, or industry. Post your resume to as many as five major job boards at no cost. Conduct special searches by these unique categories: dog-friendly employers, mom-friendly companies, employers for the 50+, and eco-friendly employers.

✑ *www.Vault.com*

You can search jobs here, but it also has one of the best libraries of career guides and employer profiles. Additionally, information on more than 3,000 companies is listed and the site's message boards offer enormous insight as to what it might be like to work at one of your target employers.

More Web Resources by Specialty or Audience

✎ *www.CollegeGrad.com*

Often called the number-one entry-level job site, this board is chock-full of advice for those ready to put their toe into the employment pool. Good info for newbies and those with limited work experience. Special features include the listing of the top entry-level employers for new grads based on the number of anticipated hires. They also offer a video component where job seekers can create a video resume, view career videos, and watch the "Job Search Minute."

✎ *www.CollegeJournal.com*

This is the sister site of *www.CareerJournal.com*. Both career sites are fueled by the *Wall Street Journal* with strong content regarding news, trends, and many excellent job search tools.

✎ *www.NACELink.com*

This site brings together students, colleges, and employers. It is a not-for-profit job board and helps students tap into the valuable resources also offered by their campus career placement centers.

✎ *www.TheLadders.com*

A resource for executive job seekers targeting positions above $100K. Visitors may view some job opportunities at no charge, but there is also a fee to join for full access to the site.

✎ *www.6FigureJobs.com*

An award-winning site aimed at senior level management. It offers a mix of openings from employer and search firms. Free membership to all visitors with full access to comprehensive resources and a feature for online networking.

✑ *www.Dice.com*

This is where those seeking computer/information technology careers go. A good resource with job tools for the high-tech professional.

✑ *www.eFinancialCareers.com*

Candidates seeking positions in accounting, finance, banking, investment banking, and the financial markets will find a wealth of information for all industries and all levels of experience.

✑ *www.careerjournal.com*

The *Wall Street Journal's* Career Journal is a multifaceted site. It contains articles, postings, resume collections, links to other sites, resume critiquing, and general advice regarding job search and careers. It is an educational and logistical support site of value for experienced candidates.

✑ *www.GovernmentJobs.com*

If you are looking for a job in the public sector, this site offers search capabilities by location, category, earnings, and keyword.

✑ *www.retirementjobs.com*

Those in the 50+ age bracket can go to this smart niche site to search jobs, take an online class, find out about companies certified as "age friendly," and read real-life success stories.

✑ *www.aarp.org/money/careers/*

AARP (formerly the American Association of Retired Persons) hosts an excellent resource for 50+ candidates which addresses occupational information, career transition, job loss, skills training, and general news for those who want to continue to work.

✑ *www.DiversityJobs.com*

Provides hundreds of thousands of job openings for candidates seeking workplace diversity. The site states its mission as one of workforce empowerment for African Americans, Women, Hispanics, Persons with Disabilities, Asian Americans, Native Americans, members of the LGBT community, and other diverse groups.

☞ *www.Net-Temps.com*

A job board focused on temporary, temp-to-hire, and full-time employment found exclusively through the staffing industry. Job information includes date of posting, duration of assignment/contract, and full work descriptions.

☞ *www.LloydStaffing.com*

A nationwide staffing service specializing in a variety of industries including office services, sales, technology, healthcare, and finance. Temporary opportunities, direct hire, and executive search positions are offered.

☞ *www.craigslist.org*

Offers classified job listings for 450 cities worldwide. Choose your location and browse what's available. Search by date or criteria such as telecommute, contract, internship, part-time, non-profit, or keyword.

☞ *www.guru.com*

Want to freelance? Find independent projects in categories such as Creative, IT, Business Consulting, and Office Administration.

☞ *www.HireVetsFirst.gov*

A site created by the government to assist veterans in finding employment opportunities. It has links to America's Job Bank and USA Jobs. It also offers advice to help transition individuals from military to civilian careers.

☞ *www.Jobster.com*

This is a good place to get your feet wet on business networking through the Internet. Read the featured profiles, do some searching, and start talking online to people who might be able to steer you toward your dream job. Good job search tips and local directory.

☞ *www.LinkedIn.com*

A major online network of more than 14 million business professionals worldwide. Identify and contact colleagues, clients, partners, and individuals who can assist with your job search.

✍ *www.Quintcareers.com*

Quintessential Careers is a favorite site for job information on the Web. It offers comprehensive career development advice, news, and tools on all topics related to the job search. Visitors receive expert guidance at all levels of their career. Outstanding content.

✍ *www.jobhunt.org*

Another favorite. One of the Web's most valuable and powerful resources for job seekers. This site brings the best Internet tools and sites to the job hunter's attention. It does not collect resumes or offer job postings, but it will direct visitors to other excellent Internet sites on virtually any area of employment.

✍ *www.chimby.com*

One more top-notch resource for job seekers. This search engine allows visitors to search more than 400 career advice sites on the Web. It covers content such as resumes, workforce topics, career management, interviewing, and on-the-job issues.

✍ *www.weddles.com*

No book could omit what is widely known as the definitive site for online job information! Founded by employment guru Peter Weddle, this outstanding site offers tips for success. More importantly, Weddle's User's Choice Awards recognize job-oriented Web sites that provide the best level of service and value to visitors. Other excellent content includes an association directory, ideal for gathering leads for networking purposes.

✍ *www.careertv.com*

Like to watch videos? This interactive site is perfect for you. Its video menu includes employers, resumes, universities, job advice, and more. A favorite resource of the YouTube generation.

Index

THE EVERYTHING SERIES!

BUSINESS & PERSONAL FINANCE

Everything® Accounting Book
Everything® Budgeting Book, 2nd Ed.
Everything® Business Planning Book
Everything® Coaching and Mentoring Book, 2nd Ed.
Everything® Fundraising Book
Everything® Get Out of Debt Book
Everything® Grant Writing Book, 2nd Ed.
Everything® Guide to Buying Foreclosures
Everything® Guide to Mortgages
Everything® Guide to Personal Finance for Single Mothers
Everything® Home-Based Business Book, 2nd Ed.
Everything® Homebuying Book, 2nd Ed.
Everything® Homeselling Book, 2nd Ed.
Everything® Human Resource Management Book
Everything® Improve Your Credit Book
Everything® Investing Book, 2nd Ed.
Everything® Landlording Book
Everything® Leadership Book, 2nd Ed.
Everything® Managing People Book, 2nd Ed.
Everything® Negotiating Book
Everything® Online Auctions Book
Everything® Online Business Book
Everything® Personal Finance Book
Everything® Personal Finance in Your 20s & 30s Book, 2nd Ed.
Everything® Project Management Book, 2nd Ed.
Everything® Real Estate Investing Book
Everything® Retirement Planning Book
Everything® Robert's Rules Book, $7.95
Everything® Selling Book
Everything® Start Your Own Business Book, 2nd Ed.
Everything® Wills & Estate Planning Book

COOKING

Everything® Barbecue Cookbook
Everything® Bartender's Book, 2nd Ed., $9.95
Everything® Calorie Counting Cookbook
Everything® Cheese Book
Everything® Chinese Cookbook
Everything® Classic Recipes Book
Everything® Cocktail Parties & Drinks Book
Everything® College Cookbook
Everything® Cooking for Baby and Toddler Book
Everything® Cooking for Two Cookbook
Everything® Diabetes Cookbook
Everything® Easy Gourmet Cookbook
Everything® Fondue Cookbook
Everything® Fondue Party Book
Everything® Gluten-Free Cookbook
Everything® Glycemic Index Cookbook
Everything® Grilling Cookbook
Everything® Healthy Meals in Minutes Cookbook
Everything® Holiday Cookbook
Everything® Indian Cookbook
Everything® Italian Cookbook

Everything® Lactose-Free Cookbook
Everything® Low-Carb Cookbook
Everything® Low-Cholesterol Cookbook
Everything® Low-Fat High-Flavor Cookbook
Everything® Low-Salt Cookbook
Everything® Meals for a Month Cookbook
Everything® Meals on a Budget Cookbook
Everything® Mediterranean Cookbook
Everything® Mexican Cookbook
Everything® No Trans Fat Cookbook
Everything® One-Pot Cookbook
Everything® Pizza Cookbook
Everything® Quick and Easy 30-Minute, 5-Ingredient Cookbook
Everything® Quick Meals Cookbook
Everything® Slow Cooker Cookbook
Everything® Slow Cooking for a Crowd Cookbook
Everything® Soup Cookbook
Everything® Stir-Fry Cookbook
Everything® Sugar-Free Cookbook
Everything® Tapas and Small Plates Cookbook
Everything® Tex-Mex Cookbook
Everything® Thai Cookbook
Everything® Vegetarian Cookbook
Everything® Whole-Grain, High-Fiber Cookbook
Everything® Wild Game Cookbook
Everything® Wine Book, 2nd Ed.

GAMES

Everything® 15-Minute Sudoku Book, $9.95
Everything® 30-Minute Sudoku Book, $9.95
Everything® Bible Crosswords Book, $9.95
Everything® Blackjack Strategy Book
Everything® Brain Strain Book, $9.95
Everything® Bridge Book
Everything® Card Games Book
Everything® Card Tricks Book, $9.95
Everything® Casino Gambling Book, 2nd Ed.
Everything® Chess Basics Book
Everything® Craps Strategy Book
Everything® Crossword and Puzzle Book
Everything® Crossword Challenge Book
Everything® Crosswords for the Beach Book, $9.95
Everything® Cryptic Crosswords Book, $9.95
Everything® Cryptograms Book, $9.95
Everything® Easy Crosswords Book
Everything® Easy Kakuro Book, $9.95
Everything® Easy Large-Print Crosswords Book
Everything® Games Book, 2nd Ed.
Everything® Giant Sudoku Book, $9.95
Everything® Giant Word Search Book
Everything® Kakuro Challenge Book, $9.95
Everything® Large-Print Crossword Challenge Book
Everything® Large-Print Crosswords Book
Everything® Lateral Thinking Puzzles Book, $9.95
Everything® Literary Crosswords Book, $9.95
Everything® Mazes Book
Everything® Memory Booster Puzzles Book, $9.95
Everything® Movie Crosswords Book, $9.95

Everything® Music Crosswords Book, $9.95
Everything® Online Poker Book
Everything® Pencil Puzzles Book, $9.95
Everything® Poker Strategy Book
Everything® Pool & Billiards Book
Everything® Puzzles for Commuters Book, $9.95
Everything® Puzzles for Dog Lovers Book, $9.95
Everything® Sports Crosswords Book, $9.95
Everything® Test Your IQ Book, $9.95
Everything® Texas Hold 'Em Book, $9.95
Everything® Travel Crosswords Book, $9.95
Everything® TV Crosswords Book, $9.95
Everything® Word Games Challenge Book
Everything® Word Scramble Book
Everything® Word Search Book

HEALTH

Everything® Alzheimer's Book
Everything® Diabetes Book
Everything® First Aid Book, $9.95
Everything® Health Guide to Adult Bipolar Disorder
Everything® Health Guide to Arthritis
Everything® Health Guide to Controlling Anxiety
Everything® Health Guide to Depression
Everything® Health Guide to Fibromyalgia
Everything® Health Guide to Menopause, 2nd Ed.
Everything® Health Guide to Migraines
Everything® Health Guide to OCD
Everything® Health Guide to PMS
Everything® Health Guide to Postpartum Care
Everything® Health Guide to Thyroid Disease
Everything® Hypnosis Book
Everything® Low Cholesterol Book
Everything® Menopause Book
Everything® Nutrition Book
Everything® Reflexology Book
Everything® Stress Management Book

HISTORY

Everything® American Government Book
Everything® American History Book, 2nd Ed.
Everything® Civil War Book
Everything® Freemasons Book
Everything® Irish History & Heritage Book
Everything® Middle East Book
Everything® World War II Book, 2nd Ed.

HOBBIES

Everything® Candlemaking Book
Everything® Cartooning Book
Everything® Coin Collecting Book
Everything® Digital Photography Book, 2nd Ed.
Everything® Drawing Book
Everything® Family Tree Book, 2nd Ed.
Everything® Knitting Book
Everything® Knots Book
Everything® Photography Book
Everything® Quilting Book

Everything® Sewing Book
Everything® Soapmaking Book, 2nd Ed.
Everything® Woodworking Book

HOME IMPROVEMENT

Everything® Feng Shui Book
Everything® Feng Shui Decluttering Book, $9.95
Everything® Fix-It Book
Everything® Green Living Book
Everything® Home Decorating Book
Everything® Home Storage Solutions Book
Everything® Homebuilding Book
Everything® Organize Your Home Book, 2nd Ed.

KIDS' BOOKS

All titles are $7.95
Everything® Fairy Tales Book, $14.95
Everything® Kids' Animal Puzzle & Activity Book
Everything® Kids' Astronomy Book
Everything® Kids' Baseball Book, 5th Ed.
Everything® Kids' Bible Trivia Book
Everything® Kids' Bugs Book
Everything® Kids' Cars and Trucks Puzzle and Activity Book
Everything® Kids' Christmas Puzzle & Activity Book
**Everything® Kids' Connect the Dots
Puzzle and Activity Book**
Everything® Kids' Cookbook
Everything® Kids' Crazy Puzzles Book
Everything® Kids' Dinosaurs Book
Everything® Kids' Environment Book
Everything® Kids' Fairies Puzzle and Activity Book
Everything® Kids' First Spanish Puzzle and Activity Book
Everything® Kids' Football Book
Everything® Kids' Gross Cookbook
Everything® Kids' Gross Hidden Pictures Book
Everything® Kids' Gross Jokes Book
Everything® Kids' Gross Mazes Book
Everything® Kids' Gross Puzzle & Activity Book
Everything® Kids' Halloween Puzzle & Activity Book
Everything® Kids' Hidden Pictures Book
Everything® Kids' Horses Book
Everything® Kids' Joke Book
Everything® Kids' Knock Knock Book
Everything® Kids' Learning French Book
Everything® Kids' Learning Spanish Book
Everything® Kids' Magical Science Experiments Book
Everything® Kids' Math Puzzles Book
Everything® Kids' Mazes Book
Everything® Kids' Money Book
Everything® Kids' Nature Book
Everything® Kids' Pirates Puzzle and Activity Book
Everything® Kids' Presidents Book
Everything® Kids' Princess Puzzle and Activity Book
Everything® Kids' Puzzle Book
Everything® Kids' Racecars Puzzle and Activity Book
Everything® Kids' Riddles & Brain Teasers Book
Everything® Kids' Science Experiments Book
Everything® Kids' Sharks Book
Everything® Kids' Soccer Book
Everything® Kids' Spies Puzzle and Activity Book
Everything® Kids' States Book
Everything® Kids' Travel Activity Book
Everything® Kids' Word Search Puzzle and Activity Book

LANGUAGE

Everything® Conversational Japanese Book with CD, $19.95
Everything® French Grammar Book
Everything® French Phrase Book, $9.95
Everything® French Verb Book, $9.95
Everything® German Practice Book with CD, $19.95
Everything® Inglés Book
Everything® Intermediate Spanish Book with CD, $19.95
Everything® Italian Practice Book with CD, $19.95
Everything® Learning Brazilian Portuguese Book with CD, $19.95
Everything® Learning French Book with CD, 2nd Ed., $19.95
Everything® Learning German Book
Everything® Learning Italian Book
Everything® Learning Latin Book
Everything® Learning Russian Book with CD, $19.95
Everything® Learning Spanish Book
Everything® Learning Spanish Book with CD, 2nd Ed., $19.95
Everything® Russian Practice Book with CD, $19.95
Everything® Sign Language Book
Everything® Spanish Grammar Book
Everything® Spanish Phrase Book, $9.95
Everything® Spanish Practice Book with CD, $19.95
Everything® Spanish Verb Book, $9.95
Everything® Speaking Mandarin Chinese Book with CD, $19.95

MUSIC

Everything® Bass Guitar Book with CD, $19.95
Everything® Drums Book with CD, $19.95
Everything® Guitar Book with CD, 2nd Ed., $19.95
Everything® Guitar Chords Book with CD, $19.95
Everything® Harmonica Book with CD, $15.95
Everything® Home Recording Book
Everything® Music Theory Book with CD, $19.95
Everything® Reading Music Book with CD, $19.95
Everything® Rock & Blues Guitar Book with CD, $19.95
Everything® Rock & Blues Piano Book with CD, $19.95
Everything® Songwriting Book

NEW AGE

Everything® Astrology Book, 2nd Ed.
Everything® Birthday Personology Book
Everything® Dreams Book, 2nd Ed.
Everything® Love Signs Book, $9.95
Everything® Love Spells Book, $9.95
Everything® Paganism Book
Everything® Palmistry Book
Everything® Psychic Book
Everything® Reiki Book
Everything® Sex Signs Book, $9.95
Everything® Spells & Charms Book, 2nd Ed.
Everything® Tarot Book, 2nd Ed.
Everything® Toltec Wisdom Book
Everything® Wicca & Witchcraft Book, 2nd Ed.

PARENTING

Everything® Baby Names Book, 2nd Ed.
Everything® Baby Shower Book, 2nd Ed.
Everything® Baby Sign Language Book with DVD
Everything® Baby's First Year Book
Everything® Birthing Book

Everything® Breastfeeding Book
Everything® Father-to-Be Book
Everything® Father's First Year Book
Everything® Get Ready for Baby Book, 2nd Ed.
Everything® Get Your Baby to Sleep Book, $9.95
Everything® Getting Pregnant Book
Everything® Guide to Pregnancy Over 35
Everything® Guide to Raising a One-Year-Old
Everything® Guide to Raising a Two-Year-Old
Everything® Guide to Raising Adolescent Boys
Everything® Guide to Raising Adolescent Girls
Everything® Mother's First Year Book
Everything® Parent's Guide to Childhood Illnesses
Everything® Parent's Guide to Children and Divorce
Everything® Parent's Guide to Children with ADD/ADHD
Everything® Parent's Guide to Children with Asperger's Syndrome
Everything® Parent's Guide to Children with Asthma
Everything® Parent's Guide to Children with Autism
Everything® Parent's Guide to Children with Bipolar Disorder
Everything® Parent's Guide to Children with Depression
Everything® Parent's Guide to Children with Dyslexia
Everything® Parent's Guide to Children with Juvenile Diabetes
Everything® Parent's Guide to Positive Discipline
Everything® Parent's Guide to Raising a Successful Child
Everything® Parent's Guide to Raising Boys
Everything® Parent's Guide to Raising Girls
Everything® Parent's Guide to Raising Siblings
Everything® Parent's Guide to Sensory Integration Disorder
Everything® Parent's Guide to Tantrums
Everything® Parent's Guide to the Strong-Willed Child
Everything® Parenting a Teenager Book
Everything® Potty Training Book, $9.95
Everything® Pregnancy Book, 3rd Ed.
Everything® Pregnancy Fitness Book
Everything® Pregnancy Nutrition Book
Everything® Pregnancy Organizer, 2nd Ed., $16.95
Everything® Toddler Activities Book
Everything® Toddler Book
Everything® Tween Book
Everything® Twins, Triplets, and More Book

PETS

Everything® Aquarium Book
Everything® Boxer Book
Everything® Cat Book, 2nd Ed.
Everything® Chihuahua Book
Everything® Cooking for Dogs Book
Everything® Dachshund Book
Everything® Dog Book, 2nd Ed.
Everything® Dog Grooming Book
Everything® Dog Health Book
Everything® Dog Obedience Book
Everything® Dog Owner's Organizer, $16.95
Everything® Dog Training and Tricks Book
Everything® German Shepherd Book
Everything® Golden Retriever Book
Everything® Horse Book
Everything® Horse Care Book
Everything® Horseback Riding Book
Everything® Labrador Retriever Book
Everything® Poodle Book
Everything® Pug Book

Everything® Puppy Book
Everything® Rottweiler Book
Everything® Small Dogs Book
Everything® Tropical Fish Book
Everything® Yorkshire Terrier Book

REFERENCE

Everything® American Presidents Book
Everything® Blogging Book
Everything® Build Your Vocabulary Book, $9.95
Everything® Car Care Book
Everything® Classical Mythology Book
Everything® Da Vinci Book
Everything® Divorce Book
Everything® Einstein Book
Everything® Enneagram Book
Everything® Etiquette Book, 2nd Ed.
Everything® Guide to C. S. Lewis & Narnia
Everything® Guide to Edgar Allan Poe
Everything® Guide to Understanding Philosophy
Everything® Inventions and Patents Book
Everything® Jacqueline Kennedy Onassis Book
Everything® John F. Kennedy Book
Everything® Mafia Book
Everything® Martin Luther King Jr. Book
Everything® Philosophy Book
Everything® Pirates Book
Everything® Private Investigation Book
Everything® Psychology Book
Everything® Public Speaking Book, $9.95
Everything® Shakespeare Book, 2nd Ed.

RELIGION

Everything® Angels Book
Everything® Bible Book
Everything® Bible Study Book with CD, $19.95
Everything® Buddhism Book
Everything® Catholicism Book
Everything® Christianity Book
Everything® Gnostic Gospels Book
Everything® History of the Bible Book
Everything® Jesus Book
Everything® Jewish History & Heritage Book
Everything® Judaism Book
Everything® Kabbalah Book
Everything® Koran Book
Everything® Mary Book
Everything® Mary Magdalene Book
Everything® Prayer Book
Everything® Saints Book, 2nd Ed.
Everything® Torah Book
Everything® Understanding Islam Book
Everything® Women of the Bible Book
Everything® World's Religions Book

SCHOOL & CAREERS

Everything® Career Tests Book
Everything® College Major Test Book
Everything® College Survival Book, 2nd Ed.
Everything® Cover Letter Book, 2nd Ed.
Everything® Filmmaking Book
Everything® Get-a-Job Book, 2nd Ed.
Everything® Guide to Being a Paralegal
Everything® Guide to Being a Personal Trainer
Everything® Guide to Being a Real Estate Agent
Everything® Guide to Being a Sales Rep
Everything® Guide to Being an Event Planner
Everything® Guide to Careers in Health Care
Everything® Guide to Careers in Law Enforcement
Everything® Guide to Government Jobs
Everything® Guide to Starting and Running a Catering
    Business
Everything® Guide to Starting and Running a Restaurant
Everything® Job Interview Book, 2nd Ed.
Everything® New Nurse Book
Everything® New Teacher Book
Everything® Paying for College Book
Everything® Practice Interview Book
Everything® Resume Book, 3rd Ed.
Everything® Study Book

SELF-HELP

Everything® Body Language Book
Everything® Dating Book, 2nd Ed.
Everything® Great Sex Book
Everything® Self-Esteem Book
Everything® Tantric Sex Book

SPORTS & FITNESS

Everything® Easy Fitness Book
Everything® Fishing Book
Everything® Krav Maga for Fitness Book
Everything® Running Book, 2nd Ed.

TRAVEL

Everything® Family Guide to Coastal Florida
Everything® Family Guide to Cruise Vacations
Everything® Family Guide to Hawaii
Everything® Family Guide to Las Vegas, 2nd Ed.
Everything® Family Guide to Mexico
Everything® Family Guide to New England, 2nd Ed.
Everything® Family Guide to New York City, 3rd Ed.
Everything® Family Guide to RV Travel & Campgrounds
Everything® Family Guide to the Caribbean
Everything® Family Guide to the Disneyland® Resort, California
    Adventure®, Universal Studios®, and the Anaheim
    Area, 2nd Ed.
Everything® Family Guide to the Walt Disney World Resort®,
    Universal Studios®, and Greater Orlando, 5th Ed.
Everything® Family Guide to Timeshares
Everything® Family Guide to Washington D.C., 2nd Ed.

WEDDINGS

Everything® Bachelorette Party Book, $9.95
Everything® Bridesmaid Book, $9.95
Everything® Destination Wedding Book
Everything® Father of the Bride Book, $9.95
Everything® Groom Book, $9.95
Everything® Mother of the Bride Book, $9.95
Everything® Outdoor Wedding Book
Everything® Wedding Book, 3rd Ed.
Everything® Wedding Checklist, $9.95
Everything® Wedding Etiquette Book, $9.95
Everything® Wedding Organizer, 2nd Ed., $16.95
Everything® Wedding Shower Book, $9.95
Everything® Wedding Vows Book, $9.95
Everything® Wedding Workout Book
Everything® Weddings on a Budget Book, 2nd Ed., $9.95

WRITING

Everything® Creative Writing Book
Everything® Get Published Book, 2nd Ed.
Everything® Grammar and Style Book, 2nd Ed.
Everything® Guide to Magazine Writing
Everything® Guide to Writing a Book Proposal
Everything® Guide to Writing a Novel
Everything® Guide to Writing Children's Books
Everything® Guide to Writing Copy
Everything® Guide to Writing Graphic Novels
Everything® Guide to Writing Research Papers
Everything® Improve Your Writing Book, 2nd Ed.
Everything® Writing Poetry Book